Textiles of the Hill Tribes of Burma

Textiles of the Hill Tribes of Burma

by

Michael C. Howard

White Lotus Press

White Lotus Co., Ltd.
G.P.O.   Box 1141
Bangkok 10501
Thailand

Telephone:	(662) 332-4915 and (662) 741-6288-9
Fax:	(662) 741-6607 and (662) 741-6287
E-mail:	ande@loxinfo.co.th
Website:	http://thailine.com/lotus

Printed in Thailand

ISBN 974-8434-84-2 pbk White Lotus Co., Ltd., Bangkok

Contents

Preface and Acknowledgments

I began work on the present book after finishing my *Southeast Asian Textiles: An Annotated & Illustrated Bibliography* in 1994. Both books are part of a larger research project that I have been engaged in for the past few years on Southeast Asian textiles and identity that has included fieldwork in the Philippines, Indonesia, Thailand, and Vietnam. It is precisely the fieldwork part of research that has been the most frustrating aspect of writing this book on Burma. Burma has been effectively closed to anthropological fieldwork by outsiders since the early 1960s and many have been the times in the course of working on this book that I would have loved to have been able to ask some villager about a particular textile rather than relying on informants well removed from the place where the textile in question came from (or presumably came from) or meager written sources of often questionable reliability. I can only hope that this situation does not persist for much longer and that within the near future a good deal more of the highland tribal areas in Burma are made available for fieldwork of a substantial nature.

By and large, my "field" in collecting information for the present study has been markets and shops in lowland Burma and northern Thailand and a handful of museums in the United States and United Kingdom. Among those associated with the markets and shops, I owe a special debt of gratitude to Laura Kan of Singapore and Chiang Mai, who has helped me as a research assistant. She has made an invaluable contribution to the present work.

One of the most pleasant aspects of my research on this project has been the visits that I have made to museums, especially to those in places that I otherwise probably never would have visited. My museum adventure began with a trip to Denison University in Granville, Ohio, in November 1995. The university's art gallery houses the largest collection of hill tribe textiles from Burma, primarily as a result of the university's association with the Baptist Church and the Baptist's years of missionary work among Burma's hill tribes. Kathy Leach of the University Art Gallery and Museum was my host and ensured that I had a very worthwhile visit.

In August 1996 I set off to visit four more museums in the United States and United Kingdom. I began with The Field Museum in Chicago. I would like to thank Bennet Bronson, the museum's curator for Asian archaeology and ethnology, and Will Grewe-Mullins, the museum's collection manager, for their assistance. Next stop was New York's American Museum of Natural History, where assistance was provided by Lisa Whittall, the museum's curator of ethnographic textiles, and Paul Beelitz, who went out of their way to ensure a successful visit.

It was then on to the United Kingdom and The Bankfield Museum of Halifax. Most textile specialists are familiar with the museum by name because of the writings of one of its early curators, Henry Ling Roth. It is a pity, however, that not more people with an interest in Southeast Asian textiles have taken time to visit the museum. Museums Officer June Hill helped me find my way to Halifax and arrange accommodation as well as spending a couple of days with me while I went through the museum's collection. My final stop was Oxford's Pitt Rivers Museum. My trail to the Pitt Rivers Museum had begun earlier when I corresponded with Ruth Barnes of the Ashmolean Museum, Oxford, who passed me on to Julia Nicholson of the Pitt Rivers Museum. Jeremy Coote, Sandra Dudley, and Marina De Alarcon provided help in preparing for my visit to Oxford. Once at the museum, additional assistance was given to me by Marina De Alarcon and Lorraine Rostant. I would also like to thank the head of conservation, Birgitte Speake.

I would also like to thank Sylvia Fraser-Lu for her encouragement throughout my work on this book. Finally, as always, I must thank the inter-library loan staff of Simon Fraser University's library for their untiring efforts on my behalf. I would also like to thank George Lee for his technical assistance in preparing the manuscript for publication.

1

Introduction

As a result of Burma's political and economic problems and its relative isolation since the 1960s, the country's rich textile tradition has been largely left out of the dramatic growth of interest in Southeast Asian textiles since the 1970s. This is a situation that is now starting to change as a result of the greater openness of Burma to the outside world in recent years and the growth of its tourist industry in particular. With such changes in mind, I felt that it was an opportune time to provide a survey of the textiles of Burma's hill tribes. No such survey has ever been attempted nor has much attention been paid to collections of such textiles that are to be found in museums scattered across Europe and North America.

The presentation of textiles in this book has been organized around ethno-linguistic groups. This is a long-standing tradition. Prior to British colonial rule, manner of dress was often used as a way of distinguishing one group from another. In fact, some peoples received their names from their style of dress. Under the British, with a desire for order in their colonial world, this notion was carried even further as efforts were made to demarcate distinctive groups and to identify their distinctive characteristics. Where possible, such characteristics included dress. Later, in an independent Burma, this tradition of linking dress style with ethnic identity continued, although acculturation and other forces of change have greatly reduced the actual wearing of distinctive costumes (at least on a daily basis) in recent decades.

Lowlanders in Burma commonly made a distinction between their own more civilized dress and the primitive dress of highland barbarians. From this perspective, part of the civilizing process was seen as adopting styles of dress associated with the civilizations of Hindu/Buddhist India, Imperial China, the European colonial powers, and lowland Burmese empires and states. In contrast, being an uncivilized hill-dwelling barbarian was associated with near nakedness or at least a presumably inferior style of dress different from that of the lowlander. An exception to this pattern can be made for the Tai-speaking Shan who are part of another civilization with a tradition of regal and other types of dress that distinguished them from their less civilized hill-dwelling neighbors. In this respect, outside observers sometimes viewed the civilizing process among these neighboring hill tribes in terms of adoption of Shan-style dress.

In general terms the notion of linking dress and ethnic identity works relatively well. It is not without its problems, however, and these need to be taken into account. First, there is the problem of identifying and delimiting specific ethnic groups. At a basic level, even an expert on Burma is often confused by the vast array of names used for different groups, and for some groups there is no widespread agreement as to what they are to be called. In addition, ethnic identities are not always rigidly demarcated and a degree of fluidity and overlap exists in many situations. Second, ethnic groups are often not homogeneous when it comes to their dress. Thus, there is a tendency for differences to exist between more isolated or separate members of hill-dwelling peoples and members of the same ethnic group who live in closer proximity to dominant groups such as the Burmese or even Shan. Third, there is a need to recognize that not all peoples have particular styles of dress. This is especially true for men's dress, but can also apply to women's dress. Fourth, it is important to view the link between dress and ethnic identity in a dynamic way that recognizes the changes a people's patterns of dress can undergo over time. Changing fashions are not a monopoly of the modern industrial world, although the changes tend to be more rapid in today's globalized world of fashion. Hill tribe fashions certainly have undergone considerable change in recent years, but they also changed in the past, albeit usually at a far slower pace.

Before detailing the textiles of each ethno-linguistic group, some background is necessary, especially in regard to Burma's linguistic mosaic. The next section in this chapter will therefore be a review of the languages spoken in Burma. This is followed by a very brief history of Burma with an emphasis on the place of the hill-dwelling peoples and their relations with lowlanders within this history. The remainder of this introductory chapter will survey the existing literature on the hill tribes of Burma with reference to their dress, provide an overview of hill tribe textiles, and briefly describe existing museum collections in North America and Europe.

Burma's Linguistic Diversity

Burma is inhabited by speakers of about 105 different languages who exhibit a variety of cultural differences that are often reflected in their traditional patterns of dress. Each of Southeast Asia's major language families are represented in Burma. Ancestors of those speaking Mon-Khmer languages of the Austro-Asiatic family were probably the earliest of presently existing peoples to arrive in Burma. Later came speakers of languages belonging to the Sino-Tibetan and Austro-Tai language families.

Speakers of Austro-Asiatic languages began moving into Mainland Southeast Asia some 6,000 years ago via northern Vietnam. They migrated south and west as far as India. The majority of languages in this family belong to the Mon-Khmer phyla or sub-family of languages. This phyla is represented in Burma by languages belonging to the Monic and Northern Mon-Khmer groups. The main Monic language is Mon. It was once spoken extensively in Thailand and Burma and is associated with the Indian-influenced Dvaravati period in Thailand and the State of Pegu (or Bago) in Burma. Today there are around one million Mon speakers in Burma living in the lowlands around Yangon and

to the east. Large numbers of Mon speakers are to be found in the towns of Martaban and Mawlamyine (Moulmein). There are also many Mon living across the border in Thailand and as far to the east as Bangkok.

Peoples speaking Northern Mon-Khmer languages are spread out from northern Vietnam to northern India and are divided into four groups: Mang, Khasian, Khmuic, and Palaungic. The Mang group are furthest to the east in China and Vietnam and the Khasian group furthest to the west in India and Bangladesh. Languages belonging to the Khumic and Palaungic groups are found in the upland areas of Burma. Speakers of **Khmu**, the most widely spoken Khmuic language, and other Khmuic-speaking peoples, live in adjacent areas of northwestern Vietnam, southern China, northern Thailand, the majority in Laos, and a small number in northeastern Burma.

Speakers of Palaungic languages are located in southwestern Yunnan and Burma's Shan State. These languages are divided into eastern and western subgroups. The eastern subgroup includes three closely related Palaungic languages found in Burma with around half a million speakers: Pale, Rumai, and Shwe. **Pale** (also known as Ngwe Palaung or **Silver Palaung**) is the most widely spoken of these languages, and Pale speakers are found in Shan State near Kalaw. There are a couple of thousand Pale speakers in northern Thailand who migrated there in recent years from Burma. **Rumai** speakers are located in northwestern Shan State (in Taungbaing). **Shwe** (also known as Ta-ang Palaung or **Golden Palaung**) speakers are found in northern Shan State near Namhsan. The eastern subgroup also includes **Riang** (sometimes known as **Black Karen**), the closely related **Yinchia** (also known as **Striped Karen** or Black Riang), and **Danau**.

The western subgroup of Palaungic languages is subdivided into Waic and Angkuic languages. These are spoken in southwestern Yunnan and northeastern Burma. The Waic languages include two **Wa** languages known as **Parauk** and **Vo** as well as Blang. Parauk and Vo speakers are often known as Wa in Burma. Wa speakers live in the upper Salween River area of Shan State. They are closely related to the Lawa of northern Thailand. There are only a few **Blang** (also known as Bulang or Pulang) speakers in Burma living in the Mong

Yawng area of eastern Shan State. There are two Angkuic languages found in Burma: **Samtao** and **Thai Loi**. These are spoken by only a couple of thousand people in the northeastern corner near the border with Laos and China.

Mon-Khmer Languages in Burma

Mon, Khmu, Pale (Palaung), Rumai, Shwe (Palaung), Riang, Yinchai, Danau, Perauk (Wa), Vo (Wa), Blang, Samtao, Thai Loi

The majority of the inhabitants of Burma speak languages belonging to the Sino-Tibetan family of languages. Of particular importance are the languages of the Tibeto-Burman phyla or subfamily. Tibeto-Burman is divided into five groups of languages: Baric, Bodic, Burmese-Lolo, Nungish, and Karen. All except Bodic are represented in Burma. The inclusion of Karen in the Sino-Tibetan family is a controversial subject among linguists. The Karen can be traced back to a region of southern Shan State and Kayah State, but where they came from before this is uncertain. Modern Karen languages also have many affinities with the Tai languages.

Speakers of the Nungish group of languages in Burma are located in Kachin State of northeastern Burma. These people also live across the Chinese border, where the Salween River becomes the Nu river. The language of most Nungish speakers in Burma is **Rawang** (also known as Nung or Nung Rawang). Rawang has between seventy-five and one hundred dialects in all, many of which are quite distinct. Mutwang is the central dialect. A language known as **Nung** (or Lutzu or Lutze) is similar to Rawang and another related language is **Norra**, spoken by a few thousand people near the border with Tibet. There are a small number of **Lama** speakers. Lama may be a separate language, but might also be a dialect of Norra.

The Baric group of languages is divided into five subgroups: Kachinic, Konyak-Bodo-Garo, Kuki-Naga, Luish, and Mirish. The Konyak-Bodo-Garo and Mirish languages are not found in Burma. There are two Kachinic languages spoken in Burma: Jingpho and Taman. These languages are spoken in Kachin State and those speaking them are some-times referred to as **Kachin**. There are over half a million **Jingpho** speakers in Burma and only a few thousand **Taman** speakers.

The Luish subgroup includes the **Kado** language and **Ganaan**. Ganaan is commonly identified as a dialect of Kado, but may be a separate language. There are about 150,000 Kado-Ganaan speakers in Burma.

The Kuki-Naga subgroup is perhaps the most diverse in mainland Southeast Asia. It is further subdivided into: Naga, Mru, Mikir-Meithei, and Kuki-Chin languages, and in all contains fifty-eight languages Speakers of these languages are located in Burma, straddling its western border from north to south, and further to the west in India and Bangladesh. There are seventeen **Naga** languages, but the majority of these are to be found across the border in India where most Naga speakers live. In Burma, most Naga-speakers live in the hills to the east of the Indian state of Nagaland. It is difficult to assess the linguistic situation of the Naga in Burma. The number of speakers is not large, but precise figures are not available. Among the Naga-speakers found in Burma are **Tangkhul**, **Yimchungru**, **Khiamnungan** (also known as Kalyo-Kengyu), and **Tase** (also known as Rangpan, a subgroup of the **Konyak** Naga). There are likely others as well.

Meithei (or Manipuri) is spoken by a large number of people in India, primarily in Manipur State, and in Bangladesh. It is also spoken by several thousand people across the border in Burma. **Mru** is spoken by several thousand people in the Arakan Hills of Burma as well as across the border in the Chittagong Hills of Bangladesh and in neighboring parts of India. The Mru live in close proximity to many Chin speakers.

The thirty-five **Kuki-Chin** languages are subdivided into Northern, Western, Central, Southern, Old Kuki, and Lepcha. These languages are found in the Chin Hills and Arakan Hills of western Burma, especially in Chin State, and in adjacent areas of India and Bangladesh. There are over 800,000 speakers of twenty-seven Kuki-Chin languages in Burma. These include languages categorized as Old Kuki, Central Chin, Northern Chin, and Southern Chin. Among the languages most widely spoken are: **Falam, Haka, Khumi, Mün** (or **Chinbok**), **Tedim**, and **Zotung**. Among the

Michael C. Howard

Kuki-Chin languages with large numbers of speakers in India and Bangladesh, but relatively small numbers in Burma, are **Paite**, **Thado**, and **Lushai**.

Speakers of the Burmese-Lolo group of languages are located primarily in China and Burma with some in northern Thailand, Laos, and Vietnam. They are divided into two subgroups: Burmish and Lolo. The Burmish subgroup is divided into northern and southern languages. The southern Burmish languages include Burmese, the most widely spoken language in Burma. In 1986 it was spoken by 21.5 million people which represented about 58% of the population of Burma. It is also the second language of many other people in Burma. In addition to standard Burmese there are a variety of important dialects such as Merguese, Yaw, Danu, Palaw, and Tavoyan. Chaungtha is probably best classified as a dialect of Burmese. Other related southern Burmish languages are: Arakanese (found mainly in Rakhine State, and a large number of speakers in Bangladesh), **Intha** (found in southern Shan State around Inle Lake), **Taungyo** (also sometimes called Tavoyan; speakers are found from Taunggyi in Shan State south to Tavoy), and Yangbye. The northern Burmish language are found in Kachin State and in adjacent parts of China, where most are included in the Jingpo nationality. They include: **Achang** (spoken by only a few people in Burma), **Atsi** (several thousand speakers in Burma), **Hpon** (a small number of speakers in Burma), **Lashi** (about 60,000 speakers in Burma), and **Maru** (about 100,000 speakers in Burma).

There are about twenty-six Lolo languages. Only seven of these are found in Burma: Akha, Hani, Lahu, Lahu Shi, Lisu, Pyen, and Sansu. There are very small numbers of **Hani**, **Pyen**, and **Sansu** speakers in Burma (but substantially more of the first two in China). There are a total of about 400,000 **Akha** speakers in Burma, China, Thailand, and Laos. About half of these live in Burma, mainly in the eastern part of Kengtung district in Shan State. There are as many as 90,000 **Lahu** (or Muhsö) speakers in Burma in the Kengtung district of Shan State. There are also a large number in China and some in Thailand, Laos, and Vietnam. Among the dialects of Lahu are: Lahu Na (Black Lahu), Lahu Nyi (Red Lahu), and Shehleh. **Lahu Shi** (or Yellow Lahu) is a distinct language. Several thousand Lahu Shi speakers live in Burma's Kengtung district as well as some in China and Thailand. Around 130,000 **Lisu** speakers are scattered across northern Burma and a larger number in China. There are a small number of Lisu in northern Thailand. Dialects of Lisu include Hwa Lisu (Flowery Lisu), Black Lisu, White Lisu, and Lu Shi Lisu.

There are over 3.5 million **Karen** speakers in Burma. They live in the hills along the eastern border with Thailand as well as in the lowlands of the Irrawaddy delta. The Karen group of languages are divided into two subgroups: Sgaw-Bghai and Pho. The Sgaw-Bghai subgroup includes **Brek**, **Bwe**, **Geba**, **Geko**, **Lahta**, **Padaung**, **Paku**, **Sgaw**, **Western Kayah** (also known as **Karennyi**, Karreni or **Red Karen**), and **Yinbaw**. Sgaw is spoken by about 1.3 million people in Burma and another 300,000 in Thailand. Western Kayah is spoken by over 200,000 people. The other languages in this subgroup are spoken by as few as several hundred to as many as several thousands. The Pho subgroup includes the **Pao** and **Pwo** languages in Burma and a few other languages in Thailand. There are about 560,000 Pao (also known as Taungthu or **Black Karen**) speakers in Burma and a small number in Thailand. There are over 1.2 million Pwo (also known as Pho Karen or **White Karen**) in Burma. There are four additional Karen languages that have yet to be classified by linguists as belonging to particular subgroups: **Manumanaw**, **Wewaw**, **Yintale**, and **Zayein**. There are only a few thousand speakers of these languages.

Tibeto-Burman Languages in Burma

Nungish: Rawang (Nung), Nung, Lama, Norra
Baric: Jingpho (Kachin), Lashi, Taman
Kuki-Naga: Khiamnungan (Naga), Tase (Naga), Mru, Meithei; Kuki-Chin: Anal, Asho, Bawm, Chinbon, Cho, Falam, Gangte, Haka, Hrangkhol, Khumi, Khumi Awa, Lushai, Mara, Mindat, Mün, Paite, Purum, Ralte, Senthang, Siyin, Tawr, Tedim, Thado, Yos, Zome, Zotung
Luish: Kado

Burmish: Achang, Arakanese, Atsi, Burmese, Hpon, Intha, Lashi, Maru, Taungyo, Yangbye

Lolo: Akha, Hani, Lahu, Lahu Shi, Lisu, Pyen

Karen: Brek, Bwe, Geba, Geko, Lahta, Manumanaw, Padaug, Paku, Pao, Pwo, Sgaw, Western Kayah, Wewaw, Yinbaw, Yintale, Zayein

Each of the phyla of the Austro-Tai family of languages is represented in Burma: Austronesian, Daic, and Miao-Yao. The Austronesian languages are represented by a few thousand Moken speakers along the coast and on the offshore islands of southern Burma. There are only a small number of Miao-Yao speakers in Burma. These include **Hmong Njua** (also known as Green Miao or Blue Miaò), who moved to Burma from China mainly during the early twentieth century with a group of them settling in Kengtung in 1917. Larger numbers of Hmong Njua live in Laos and Thailand and many of the Hmong Njua in Burma have subsequently moved to northern Thailand. Some time around 1900 a small number of **Mien**-speakers, also known as Yao, settled in Kengtung. There is very little documentation on the Mien in Burma.

Austro-Tai Languages in Burma

Austronesian: Moken
Miao-Yao: Hmong Njua, Mien
Daic: Khamti, Thai Khun, Lu, Shan, Thai Nua

The Daic languages are represented in Burma by five closely related southwestern Tai languages: Khamti, Thai Khun, Lu, Shan, and Thai Nua. Speakers of these languages are found largely in Shan State and to the west. **Shan** (or **Thai Yai**) is the most widely spoken of these languages. There are approximately 2.5 million Shan speakers in Burma, representing about 6% of the country's population. There are about 75,000 **Thai Nua** speakers in Burma (also known as **Chinese Shan**) and a much larger number of them in Yunnan, and there are several thousand Thai Nua speakers in northern Laos. Over 100,000 **Thai Khun** speakers live in the Kengtung valley in Shan State. They are also known as Khun Shan and are linguistically close to the Lan Na Thai of northern Thailand. There are about 200,000 **Lu** (also known as Thai Lue) in Burma living in the Kengtung district of Shan State. There are also a large number of Lu in China and in northern Thailand as well as a smaller number in northern Laos and northern Vietnam. Around 70,000 **Khamti** (or Khamti Shan) live in northwestern Burma and across the Indian border in Assam.

A Very Brief History of Burma

Lowland Burma consists largely of a region adjacent to the Irrawaddy River and to the lower reaches of the Salween River. To the west, east, and north are hills, mountains, and upland valleys. The archaeological and historical records of Burma focus on the lowland region around the Irrawaddy River. Very little is known of the early prehistory of Burma as little systematic archaeological research has been conducted relating to these years, although finds of stone tools indicate that the lowland area was occupied for many thousands of years prior to the emergence of the earliest states.

The Mon-Khmer languages split from the Viet-Muong languages between 2000BC and 1000BC and between 1500BC and 1000BC Mon-Khmer-speaking peoples identified with the Eastern Neolithic Culture were found in eastern India. Thus, sometime between 2000BC and 1000BC early Mon-Khmer speaking peoples settled in Burma, probably along its main river systems. Much later the Mon founded the Kingdom of Ramanadesa in the lower reaches of the Irrawaddy. The earliest Tibeto-Burman speakers to enter Burma appear to have been the Pyu who arrived from the eastern Himalayas and settled along the Irrawaddy around 200BC. The Pyu had come under Indian Buddhist influence by the first century AD. They developed a stratified society and built fortified towns. The Pyu were followed in the second century AD by the Mranma, ancestors of the Burmans, who also settled along the Irrawaddy. The Burmans began to build Pagan in 849.

The Mon, Pyu, and Burman kingdoms were lowland kingdoms. It was the Tai speaking Shan who established the first upland kingdom in the early

1200s, after apparently living in the Shan State area for a few centuries. Many Shan also moved into the lowlands around the present city of Mandalay and for a period exerted political influence over this lowland area. The Shan State for the most part was comprised of a group of small principalities.

The Burman Kingdom of Ava established control over much of lowland Burma during the late 1300s. During the latter part of the 1500s the Burmese had extended control over the Shan and over many neighboring peoples. For most of the next couple of centuries the Burmese controlled a state that incorporated most of what is today lowland Burma as well as some upland areas. In addition, several important neighboring areas, such as Shan State, were vassals of the Burmese. Burmese control, however, was constantly challenged by the Mon, Shan, and others.

Burma was the first country in mainland Southeast Asia to experience European conquest. Burmese expansion into Manipur in 1813 and Assam in 1820 brought the Burmese into conflict with the British. The first Anglo-Burman War (1824-26) resulted in the Burmese giving Assam, Manipur, Arakan, and Tenasserim to the British. Following further conflict, the British annexed the Irrawaddy delta region in 1862 and formed an administrative unit known as Lower Burma. This was of little direct relevance to the upland areas and primarily influenced lowland-dwelling Burmese, Mon, and Arakanese. Following a third war, the Burmese king was deposed by the British in 1885 and Upper Burma, as it was called by the British, was annexed in 1886. Some Burmese resistance continued until 1891.

With the annexation of Upper Burma the British set about to establish some form of administrative control over the upland peoples who had been loosely part of the Burmese kingdom. Unlike lowland Burma (sometimes referred to as "Burma Proper"), where the British established direct rule, in the upland areas (sometimes referred to as the "Frontier Areas") they tended to rely more on indirect rule. Karenni State had already come under British administration in 1875. Between 1888 and 1890 the British established an administrative presence in the Shan States. In 1892 the British recognized Sipsongpanna, the home of the Tai Lu, as Chinese territory. In 1895 the British sought to establish an administrative presence in the Chin Hills and between 1896 and 1898 did so in the Kachin Hills as well. It is important to note that the British presence in these hill areas was often very limited and some areas (such as the Wa States, large portions of Kachin State, and the southern Chin Hills) were largely outside of British administrative control for at least another couple of decades. In fact, many Naga and Wa were never brought under effective British rule. In addition, the Shan rulers of Shan State and Karenni State were allowed to function under a system of indirect rule.

Much of Burma was occupied by the Japanese during the Second World War. During the war many of the hill tribes resisted the Japanese, with British support. Following the granting of independence in 1948, there were serious divisions between the Burmese majority, keen on creating a relatively unified independent state largely under their control, and the non-Burmese minorities, who favored a less unified state in which they were granted considerable autonomy. This soon resulted in an outbreak of conflict between some minority groups and the central government. Among those active in their opposition to the central government were the Arakanese, Karen, Karenni (Western Kayah), Mon, Kachin, Shan, and Wa. Among the Chin opposition developed only to a very limited extent.

The military overthrew the elected government in 1962 and imposed a form of isolationist socialism that greatly reduced the country's contacts with the outside world. During the years that followed the country's economy declined and ethnic conflicts persisted. Following anti-government demonstrations in 1988, a new military-dominated government was formed. Since 1988 agreements have been reached by the government to end hostilities with some ethnic groups, but fighting continues with others. There have also been economic reforms that have resulted in at least some openness in the economy.

Previous Studies of Burma's Hill Tribes and Their Textiles

The existing literature on the textiles of Burma's hill tribes is relatively sparse. This is especially evident when compared with writings on the textiles of ethnic minorities in other Southeast Asian countries. Moreover, because of the political situation in Burma, most of what had been written dates from the early 1960s or before. Literature on the textiles of Burma dating from the 1960s focused on lowland textiles.

The initial ethnographic writing on the hill tribes of Burma is comprised of works by a handful of government colonial officers and Christian missionaries. Even works of this nature, however, are relatively scarce. Reginald Hugh Dorman-Smith, Governor of Burma around the time of the Second World War, remarked on the lack of literature on the hill tribes and notes that, for the most part, information on these peoples is "locked away in the minds of those devoted Frontier Service Officers who have lived their lives among the hill tribes" (Stevenson 1968: foreword). Unfortunately, few of these colonial officers ever published detailed accounts of what they knew. Moreover, after the war, when there was potentially greater scope for systematic research by anthropologists among the hill tribes, few anthropologists availed themselves of this opportunity, and after 1962 the country was effectively closed to such research.

Unsettled conditions in the frontier areas between lowland Burma and neighboring India, China, and Siam in the nineteenth century severely limited the scope for systematic observation of the hill tribes. The accounts that we have from this period are associated with expeditions that tend to have military overtones. Among these are accounts by John Anderson (1871, 1876) of his travels in northern Burma and Yunnan that contain occasional mention of the dress of the different peoples he encountered. Another is a study of the Karen within the area of British administration in the 1860s by the deputy commissioner in charge of Toungoo District, Lt.-Col. A.R. McMahon (1876). By and large, these accounts contain only very limited descriptive information on dress.

As British administration spread, efforts were made to provide systematic surveys of the peoples inhabiting or adjacent to the areas under British rule. The most important of these works in regard to the hill tribes were a series of government published gazetteers and handbooks. The first of these was the *British Burma Gazetteer,* compiled by H.R. Spearman, published in 1880. While most of the information contained in this gazetteer is on the lowlands, there are some useful passages on the dress of hill-dwelling peoples. Of more relevance are gazetteers dealing with specific regions, especially the *Gazetteer of Upper Burma and Shan States,* compiled by James George Scott and J.P. Hardiman published in 1900. This work delineates the different ethnolinguistic groups within the area they cover and includes brief descriptions of the costumes of many of these groups. Such material is presented in revised form in James George Scott's, *Burma: A Handbook of Practical Information.* This handbook, first published in 1911, became the standard reference work on Burma, and was subsequently republished in revised editions. It provides surveys of ethnolinguistic groups with attention to their costumes and includes photographs of people representing the major groups. The descriptions of dress included in these works, while useful, are relatively brief and contain little information on the sociocultural uses or economic aspects of textiles. Mention should also be made of W.J.S. Carrapiett of the Frontier Service of Burma, who wrote *The Kachin Tribes of Burma* (1929). This work contains a few passages relating to Jingpho dress.

Christian missionaries, mainly American Baptists, were active among the hill tribes of Burma from the nineteen century and have left us the most informative ethnographic accounts from the pre-war period. The American Baptist Mission to Burma began work in 1813 and by 1925 the number of Baptist missionaries in the country had grown to 220. During the Second World War most missionaries were forced to leave. They returned in smaller numbers after the war, but were soon forced to leave again. The last one departed Burma in 1960. They left behind some 250,000 Burmese Baptists. A list of Baptist missionaries contributing textiles to the Denison University collection (*Burmese Art Newsletter* 1969: 2-3) provides an indication of the relevant hill peoples among whom the Baptists worked. The locales listed where the Baptist missionaries were stationed includes: Bhamo, Maymyo, Sandoway, Thayetmyo, Bassein, Toungoo, Haka, Tiddim, Kengtung, Namkham, and Kalaw. The ethnolinguistic groups among whom they worked include the Haka and Tiddim Chin, various Karen, Tai speakers, and others in the Kengtung area.

Only a few Baptist missionaries provided written descriptions of textiles and their use. An important early twentieth century study of the Karen is that of American Baptist missionary Rev. Harry Ignatius Marshall. His 1922 monograph, *The Karen People of Burma: A Study in Anthropology and Ethnology,* provides the most detailed description written of Karen dress in Burma. Another Baptist missionary, O. Hanson, wrote an important monograph on the Jingpho, *The Kachins: Their Customs and Traditions,* published in 1913. Unfortunately, Hanson's work provides only a very basic description of Jingpho dress.

There were also Catholic missionaries, but they published little on the costumes of the hill tribes. Charles Gilhodes was a Roman Catholic missionary who lived among the Gauri Jingpho for many years during the early part of the century. His 1922 monograph, *The Kachins: Religion and Customs,* focused on Jingpho religion and provides only passing mention of the people's dress (see pages 111-114).

Quite a few travel accounts were published during the period of British rule, although only a handful of these provide significant information on the hill tribes. Prince Henri d'Orléans, in his *From Tonkin to India by the Sources of the Irawadi, January '95-January '96* (1898), provides some useful information on the peoples of northern Burma. Probably the most relevant of these travel accounts are those by Captain F. Kingdon Ward. While concerned primarily with botany, Ward also recorded useful information on the hill tribes of northern Burma. The most significant of his works in this respect are *In Farthest Burma: The Record of an Arduous Journey of Exploration and Research Through the Unknown Frontier Territory of Burma and Tibet* (1921) and *From China to Hkamti Long* (1924). In these works, Ward reports scraps of information about the various groups of Lisu, Jingpho, Nung, Maru, and Khamti with whom he came into contact.

There are only three modern anthropological works of relevance to the present subject: two on the Chin and one on the Kachin or Jingpho. While modern anthropology led to a vast improvement in the recording and analysis of many aspect of the lives of Burma's hill tribes in general, it tended to pay less attention to material culture than had previ-

ous studies and, as a consequence, to the role of items of material culture in the overall lives of people. This was in part a reaction to the perceived over-emphasis on material culture by earlier ethnographers. Interest in material culture has grown considerably among anthropologists over the past decade, but the inability to conduct fieldwork in Burma has meant effectively that study of the material culture of Burma has not been a part of this new trend. Thus, the three works in question, while very good anthropological studies, are of limited use for the study of textiles.

Modern anthropology in Burma can be said to have begun with the publication of H.N.C. Stevenson's *The Economics of the Central Chin Tribes* in 1943. Stevenson served as a Frontier Service Officer in the Falam Subdivision during the 1930s and 1940s and produced his monograph as a contribution to applied anthropology influenced by anthropologists at the University of London such as Bronislaw Malinowski, Raymond Firth, and Lucy Mair. Unfortunately, while the manuscript was saved, the author lost his field notes when the Japanese overran his home. The monograph is devoted mainly to such economic aspects of Chin life as agricultural production, animal husbandry, and land tenure, but throughout there are scattered bits of useful information on trade in textiles and their use on ceremonial occasions.

The second work is E.R. Leach's anthropological classic, *Political Systems of Highland Burma,* published in 1954. This is the only anthropological study of Burma that anthropologists not specializing in mainland Southeast Asia are likely to have read, since it has assumed importance as a theoretical work within anthropology. Leach changed careers to study anthropology at the London School of Economics in the mid-1930s. He began fieldwork in Kachin State just before the start of the Second World War. When war broke out he joined with various irregular military units in Burma. During the war he also lost his field notes, but was able to assemble sufficient material after the war to complete his Ph.D. thesis, which formed the basis for the monograph on political systems in northern Burma. In his work, Leach argued that the complex ethnolinguistic setting in highland Burma should be seen as part of a comprehensive system that was full of inconsistencies, rather than as being divided into tribal units. The work contains a number of passing references to dress, but no detailed discussion of the relevance of dress to identity or other aspects of sociocultural life. Leach moved from the London School of Economics to Cambridge University in 1953 and his fieldwork interests shifted to Sri Lanka.

The third work is F.K. Lehman's *The Structure of Chin Society: A Tribal People of Burma Adapted to a Non-Western Civilization,* published in 1963. Lehman's fieldwork among the Chin, conducted in the latter part of the 1950s and early 1960s, while not focusing on Chin material culture, does provide important background material on Chin society that complements the earlier work of Stevenson. Especially important in this regard is Lehman's material on the Southern Chin. Lehman's monograph contains several useful photos of Southern and Northern Chin that illustrate their dress and there are a number of passages that deal with clothing styles and trade in cloth. His discussion about Ng'men, M'Kang, and Daai cultural differences in particular includes attention to clothing and possibly the only published reference to the Southern Chin man's sitting cloth (1962: 84).

Mention should also be made of a number of other works describing Burma hill tribe textiles. The most relevant of these are catalogues of textiles from Burma in the collections of The Bankfield Museum in the United Kingdom and The Ethnografiska Museet in Sweden, as elaborated on below. The Bankfield collection is featured in the catalogues by Laura Start (1917) and R.A. Innes (1957). The Ethnografiska Museet collection is described in Henny Hansen's (1960) catalogue. These works focus on technical descriptions of pieces in these collections, which come mostly from Shan and Kachin States, rather than the broader ethnographic aspects. Two recent books by Sylvia Fraser-Lu contain two chapters on the textiles of Burma (1988: 84-103; 1994: 252-277). Both focus on lowland textiles, but also include brief descriptions of hill tribe textiles.

Collections of Textiles from Burma

In addition to a handful of museum collections of textiles in Burma itself, there are a few noteworthy collections of hill tribe textiles from Burma in

Europe and North America. The latter collections reflect colonial and missionary activities: Britain's colonial rule and American Baptist missionary work among certain hill tribes. Within Burma the museum collection of most relevance is that of the Shan State Museum in Taunggyi.

There are three good collections of textiles from Burma's hill tribes in the United Kingdom. The first of these is at The Bankfield Museum in Halifax (east of Manchester). Descriptions of many of the older pieces in this collection are included in Start (1917) and Innes (1957). The core group of textiles is included in the George Collection. This is a group of textiles collected by Mr. E.C.S. George during the late nineteenth century when he was employed by the commission responsible for delineation of the boundary between Burma and China. This collection includes textiles from the Taungyo, Riang (Yang Lam or Black Karen), Lahu Nyi (Muhso or Red Lahu), Lu, Shan, Akha, Thai Nua (Chinese Shan), and Jingpho (Kachin). The museum also has a collection of Naga textiles from India.

The second significant collection in the United Kingdom is that of Oxford University's Pitt Rivers Museum (see Dudley 1996 for an overview of the museum's collection of materials from Burma in general). The museum has about seventy-eight textiles from Burma in its collection. Eighteen of these pieces are unidentified as to ethnic group. There are thirteen Jingpho, eleven Burman, eleven Shan, ten Karen, seven Shan, seven Chin (mostly Khumi), four Nung, two Intha, one Maru, and one Kayah textiles in the collection. Twenty-one of the textiles in the collection are bags. Many of the oldest items were donated by military officers who served in Burma. The oldest pieces in the collection are a coat and cape of royal origin obtained by Lt. F. Abbott after the Battle of Rangoon in 1824. There are several textiles from the Chin Hills donated to the museum by Captain Hastings in 1892 and Colonel L.W. Shakespear in 1923. A number of the pieces from northern Burma (Nung, Maru, Jingpho) were collected by Col. James Green of the Burma Rifles in the 1920s and donated to the museum in 1934. The museum also has an extensive collection of Naga textiles from India.

The third noteworthy collection is at The Brighton Museum. This is contained in the Burma Rifles

Collection. These are pieces collected by Col. James Henry Green of the Burma Rifles during recruiting tours and expeditions to northern Burma during the 1920s. The collection includes twenty-seven bags and a number of Burman, Shan, and northern hill tribe costumes. In addition to textiles, Col. Green's collection include around 1,500 photographs (there is also an unpublished manuscript by Green).

In the United Kingdom additional textiles from Burma are to be found in the collections of The Gulbenkian Museum of the University of Durham, The Horniman Museum and Library in London, The Victoria and Albert Museum in London, and The Ashmolean Museum in Oxford.

Elsewhere in Europe the only other important collection of textiles from Burma is that of the Ethnografiska Museet in Gothenburg, Sweden. Henny Harald Hansen (1960) provides detailed descriptions of many of the sixty-seven textiles from Burma in the collection, but with relatively little background information. The core of this collection is a group of textiles obtained by Ebba and René Malaise in Shan State in 1934. There are textiles in this collection from the Jingpho, Maru, Lisu, Riang, Intha, Taungyo, and five Karen groups (Sgaw, Pa'o, Western Kayah, Zayein, and Padaung). The museum's displays illustrated in Hansen include several mannequins wearing costumes. There are a few textiles from Burma in the collections of the Museum für Völkerkunde in Basel, Switzerland, and in the Musée de l'Homme in Paris, France.

The largest museum collection of textiles from Burma is to be found at Denison University in Granville, Ohio. Denison University has a history of association with the Baptist Church and its collection reflects extensive missionary activity among the hill tribes in Burma by Baptists from the mid-nineteenth century until the early 1960s. There are over four hundred textiles from Burma in the collection, which includes a large number of Karen pieces, as well as Arakanese, Chin, Jingpho, Mon, Naga, Shan, Wa, and Taungyo textiles. The Wa and Naga pieces are especially noteworthy, since pieces from these two groups are rarely encountered in museum collections. There are also a number of lowland Burmese textiles in the collection.

There are two other important collections of textiles from Burma in the United States. The first of

these is in The American Museum of Natural History in New York. The museum's collection includes ninety-five textiles from Burma. Among these is a small group collected by an American missionary around 1900, several pieces collected by Vernay Hopwood in 1935 in conjunction with an American Museum of Natural History Expedition to Burma, a group obtained from a Mrs. G.E. Blackwell in 1963, another group from a 1958 Burma American Institute exchange, and several pieces obtained from the American anthropologist F.K. Lehman. There are twenty-seven Chin textiles (generally the specific group is not distinguished), twenty-five Karen textiles (Pwo Karen, Sgaw Karen, Paku Karen, and Bwe Karen), six Jingpho (Kachin) textiles, six textiles from Shan State (variour Tai groups), two Naga textiles, and twenty-seven textiles with no specific group identification (some of these are Burmese).

1.1. Display of textiles from Shan State in Bankfield Museum, Halifax, United Kingdom
[photo by author]

The other collection of note in the United States is that of The Field Museum of Natural History in Chicago. The museum's collection includes thirty-five textiles from Burma. There are twelve Karen textiles in the collection (many obtained in 1962 from the same Mrs. Blackwell mentioned above). These includes examples from the Western Kayah or Red Karen, Paku Karen, Bwe Karen, and Sgaw Karen. There are two Jingpho textiles also obtained from Mrs. Blackwell. Four especially interesting pieces from Shan State collected by Alleyne Ireland, a British official, around the turn of the century, were sold to the museum in 1905. There are four Burmese textiles, including one piece given to the museum in the 1960s by Capt. A.W. Fuller and said to have been collected during the first half of the nineteenth century by William Pitt Amherest (who died in 1857) .

Additional small American collections of textiles from Burma are to be found in Harvard University's Peabody Museum (Cambridge, MA), the Smithsonian Institution's National Museum of Natural History (Washington, DC), The Textiles Museum (Washington, DC), The Metropolitan Museum of Design (New York), and The Metropolitan Museum of Art (New York).

Finally, there are also a few textiles from Burma in collections of the Museum for Textiles in Toronto (Ontario, Canada), the National Gallery of Australia (Canberra), and the Art Gallery of South Australia (Adelaide).

An Overview of Burma's Hill Tribe Textiles

The traditional textiles of highland Burma reflect the region's cultural diversity, adaptations to differing environments, and varying external influences. This section presents a general picture of the types of materials used, techniques of producing and dyeing cloth, and types of clothing made in the mountain regions.

Traditional Materials

Barkcloth. Barkcloth use is undoubtedly of great antiquity in Burma. Unfortunately, reports of its use are few, and there appear to be no examples in museum collections. Parry (1932: 31-32) mentions a report of some isolated Mara wearing barkcloth

and Bernatzik (1947: 418) reports barkcloth making among the Akha. The only detailed description we have of barkcloth among peoples associated with Burma is one by Fürer-Haimendorf (1969: 13) of the Konyak Naga of Thendu in Nagaland (see the section on the Naga in chapter 4).

Grasses. Wild grasses are reported to have been used for the manufacture of clothing among a few groups. Konyak Naga women are known to have worn skirts made of dried grass. The Matu Chin (and perhaps other Southern Chin) made woven cloth from wild flax. Rowney (1882: 173) reports Naga women weaving cloth made of "nettle fibres."

Hemp. Hemp (*Cannabis sativa*) appears to be a fiber of greater antiquity than cotton in the area and may have once been much more widely used than reported over the past century or so. Hemp can be grown at higher altitudes than cotton and thus more easily obtained by those living at heights above those where cotton can be grown (Adams 1974: 54). During the twentieth century hemp has been used in clothing manufacture by only a few of the more isolated uplands peoples. These include a few groups of Chin, Hmong, and Lisu. Rose and Coggin Brown (1911: 258-260) reported that hemp was once widely used among the Lisu, but by the time of their research had been replaced by cotton except for a small number of the more isolated northern groups. Among the Hmong in Burma, strips of hemp cloth are included in skirts that are otherwise made of cotton. Some groups of southern Chin used hemp to manufacture blankets and other item, of clothing.

Producing hemp cloth is a fairly time consuming process. First the stems of the plant are cut and the leaves removed. They are then dried for a few days. Once dry, the stalks are split into fine strips. Often this is done with a long thumbnail grown specifically for this purpose. The ends of the fibers are frayed, and the fibers are folded together to form a long strand. These strands are placed in boiling water which contains ashes to bleach them. The bleached strands are twisted to form yarn for weaving. The yarn is often used in the brown or brownish-white color resulting from the boiling without further dyeing, but sometimes it is dyed indigo or, rarely, another color.

Cotton. Cotton is the most important material used for making clothing among Burma's hill-dwelling peoples. The main variety of cotton found in Burma is *Gossypium herbaceum*. It is grown in lowland Burma around Mandalay and Sagaing and also in Pakokku area of central Burma. It was an important export crop to China during the eighteenth century. Cotton growing in the lowland areas went into decline in the nineteenth century as large quantities of commercial cotton cloth were imported under British commercial influence. Cotton has also long been an important crop among many of the highland peoples. In addition to growing cotton for domestic use, it was often traded with those living at even higher elevations than the growers, as well as to merchants from the lowlands. There are numerous early reports, for instance, of Karen providing cotton to Chinese traders. Upland peoples also sometimes provided cotton as tribute to rulers claiming some sort of authority over them.

The method of processing cotton is fairly uniform among highland peoples. After it is picked, the pericarp is removed and the cotton is allowed to dry in the sun for a few days. It is then put in a gin to separate the seeds and fibers. The gin usually consists of an upright wooden frame with rollers that are turned by a handle. The fiber is then pulled apart and fluffed in preparation for spinning. Spinning wheels are employed to twist the cotton fiber into yarn. The wheel is either spoked or drum-shaped and turned by a handle to rotate a mounted spindle attached by a cord. Pieces of cotton are attached to the spindle and played out as the spindle turns. The yarn is then looped around a frame to form skeins, which may be dipped into a starch solution to stiffen the yarn for ease of handling. They are then put on a swift. This is an implement with rotating arms from which thread is drawn as needed.

The British took an interest in Burma's indigenous cotton industry and market—sometimes in an effort to promote local economic growth and sometimes looking for ways to expand the sale of Britain's own cotton goods. Scott and Hardiman, in their 1900 *Gazetteer of Upper Burma and the Shan States* (1900, I/II: 363-365), provide a useful survey of cotton growing and manufacturing in Burma in the late nineteenth century by G. F. Arnold:

> …cotton is cultivated in almost every district of Upper Burma, and in about half the Lower Burma districts. In most of the latter only very little is now grown, in out-of-the-ways parts for home consumption, and the area of cultivation is yearly contracting. Since cotton goods are now imported in such large quantities in most parts, cotton-weaving has become more of a pastime than an industry… In Upper Burma the conditions are slightly different. In some districts, *e.g.,* in Meiktila and Myingyan, cotton is grown largely and exported raw to China and India; there are also more weavers, men and women alike pursuing the trade, though the imported yarn ready-dyed, is used largely in preference to the native home-spun.
>
> This, however, is not everywhere the case. It is recognized in some parts, *e.g.,* in the Mogôk district and in the Shan States, that coarser native yarn makes a cheaper and more durable material: in others, especially among the Kachins and Shans of Hsen Wi and Kengtung, there exists a national costume woven from home-grown sources, and the people wear no other. In Upper Burma also, while the physical features of the land are more favourable to cotton cultivation, there are more regions as yet only partially opened to trade and to which the journeyman clothes-seller does not penetrate with his wares. Her cotton is much grown and weaving flourishes, protected from competition, temporarily at least, by nature's barriers. . . .
>
> In Katha, the Kachins and Kadus still very generally make their own clothing. Weaving is carried out for home use only, the instruments being very rude and the method laborious. The threads made from home-grown cotton are being rapidly ousted by the common threads of European manufacture. Threads equally cheap and dyed more brilliantly can be had in nearly all the bazaars….

Scott and Hardiman (1900, I/II: 366) provide more specific information regarding cotton growing and manufacture in Shan State and indicate the extent to which indigenous cotton was being replaced by imported cotton:

> In the Southern Shan States a considerable quantity of cotton is exported in pressed bales

to Yunnan, and caravans from China, coming round with wares, collect cotton and European and Indian cotton fabrics for their return journey. ...the raw cotton is obtained from the hill villages and local bazaars.... In Kengtung State cotton is grown almost exclusively by the hill tribes. They make their clothes of it and sell their surplus to the Shans of the villages and to the Chinese caravans.

In Shan villages nearly every house has a loom, and the women clean, dye, spin, and weave their own cotton. The hill-people, the Shans of the more remote villages, and generally the poorer sort still wear clothing of home manufacture. There can be no doubt, however, as to the popularity of the finer imported stuff.

In Kengtung State tribal custom prescribes a certain style of dress and especially the women have a distinctive costume, as have also the Shan-Chinese community and the Lu men and women. Such dresses are now home-spun, but custom will only delay, not prevent, the use of imported fabrics as soon as traders can sell them at a less cost.

Already the people of the Kengtung valley have adopted imported stuff for turbans, and the Lu women freely use imported fabrics for their jackets, after dyeing them to their own taste. So far the Shan-Chinese have adhered to their home-spun but this is due as much to economy as to conservatism....

In the Hsi Paw State the villages on the main road used to weave their cloth, but now most people buy cotton goods which come up from below. There was formerly a fine sort of *hpyin* manufactured for making jackets and *thingans,* but now that finer cloth can easily be obtained in every bazaar, only the coarse *hpyin* is woven. There is a considerable amount of cotton cultivation around Lashio, but clothes are often made from imported calico of Manchester manufacture, and the cotton yarn used for weaving is not always locally produced.

The Palaungs of Tawng Peng Loi Long buy their threads already dyed from the hawkers, or traders, or in a bazaar. Imported fabrics have certainly reduced the amount of weaving done, and as the country becomes civilized the weaving will still further decrease. The locally-made cloth being infinitely more durable, it is cheaper to wear clothes made from it, but the richer Palaungs of Nam San and the surrounding villages that are nearer civilization prefer something finer in appearance. It is only amongst the poorer classes that weaving is now done.

The extent of replacement of indigenous cotton by imported cotton is further highlighted in a report from the Deputy Commissioner of Bhamo (Scott and Hardiman 1900, I/II: 366):

> The cotton-manufacturing industry is now passing out of the primitive phase where every household manufactured its own garments and cloths from the crop grown on its own piece of ground. This state of affairs was general in the Bhamo district only fifteen years ago, and, in the hills, the Kachins, and, to a lesser extent, the Shans, are still in the same stage of development. In Bhamo itself, there are few indications left of this condition of things.

Silk. Silk cultivation has never been widespread in Burma and imported silk thread or cloth is often used. A cultural constraint on the production of silk is the Buddhist prohibition against taking life, and some Buddhists in Burma formerly obtained their raw silk from neighboring animists. Silk is used among the upland Burmish-speaking Intha and Taungyo for certain types of clothing, but they do not produce their own silk and must obtain it through trade. Silk is also used among the Shan and other Tai groups for some items of clothing, especially among elites. Among the items in which silk is used by Tai speakers are Shan bags and skirts and Lu turbans. Again, these groups do not produce their own silk, but obtain it through trade. The Shan in particular traditionally obtained silk from the Riang, who produced silk for commercial purposes, but whose own clothing was made of home-spun cotton. Among the Chin, silk is primarily known among the Haka, but it is also used among other Chin groups such as the Mara. A little silk is produced among the Chin, but most is obtained through trade with the lowlands. The Jingpho sometimes use small amounts of silk thread in their cloth.

1.2. Burmese spinning wheel [Scott and Hardiman 1900, I/II: fig. V, f.pg. 368]

1.3. Cotton caravan at Saó-mao near the China-Myanmar border [Davies 1909: f.pg. 98]

1.4. Karen woman weaving on a backstrap loom [Marshall 1922: 114]

This silk is also acquired through trade. Some groups of Karen embroider silk thread into their cotton clothing, including the Bwe, Geko, and Kayah. They too obtain their silk through trade with the lowlands.

Metallic Threads. Metallic threads of gold and silver (or other metals made to look like gold or silver) are widely used to decorate traditional ceremonial silk clothing throughout Southeast Asia, especially where Indian influence is evident. In the past metallic threads were made by winding thin strands of gold or silver around a fine silk thread. For the past century, threads generally have been made entirely of a strand of metal (initially imported from Europe). In Burma, such textiles are associated almost entirely with lowland peoples, although upland elites sometimes wore clothing made of such elaborate cloth which was obtained through trade. Among the upland Burmish and Tai peoples, in particular, small amounts of metallic thread were sometimes used in clothing and on shoulder bags used by those of the more common classes.

Dyes

A wide range of materials were used in the past by weavers in Burma to produce natural dyes and, fortunately, there are several good surveys of these dyes dating from the late nineteenth century. Scott and Hardiman (1900: I/II: 377-399) provide a very useful survey of natural dyes used in Burma based on a monograph prepared by J.D. Fraser in 1896 on Burmese natural dyes. Accounts by H.G.A. Leveson on dyes in the Shan states and T. Giles on dyeing practices of the Kayah (or Karenni). Spearman (1880) also provides a lists of over thirty local plants used in southern Burma for dyes. Fraser's survey provides a list of seventy-four barks, woods, and other items used in making natural dyes. A few of the more common dyes are described below.

Indigo. This is easily the most widely used dye among the hill-dwelling peoples of Burma and is used to produce a dark blue color. Among the lowland peoples the cultivation and use of indigenous indigo was in decline by the latter part of the nineteenth century and was being replaced by indigo imported from Bengal (Scott and Hardiman 1900, I/II: 378). Nabholz-Kartaschoff

(1985: 156, 158) discusses the use of *Indigofera tinctoria* and *Strobilanthes flaccidifolius.* for indigo dyeing among the Akha. Shakespear (1880: 30-31) describes the use of *Strobilanthes flaccidifolius.* for indigo dyeing among the Angami Naga in India and this plant is also used for indigo cloth among the Naga in Burma.

Lac. Lac produces a red color. Its source is a deposit left by an insect (*Coccus lacca*) on the branches of certain trees. Sticks of the deposit are removed, dried, and made into powder. The powder is placed in a basket, and water is poured into the basket and allowed to drain into a container. This water serves as the dye into which cloth is placed.

Jackfruit. Chipped wood of the jackfruit tree (*Articarpus integrifolia L.*) is used to produce yellow. This dye is for the robes of Buddhist monks.

Betel nut tree. Wood chips from the betel nut tree (*Areca catechu*) are boiled in water to produce a brown color.

Leveson comments that indigo and lac are the only dyes produced in the Shan states in relatively large quantities (Scott and Hardiman 1900, I/II: 394) and notes that most dyes are found in the wild rather than being produced from domestic sources. Indigo is commonly grown in people's gardens while the Kayah alone seek to stimulate the production of lac artificially by grafting the insects on to appropriate trees (Scott and Hardiman 1900, I/II: 393-394).

Fraser's 1896 report opens with a comment on the spread of aniline dyes among Burmese weavers (Scott and Hardiman (1900, I/II: 377):

> The colours, for the most part very pure and beautiful, are combined by the weavers with the most harmonious effect. Bright or gaudy colour is used sparingly and then only to produce the contrast which may be necessary. Unfortunately native dyes are being rapidly ousted by the common aniline dyes of European manufacture, which give a bright and gaudy colour, instead of the subdued and artistic tones obtained from native ingredients. Besides the meretricious results most of the aniline colours give they have not the important merit of permanence, but fade rapidly when exposed to the sun... In Mandalay, the headquarters of the silk-

weaving industry, aniline dyes have displaced all except three or fours sorts of Burmese dyestuffs.... Dying with other indigenous products is still carried on in out-of-the-way parts, but usually only for domestic use.

Gradually in the twentieth century such aniline dyes have replaced most natural dyes among many of the hill-dwelling peoples as well. Modern aniline dyes are often viewed as being easier to prepare, able to provide more predictable results, and better able to resist sunlight and washing than local natural dyes. Many weavers also purchase pre-dyed threads that employ aniline dyes. The results, as noted by Sylvia Lu (1988: 31), tend to be "harsh and jarring" since, as she notes, "being relatively new to chemical dyes, many dyers in South-East Asia have not yet acquired consummate skill in mixing and blending these powerful agents to get a range of rich subtle shades."

Looms

Several of the hill-dwelling peoples in Burma employ body-tension or backstrap looms. The simplest form of such a loom has a continuous warp with one end supported by the weaver's feet. This type of backstrap loom does not, however, appear to have been used in Burma. A more complex type of backstrap loom employs a continuous warp that is attached to some fixture, such as a wall or a tree. Looms of this type are used among the Naga, Jingpho, Karen, and some Chin, and may have been the original type of loom employed by most of the hill peoples. One important feature of such looms is that they restrict the possible width of a piece of cloth so that wider types of clothing, such as the shoulder cloths or blankets widely worn in the region or tubeskirts, if made on such a loom must be made of a few separate pieces of cloth sewn together.

Frame looms are also employed by some hill-dwelling peoples, although in general these are associated with lowland societies and their use can be associated with the integration of highland peoples into the dominant lowland society. The frame looms employed in the highlands are commonly of a type typically referred to as a Burmese loom. Simple versions of frame looms are

used by the Hmong Njua, Akha, and Lahu (see Lewis and Lewis 1984, Ling Roth 1918: 92, and Fraser-Lu 1988: 35-37, for descriptions of these looms). The Hmong Njua employ a backstrap loom that has some features of a frame loom.

In this loom the warp threads are wound around a beam that is supported by upright beams while the weaver sits on a bench in front of the frame with a backstrap fastened around the waist (see drawing in Fraser-Lu 1988: 35). The Akha frame loom features four two meter high posts sunk into the ground at each corner with supporting cross poles. The weaver sits inside this frame with the warp threads attached to one end of the frame. The Lahu loom is a somewhat more advanced version of the Akha loom.

Finally, band and card looms are sometimes employed among the various highlands peoples for tablet weaving. These are used for making belts or sashes and other narrow pieces of cloth.

Techniques

While much of the clothing worn by the hill peoples of Burma is plain and uniform in color (usually dark blue), a variety of decorative techniques are employed on some of the cloth and even relatively plain pieces of clothing often feature at least a few decorative embellishments. Burmese weaving sometimes employs a tapestry weave to create brightly colored patterns on skirts. This technique, however, is rarely found among highland peoples. Decorations are often made in the case of the latter's clothing through the use of embroidery, appliqué, and beading. Such techniques, for example, are used by the Akha, Lahu, Lisu, Hmong, and Mien.

Supplementary weft weaving is especially noteworthy among the Tai speaking Lu. Other Tai speakers, Jingpho, some Karen, Arakanese, and some Chin also employ supplementary weft techniques on some cloth.

Weft ikat weaving was probably introduced to Khmer weavers from India by Indian and Arab traders during the fourteenth and fifteenth centuries. Khmer weavers in turn seem to have introduced the technique later to some of the peoples currently living in Burma, such as the Intha, some Tai-speaking peoples, and some of the Sgaw Karen.

Other techniques encountered in highland textiles are the tabby weave, float weave, and satin weave.

1.5. Burmese loom
[Scott and Hardiman 1900,
I/II: fig. X, f.pg. 368]

1.6. Plains Karen woman weaving on a Burmese
type of loom. The use of such looms is common
among plains Karen [Marshall 1922: 112]

1.7. Thai Mou (Shan) woman weaving [photo by
Raynou Athamasar]

Types of Clothing

Within recent history there has been considerable variation in the patterns of dress of the various highland peoples of Burma. During the early part of the twentieth century one could still find people wearing no clothing at all as well as others wearing sumptuous regal costumes of silk and gold. Altitude and other environmental factors were not overly important, beyond the fact that cotton was difficult to obtain at higher altitudes and certain hill tribes wore blankets during the colder months, although the latter in some instances appears to be a relatively recent innovation reflecting growing outside influence rather than cold weather.

In providing a short summary of the types of clothing found among the hill tribes, it is important to note that many of these groups have different types of everyday dress and dress for special occasions. What is sometimes presented as representative clothing of a particular group are their party clothes rather than what they wear when at work or at home.

Turning first to men's clothing, the most widespread and basic traditional form of dress in the hills was a loincloth. In many instances in the past this would be all that a man would wear. The dimensions and amount of decoration of loincloths varies a good deal, ranging from very tiny plain pieces of cloth that barely cover the genitals to relatively wide lengths of cloth that are wound many times around the waist and are highly decorated at the ends. The latter tend to be worn only for special occasions, along with various other decorative items. The men of several groups traditionally wore trousers instead of loincloths. Among some Karen these are relatively short, but more common are the familiar Chinese-influenced longer bell-bottoms. Traditionally hill tribe men often went bare chested, wearing a blanket when it was cold or for special occasions to indicate the status of the wearer. There are also a variety of smocks, shirts, and jackets worn by men. Men in a few tribes also wore turbans or headcloths. Finally, shoulder bags were widely distributed throughout the region. These are sometimes relatively plain, but often are highly decorated. Such decorated bags often were gifts from girl friends or wives.

Some hill tribe women traditionally also wore loincloths, but more common were various type of wrap-around skirts or tubeskirts. Among the tribes living along the Indian border, these skirts could be quite short. Elsewhere they tended to be much longer. Everyday skirts were often rather plain, while many groups had more elaborate skirts for special occasions. In some instances women traditionally wore no blouse; but the women of many groups, at least within the past century, did wear blouses or long or short jackets, although sometimes only for special events. Women in a few groups wore smocks instead of skirts and in some cases wore trousers. Although less common than with men, women sometimes wore blankets. Other items of attire included turbans or headcloths, leggings, waist sashes or aprons, and shoulder cloths.

It is clear from early accounts of the hill peoples that the nineteenth and early twentieth centuries were periods of considerable change in patterns of dress as a result of greater external influences. In some cases this meant the adoption of forms of clothing where none had been worn before, while for many others it was a matter of adopting more elaborate forms of dress either by embellishing traditional styles of dress or by replacing relatively simple traditional dress with a more complex type adopted from others.

There have been various of external cultural influences on the dress of the hill peoples. Dress styles from neighboring lowland Indians, Chinese, and Burmese had some influence on peoples living in closest proximity to them. British influence was mainly in terms of making a wider variety of commercial cloth and dyes available which were usually incorporated into more traditional forms of dress, although some individuals adopted Western dress. Christian missionaries sometimes influenced the dress of those coming most directly under their influence in terms of notions of modesty, adoption of Western dress, or Western materials or patterns being employed in textiles. In recent years many upland people have adopted either Burmese dress or Western clothing such as T-shirts and blue jeans. Warfare related to separatist movements and drugs has also influenced dress as men in particular have come to wear military-style uniforms.

2

Upland Burmish Groups

The Upland Southern Burmish Peoples

The Southern Burmish languages include Burman, Arakanese, Intha, Taungyo, and Yangbye. The Burmese, Arakanese, and Yangbye are essentially lowland peoples, although today Burmese are to be found living throughout the country. The Burmese are of interest for the present study because of their acculturative influence on hill-dwelling peoples. In particular, their patterns of dress (see Fraser-Lu 1988: 88-92; Fraser-Lu 1994: 252-277) are widely viewed as setting national standards. Danu is a dialect of Burmese spoken by a group living in southwestern Shan State (see Scott and Hardiman 1900, I/I: 562-564; Scott 1911:69). The Intha and Taungyo also live in the southwestern corner of Shan State. The Southern Burmish peoples of relevance for the present study are the Arakaanese, Intha, and Taungyo.

Arakanese

The majority of Arakanese live in the lowlands, but some live in the upland portion of which the British referred to as the Arakan Hill Tracts. Spearman (1880, II: 64-65) refers to these hill-dwelling peoples as Rakhaing, noting that they speak a dialect of Arakan and that their cultural practices differ little from other Arakanese. He states that "their dress consists of the Arakanese waist cloth of dark home-spun cotton and a white turban…. the women wear the Arakanese petticoat which is the same as the Burmese save that it comes further round so as not to expose the leg in walking" (p. 65). Spearman seems to have little regard for

this petticoat, finding the colors "sad", the Arakanese seeming to lack an "appreciation of the harmonious blending of gorgeous colours so dear to the eastern Burman's eye" (p. 65). It is an interesting commentary on the author's own taste.

Intha

The Intha, also referred to as Ang-hsa or Dawè, live around the shores of Inle Lake (also known as Yawng Hwe Lake) in southern Shan State. The 1901 census gave their population as 5,851. Today there are around 150,000 Intha. They migrated to the area from the Tavoy region of southern Burma. According to their own accounts (Scott 1911: 68), they were brought to the Inle Lake region in 1353 by a Burmese prince to build religious structures.

Scott (1911: 68) states that both men and women dress like the Shans, but that women "wear black-lacquered string garters to show off the whiteness of the leg, which Shan belles do not think necessary." Lewis (1911: 30) comments that "the Inthas have practically adopted Shan dress and, but for their dialect and aquatic mode of life would in all probability have been looked upon as Shans; but they are undoubtedly of Burmese stock." The best known Intha textiles are the *zin me longyi*. *Zin me* is a Burmese rendering of the name Chiang Mai, the town in neighboring Thailand. It appears these textiles started to be woven only in the early part of the twentieth century. These are weft ikat patterned silk cloths produced in the village of Inpawkhon (Fraser-Lu 1988: 97). The silk thread is imported, and the cloths traditionally bore designs influenced by Cambodian and Thai textiles. Later, bird and flower patterns were introduced as was the use of metallic thread. The older cloths usually were dyed red, yellow, and green. Initially, locally produced natural dyes made from bark and seeds were used; but these came to be replaced by aniline dyes, although still using the same three colors. After two weavers were sent to northeastern Thailand in 1936 to study Thai weaving several innovations were introduced, including the use of a wider range of colors and motifs.

Taungyo

There are over 450,000 Taungyo (sometimes called Tavoyans) living as far north as Taunggyi in southwestern Shan State and to the south as far as Tavoy. Those living in Shan State migrated there from Tavoy. Scott and Hardiman (1900, I/II: 561) describe them as "pure spirit-worshippers," implying that they are not Buddhists. Their chief crop is paddy rice.

TAUNGYO WOMAN.

2.1. Taungyo woman
[Scott and Hardiman 1900, I/II: f.pg. 370]

Scott (1911: 68) states that "the men dress like Shans, and the women have a picturesque dress, suggestive of the Karen fashions." Lowis (1911: 30) describes the dress of Taungyo women as comprised of "a smock, head-dress and garters of brass wire." The so-called smock is similar to that worn by the Pao Karen, but differs in color, the Taungyo smock tending to be of a reddish color and the Pao Karen one being black (Scott and Hardiman 1900, I/II: 554).

The collection of the Ethnographical Museum in Göteborg includes two Taungyo textiles. These are described in Hansen (1960) as: (1) a woman's tubeskirt made of two different pieces of cloth sewn together, the upper portion is brown cotton and the lower portion black hemp (Ac# 35.39.399); and (2) a woman's open, draped leggings made of plain indigo-dyed cotton (Ac# 35.39.400).

The Northern Burmish Peoples

Peoples speaking Northern Burmish languages are found in Kachin State and adjacent parts of China. They include the Achang, Atsi, Hpon, Lashi, and Maru. These are all hill dwelling peoples.

Achang

There are only around 1,700 Achang in Burma, and about 27,000 of them in China living in southwestern Yunnan. The Chinese consider them an official nationality. They are also known as Maingtha or Monghsa. Their main habitant is just east of the Burmese border and in the valley of a southern tributary of the Taping river in two Shan states: Hohsa and Lahsa. This area is called Monghsha by the Shan. The Achang may be Atsi who moved to the east and fell under Shan influence. In Monghsha they formed part of the commoner population under Shan rulers. They are nominally Buddhist. The Achang work in other parts of Shan state as seasonal laborers employed as carpenters and blacksmiths.

Davies (1909: 395) comments that "to such an extent have A-ch'angs adopted the dress, customs, and Buddhism of the Shans, that they will even sometimes speak of themselves as Shans, though on closer questioning they will admit that they really belong to a distinct race." Scott and Hardiman (1900: I/I: 618) report that "the men dress like Chinese-Shans, while the women more frequently seem to wear trousers after the Chinese feminine fashion."

Contemporary Achang dress in China is described in *Ethnic Costumes and Clothing Decorations from China* (Shanghai Theatrical College 1986: 202-203):

Young men wear short blue, white or black jackets open in the central front, and black long trousers with broad legs. Under the jackets are white shirts with turned-down collars, and around the waist are belts with knives hanging from them.... On festivals, Achang men wear... long turbans of white gauze with woolen balls at one end falling from the right shoulder down to the waist and the tops decorated with red and green balls at one end falling from the right shoulder to the waist and the tops decorated with red and green balls of wool. In Husa area, most old and middle-aged men wear low-collared jackets open at the right side and long turquoise turbans around their heads.

The costumes and headresses of women vary with the age and locality. In most cases, married women wear skirts and narrow-sleeved long garments open from the central front. They wear tall and round black or blue turbans and big earrings. Some wear their turbans like basins with butterfly-like knots above the foreheads. Nowadays, most young and middle-aged women wear white jackets buttoned down the front, blue waistbelts and long trousers. With the front hem covered with blue aprons, the jackets look neat and smart....

In Husa area, women's attire includes a jacket open from the central front, long trousers and leggings. The jacket is rather short and decorated with a light-blue strip around the lower part of its sleeves. To make their headress bigger and nice-looking, they coil their braids on top of their heads first, then wrap them up with turquoise gauze of five or seven meters long, and decorate them with colourful threads, pearls and flowers.

For the lower part, they wear long trousers and leggings embroidered with various patterns. They also wear 30-centimeter-long aprons, around which are silver chains.

There are thus two different patterns of dress among the Achang in China. Unfortunately, inadequate descriptions from Burma make it difficult to determine which pattern prevails there.

Atsi

There are some 13,000 Atsi (also referred to as Zi, Szi, or Asi) in Burma and a larger number in China, where they are included in the Jingpo nationality. In Burma they live in widely dispersed villages mainly in the hills near Mogaung. The Atsi are generally hierarchically organized with recognized chiefs. Scott (1911: 70) stated that they were "very much mixed up" with the Lashi. Moreover, he notes

2.2. Achang man
[Davies 1909: f.pg. 26]

that they and the Lashi and Maru "are mixed up with pure Kachin septs, and their dress, religion, and customs are those of the Chingpaw." Carrapiett (1929: 17) quotes T.F.G. Wilson, who states that Atsi and Lashi women "wear short skirts which do not extend below the knees."

Hpon

The Hpon live in Kachin State on the Irrawaddy between Bhamo and Sinbo. The 1931 census enumerated 1,000 of them. Today there are about 1,500 Hpon in Burma, in two divisions reflected in dialects: the Hpon Hpye or Mong Ti Hpon and the Hpon Samong or Mong Wan Hpon. They practice slash-and-burn agriculture. Prior to the Second World War they were rapidly becoming like the Shan (Leach 1954: 30). Scott (Scott and Hardiman 1900, I/I: 655-569; Scott 1911: 70) briefly discusses them, but provides no description of their dress.

Lashi

There are over 60,000 Lashi in the Htawgo subdivision of Kachin State in Burma and some in China, where they are included in the Jingpo nationality. The Lashi are generally organized along egalitarian lines without recognized chiefs. As noted with reference to the Atsi, Scott (1911: 70) reports that their dress is that of the Jingpho. Also as noted above, Carrapiett (1929: 17) quotes Mr. T.F.G. Wilson, who states that Lashi and Atsi women "wear short skirts which do not extend below the knees."

Maru

Maru is a Jingpho name for these people who refer to themselves as Lawng. The Maru live in the border area between China and Burma, primarily near the 'Nmai Hka River and its tributaries. There

2.3. Maru woman. The headcloth shows that she is married [Ward 1924: f.pg. 72]

2.4. Lashi woman. Near Myitkyina, Kachin State [photo by Laura Kan]

are about 100,000 Maru in Burma's Kachin State and some in neighboring areas of China, where they are included in the Jingpo nationality. There are a number of dialects. The Lisu live in higher areas between the Maru and the China border. Most Maru groups are relatively egalitarian (following the *gumlao* pattern), but some have chiefs.

In his description of the Maru living in and around the 'Nmai Hka River valley, Ward writes (1921: 150) "the Marus down in the valley are better dressed, live in bigger huts and are better off in all respects than those higher up in the mountains." As mentioned about the Atsi, Scott (1911: 70) and Davies (1909: 397) report that the Maru dress like the Jingpho. Ward (1921) provides a description of Maru dress as well as several photos. He describes the men as wearing "a brown or blue striped kilt, like a Burmese *lone-gyi,* dyed locally with jungle dyes" (1921: 137). "As for unmarried girls...their tight skirts of white hemp cloth, home woven, reach

2.5. Maru women. Skirts are dyed dark blue and red [Ward 1924: f.pg. 52]

just below the knee, and they wear a low-necked blue cotton jacket with short sleeves, embroidered with cowrie shells, or buttons, according to the state of the market" (Ward 1921: 137-138). Young women often also wear "a cloak of native manufacture" that "is thrown over the head and hangs down behind" (Ward 1921: 150). Married women are distinguished by wearing "a sort of white turban, like a dirty pudding-cloth after a suet dumpling has been boiled in it" (Ward 1921: 152).

During the early twentieth century, Ward (1921: 136) reports that the Maru obtained Chinese clothes and other goods from the Lisu, but thought he saw relatively few such goods. He also describes a village headman "dressed like a Burman, with *in-gyi* and silk *hkoung-boung* in addition to his *lone-gyi"* (1921: 178-179).

There are a few Maru textiles in museum collections. Göteborg's Ethnographical Museum (see Hansen 1960) has three Maru textiles that were collected in 1934. They are all part of a woman's costume: (1) a woman's jacket with sleeves and collar made of black cotton with bottons; with a strip of Chinese brocade cloth attached to the bottom (Ac#35.39.270); (2) a woman's tubeskirt made of cotton with black and brown horizontal stripes (Ac# 35.39.269); and (3) a pair of tube leggings made of undyed white cotton cloth with facing made of plain blue cotton at the bottom (Ac# 35.39.271). The Pitt Rivers Museum has one Maru textile, a jacket, in its collection, donated by Col. Green in 1934 and presumably collected some time in the 1920s. It is from the Ngawchnag valley of the lower 'Nmai Hka River. The textile shows signs of being strongly influenced by the Jingpho. The upper part of the body is of handspun cotton dyed with indigo. The lower portion is made of dog's hair woven on an indigo cotton warp. The dog's hair is dyed red much like Jingpho skirts.

3

The Tai

Five closely related Tai groups are found in Burma: Khamti, Khun, Lu, Shan, and Thai Nua. These Tai live mainly in Shan State and to the west toward India. The Tai are not, strictly speaking, hill tribes like the other upland groups discussed in this book. The Tai tend to live in mid-level valleys in the mountains, where they practice terraced rice production. Traditionally they comprise small states or principalities and in some cases larger states more like the lowland Burmese, Arakanese, and Mon. The Shan, like the lowland Burmese, served over many centuries as a point of reference in respect of cultural change processes among neighboring hill tribes. Hence such hill tribes evolved from being referred to by the British as still wild to tame tribes or to losing their identity altogether. The Tai certainly do not consider themselves to be hill peoples. In these respects, therefore, the Tai, especially the Shan, should be classified alongside the lowland Burmese, Arakanese, and Mon. On the other hand, the Tai are more often closer to the hill tribes than the Burmese and other lowlanders, as the tend to live at higher altitudes. In the past non-hill people often placed the Tai alongside the hill tribes, rather than among the dominant lowland Burmese. In recent times the Shan have joined other hill tribes in opposing the Burmese-dominated central government. In the present study the various Tai groups will be included in considering hill tribe dress, although it might be more correct to classify them with Burmese and other lowlanders.

By the tenth century there were numerous Tai speaking chiefdoms located in the valleys between the Yunnan plateau and the mainland Southeast Asian lowlands. During the eleventh and twelfth centuries an increasing number of Tai speaking peoples moved into the lowland frontier areas of the Angkor and Pagan empires, where they came under the influence of Theravada Buddhism and other Indian-derived beliefs and practices. With the decline of Angkor's influence in Thailand and Pagan's influence in Burma in the thirteenth century, the Tai began to assume political prominence in these areas. The Tai-speaking peoples of Burma today are the descendants of such earlier migrants who settled in what is today northern Burma, some of whom formed states that were subsequently incorporated into Burmese and Chinese states.

The Shan

The Shan, also known as Thai Yai, form the largest group of Tai in Burma, with a population of over 2.5 million. The present Shan State within which they mainly live, used to be the former Shan states made up of a number of smaller principalities.

The Shan established the Kingdom of Mao about 1215. This polity grew out of the chiefdom of Muang Morong, that may date back to the sixth century. The Kingdom of Mao held influence over portions of southern Yunnan, northern Burma above Shwebo, and Shan State. Throughout its history the Tai Kingdom of Mao was under frequent attack from the Chinese. After driving off the Mongols towards the end of the thirteenth century, Mao was attacked again by Chinese armies in 1343. Between 1395 and 1515 they were attacked six more times by Chinese armies. Mao was finally defeated by the Chinese in 1604.

After the fall of Pagan and the expulsion of the Mongols, Tai from Mao spread into the lower areas of northern Burma and in so doing appear to have assimilated many Burmese ideas and practices. Burmanized Shans established a capital at Ava, near Mandalay, in 1364. Ava became an important

3.1. A trans-Salween Shan *sawbwa* in *hkön* dress [Scott 1906: f.pg. 147]

3.2. Shan *sawbwa* and his wife in court dress [Scott 1906: f.pg. 114]

3.3. Shan commoners of Kengtung area [Ferrars 1901: f.pg. 143]

regional power that ruled over Tai and Burmese until Ava fell to the Burmese of Toungoo in 1555.

Throughout this period there had been many small autonomous or semi-autonomous Shan principalities. After the fall of Ava and Mao, those Shan who did not fall directly under Burmese or Chinese control were divided into small principalities under the rule of local *sawbwas.* The fortunes of these principalities and the degree to which they were subject to external control, fluctuated over time. The Burmese sought to exert control over the Shan states from their administrative center at Mong Nai. The extent of this control varied, with states to the north and east generally being the most independent. During the latter part of the nineteenth century political turmoil in Burma weakened Burmese control over the Shan states and by 1885 the Burmese had been pushed out of most Shan territory by a group of allied princes. At this same time, however, the Shan suffered from aggression by Jingpho invaders from the north.

After the capture of Mandalay in 1885, the British began asserting control over neighboring Shan territories. By 1887 the Southern Shan states were securely under British influence. A military expedition visited many of the other states in 1887-88 and established British control. Following disturbances involving the Kayah (or Karenni) in 1888, a British civil officer was permanently stationed in Mong Nai. By and large, British authority was established without outright opposition. As noted by Scott and Hardiman (1900, I/II: 302): "the intention of the Government [was] to maintain order and to prevent private wars between the several States, while at the same time allowing to each Chief independence in the administration of his territory to the fullest extent compatible with the methods of civilized government...." In short, the British established a structure of indirect rule over the Shan states. The Shan states were demarcated by the British between 1887 and 1895 as follows:

I. *The Northern Shan States:* Tawng Peng, North Hsen Wi, South Hsen Wi, Hsi Paw, East and West Mang Lon, and territories east of the Salween River (the various Wa states)

II. *The Southern Shan States:* Mong Nai, Mong Pan, Lawk Sawk, Yawng Hwe, Mong Kung, Lai Hka, Mong Pawn, Mawk Mai, Mong Pai, Keng Tung, and fourteen *myozaships*

III. *The Myelat* (administered along with the Southern Shan States): one *myozaship* (Maw Nang) and fourteen *ngwekunhmuships*

IV. *States* under the supervision of the Commissioner, Northern Division: Mong Mit

V. *States* under the supervision of the Commissioner, Central Division: Hsawng Hsup, Singkaling Hkamti

Because of their history, with the formation of small states and social stratification, the Shan have a tradition of common as well as courtly dress. Most Shan clothing is made of cotton. Silk was extensively used in courtly dress and less often for special dress among commoners. Much of this silk material was imported, although some was produced locally: in "a few restricted localities in the south-east part of the Lai Hka State, in the Laklai circle of Mong Sit State, and in the south-west of the Myelat" (Scott and Hardiman 1900, I/II: 395).

Scott and Hardiman (1900, I/II: 319) describe the dress of Shan men as follows:

> Their dress is a pair of trousers and a jacket; the pattern of the trousers varies considerably. Sometimes they are practically of the Chinese pattern with well defined legs, but among the better-to-do classes the seat is frequently down about the ankles and the garment generally is so voluminous as to look more like a skirt than a pair of trousers. The turban is usually white in the north, of various colours in the south, while the Shan-Chinese wear blue....

Seidenfaden (1967: 32) describes the common dress of Shan women thus:

> The fair skinned women, who are less coquettish than their Burmese sisters, dress in skirt (the *pha sin* in North Thailand and Laos), and some use a scarf folded cross wise over the bosom, others, like the Thai Lu and Thai Khun (Chinese Tung), wear a white bodice with long and tight sleeves. In the north they wear very voluminous turbans while in the south a scarf, wrapped round the chignon, must serve as a turban. At festivals the young girls dress picturesquely in gaudy colours, pale blue jackets, and paneled skirts of every hue interwoven with gold thread.

27

Scott and Hardiman (1900, I/II: 371) also describe another type of cloth produced: "among the Shans of the Hsen Wi State some curious sleeping-mats or cloths are made. They are described as being of zig-zag or diamond shaped pattern, woven usually in black or red on a white ground, and carried out with the nicest exactness and regularity of detail." Such cloths appear to have been produced solely by the Thai Mao (see Athamasar 1997), a sub-group of Shan, but may also have been produced by other groups of Tai.

Leslie Milne (1910: 121-23) provides a description of ceremonial banners or *tung* which were made by the Shan for *thawt kathin,* lasting from mid-October to mid-November, to celebrate the ending of Buddhist lent (*phansaa*). At this time new monastic robes are offered to monks, and new clothes are prepared for all members of the family. She notes that during this time: "the stalls of traders in silks and velvet are thronged by villagers, waiting to buy or barter their goods. Materials for the skirts and turbans of the women are woven at home, but jackets are of imported stuffs." *Tung* are also prepared at this time:

> Women besides fashioning pretty clothes, prepare great streamers, which, when attached to bamboo, are raised in remembrance of dead relatives or friends. These streamers are from one to three feet wide, and are often many yards in length. They may be of plain cloth, but some are ornamented with geometrical designs cut out of gold paper; others are of thin white cotton cloth, covering many small hoops of bamboo.... Sometimes the streamers are not white, but are embroidered with elaborate designs. Pagodas and birds are represented; there is generally a boat, in which a passenger is being rowed across a river by one or more boatmen, and the water is full of fish.

Shan clothing was influenced by industrially produced cloth and dyes from the early days of British colonial rule. H.G.A. Leveson (Scott and Hardiman 1900, I/II: 391) provides an account of the situation during the late nineteenth century:

Made-up clothing and Manchester goods, white and coloured, constitute a large portion of the annual imports into the Shan States; aniline dyes also are now imported in considerable quantities, and used in all parts of the country. So far east as Kengtung, tins of dyes of all colours are exported for sale in every large bazaar.... In the neighbourhood of all the large centres of population and trade, the ordinary Shan wears nothing but imported goods, so that dyeing as an industry is practiced chiefly by the comparatively less civilized hill tribes, and by the Shans proper only in outlying districts... The Shans of the Northern States and the Hköns or Eastern Shans of Kengtung wear, as a rule, either undyed or indigo-dyed home-spun.... In Möng Nai or Mawkmai, on the other hand, home-dyed clothes are seldom or never to be seen, except on bazaar days when the Yangs come from the surrounding hill villages, nor would many purely native-dyed garments be met with in

3.4. Contemporary Thai Mou (Shan) woman
[photo by Raynou Athamasar]

a tour round the bazaars of the Inleywa lake in Yawnghwe State.... Even in Möng Pawn, although indigo is grown in the hills overlooking the State, foreign dye is imported and used....

One problem in identifying the textiles of the different Tai groups in Burma is that the British tended to use the term Shan in a few different ways: (1) for the Tai Yai alone, (2) for all Tai-speaking peoples in Burma (sometimes including what is now northern Thailand as well), and (3) for most of the peoples living in Shan State (including non-Tai). In museum collections of textiles from Burma the term Shan can be used for purposes of identification in any of these three senses and thus must be treated with care. The problem is particularly acute in the case of textiles from non-Thai Yai Tais, whose textiles are generally referred to simply as Shan. These may or may not show similar dress designs.

The Thai Khun

The Thai Khun, also known as Khun Shan, live in the Kengtung valley of Shan State. Culturally and linguistically they are close to the Lan Na Thai of northern Thailand. They appear to be generally treated as Shan, hence no separate description of their dress appears in the literature.

The Lu

There are about 200,000 Lu (or Lue) in Burma living in the Kengtung district of Shan State. The Chinese called them Shui Pa-yi or Water Barbarians and at present the Chinese include them in the Dai nationality. They originally came from the Sipsong Pannas or twelve *pannas* (countries) region. Eleven of these *pannas* are on the west bank of the Mekong in China and the twelfth is in Laos. There are also many Lu living outside of this area in northern Laos, northern Thailand, and northern Vietnam, in addition to northern Burma. Seidenfaden (1967: 25) estimates that in 1918 there were about 50,000 Lu in Kengtung.

The dress of Lu men is described by Davies (1909: 382) as follows: "the men wear blue clothes, but the bottom of the legs of their trousers and the sleeves of their jackets are ornamented with stripes

of some lighter colour, and on their heads they usually wear yellow silk turbans." Izikowitz (1944) describes the stripes as being red, yellow, or white and the turbans as being white. Davies (1909: 382-383) says of the dress of Lu women: "the Lu women wear light blue or dark blue jackets, and skirts striped horizontally with various colours, generally green or light blue at the bottom" and they wear turbans that are "dark blue with a gold fringe." Izikowitz (1944) says that the women's dress consists of "sky blue double breasted jackets, embroidered and adorned with small pieces of silver," skirts that are "red or even a scarlet colour" and "very large turbans." Scott and Hardiman (1900, I/II: 371-72) remark that "the Lu women of the Trans-Salween Shan States wear a turban fashioned like a tea-cosy. It is always dark blue and ornamented with real or imitation gold and silver thread, which is interwoven with the cotton, and when on the head, the ornamental portion is outside and to the front... Hitherto this has been preserved, but in the weaving of their embroidered petticoats and the border on the trousers of the Lu men pieces of coloured imported stuff are now added."

3.5. Chinese Shan woman of Namh Kam (northern Shan State near the Chinese and Kachin State borders) [Scott and Hardiman 1900, I/II: plate 26, f.pg. 307]

The Thai Nua

The Thai Nua or Northern Shan are also referred to as Thai Che or Chinese Shan. The majority of them live in Dehong prefecture in Yunnan. In China they are included in the Dai nationality and referred to as Dehong Dai. There are also a number of Thai Nua in northern Laos, known there as Thai Neua (see Chazee 1995: 50). The Thai Nua in Burma migrated to the Shan states from China. They are primarily rice farmers and Davies (1909: 380) comments that they "seem to be poorer than the Shan State Shans, and do not trade on the large scale of the latter." This lack of trading he links to competition with the Chinese.

Leslie Milne (1910: 135-136) describes their dress:

> The men wear garments cut in the usual Shan fashion, but always dark blue in colour.... Their women dress as British Shans, with the exception of the turban, which is made of a very long piece of thin black cloth, wound round and round the head in a tall cylindrical shape. They also wear coloured gaiters. The young girls among them have paneled skirts of bright hues, but they lay aside their gay clothes when little more than children, dressing themselves in sober colours at an earlier age than their sisters in British territory.

Davies (1909: 381) observes that the turban of Thai Nua women varies according to locality: "west of the Salween, the women are conspicuous by the size of their turbans, which appear to be nearly a foot high and get broader at the top," while east of the Salween the turban "is about the same size as that worn west of the river, but is put on in a different way, in a low oval shape, with ends of the oval sticking out at each side."

Seidenfaden, differentiates Chinese Thai or Tayok from the Thai Nua. He states that the Thai Nua inhabit the valley of the Mekong, part of the Salween valley, and the mountainous area in between. He describes the dress of the Thai Nua as follows (1969: 24): "their women wear vertically striped white or black skirts, and the well to-do women dress coquettishly in rich divided silken skirts. The men dress somewhat like the Shans."

3.6. Chinese Shan. [Ferrars 1901: 149]

The Khamti

The Khamti are also known as Khamti Shan or Hkhamti Shan. There were an estimated 70,000 of them in total in 1990. The Khamti live mainly in a large plain known as Khamti Long at the headwaters of the Irrawaddy River, but are also found in the Hukawng valley and the upper Chindwin River valley. There are also 22,000 Khamti living in eighty-five villages across the border in India, in Assam and Arunchal Pradesh States. They have close social and political relations with neighboring Jingpho.

The Khamti initially lived within territory under the sovereignty of the Shan State of Mueng Kong or Mogaung, within which their own principality or sub-state was known as Munche or Pong. The Burmese deposed the local Tai rulers of Mogaung in the eighteenth century and some Khamti moved westward to Assam, where they established themselves as local rulers, migration continuing sporadically from 1750 to 1850.

Khamti culture is similar to that of the Shan, having a hierarchical society with exogamous clans. They are wet rice cultivators, whose religious beliefs are a mixture of Theravada Buddhism and spirit worship.

Ward (1921) provides a brief description of Hkamti dress in the early twentieth century: "the dress of the Hkamti Shans differs considerably from that of the southern Shans inhabiting the country round Bhamo and Myitkyina, as well as the Shan States proper; the latter have been influenced by the Burmans" (1921: 238). He describes women's dress as follows (1921: 238-239):

> …they are very dainty, in tight skirt of dark blue cloth relieved with a few stripes of red or brown, reaching to the bare ankles, and close-fitting, short-sleeved jacket. Perhaps they are proud of their neat figures…. for their clothes are always tight-fitting, and the trick of edging the trim sleeves of their dark coloured jacket with brighter red, and wearing a low turban of white or bracelet, draws attention to just those points they would have you look at. Often a white wrap with coloured stripes at each end is flung loosely across the breast, over the left shoulder.

By way of comparison, Gogoi (1996: 125-126) provides a contemporary description of Khamti dress from Assam. He describes the women's dress, or *pha chien,* as being indigo or black with no de-

3.7. Khamti (Hkamti Shan) women of Khamti Long [Ward 1921: f.pg. 216]

31

signs. They wear blouses bought commercially. Over the blouse they wear a *nang wat* or *lang wat*, a scarf-like cloth used to wrap over their breasts. This cloth is green with designs. They also wear a waist cloth or *chai chien*. Khamti men in Assam are described by Gogoi as wearing commercial shirts and a chequered *lungyi* (referred to as a *pha nung*). Such men's dress clearly has been adapted from non-Tai. Both men and women are described as wearing a *fa mai* or shoulder-cloth. This is usually plain white. There are also shoulder-bags called *thung,* which are made of cotton and wool and feature embroidered designs and other decorations. Other types of cloth include *pha chiet* (towel), *tan khan* (sacred hanging), *chankanfra* (a type of sacred cloth), and *pha chang long* (a sacred shoulder-cloth).

The Khamti black dye come from *Baphisacanthus cusia,* known as *tun hom* or *tun rom,* which is grown around the home compound (Gogoi 1996: 161). The leaves are crushed and soaked in water for four to five days. An alkali solution is added before using the dye by pouring the water in which the leaves have been soaking through banana ash and adding lime. The yarn to be dyed is then dipped in the solution for two to three hours. The process is repeated two to three times. This dye is also used for tattooing.

4

The Chin, Naga, and Mru

The Chin, Naga, and Mru speak languages belonging to the Kuki-Naga subgroup of the Baric group of Tibeto-Burman languages. They are basically hill-dwellers who live in the mountains that straddle Burma's western border with India and Bangladesh. Their most prominent textiles are blankets or shawls that often serve as important indicators of status and ethnic identity. Naga and Chin men were also known in the past for their relative lack of clothing besides such shawls.

The Chin

There are around one million speakers of twenty-seven Kuki-Chin languages in Burma. Many of those identified as Chin live in Chin State. This includes the Chin Hills, Arakan Hills, and adjacent lowlands of western Burma. The point furthest north occupied by the Chin in Burma is the Namwe Chaung in the Somra Tract of the Naga Hills district. Chin are found as far south as the hills west of the Prome district. Members of Chin groups are also located in neighboring areas of India and Bangladesh. The Chin are often divided into Northern, Central, and Southern groups or, following Lehman (1962), only into Northern and Southern groups. I shall follow the latter division. Essentially, most Northern Chin had a more elaborate material culture and more complex social structure, while most Southern Chin had a relatively poor material culture and simpler social structure. Northern Chin societies generally were hierarchical with headmen and chiefs, while Southern Chin societies for the most part were egalitarian with only informal leaders.

Northern Chin external relations were historically with Manipur and Tripura to the west and with Ava to the east. The area that they occupied formed something of a frontier between Manipur and Ava, so Chin were often caught up in the fighting between the two kingdoms. External relations of the Southern Chin were mainly with Arakan. Such relations took the form of raiding as well as more peaceful forms of trade and occasionally payment of tribute by Chins to adjacent kingdoms. Burmese and other lowlanders would sometimes raid the Chin for slaves and various Chin groups would in turn raid lowlanders (as well as one another) to seize slaves and other desired goods. Relations among groups of Chin featured uneasy alliances and established trade networks, as well as blood feuds and other forms of aggression. Some Northern Chin were head-hunters who mounted their trophies on posts outside the villages like the Wa. Wars among the Northern Chin in the early eighteenth century led to the expansion of the tribal realms in the Falam and Haka areas. During the mid-nineteenth century the Lushai pushed the Thado out of the Chin Hills into Manipur and the Naga Hills. Movement, often as a result of aggression, was a common feature of the history of the Chin into the present century.

The Northern Chin had dispersed patrilineal clans and patrilineages that were more demonstrably based on genealogical links. Their societies were stratified into aristocrats, commoners, and slaves. This hierarchy was reflected in their clans and lineages, which were also ranked into aristocratic and commoner strata. Northern Chin societies generally had hereditary village headmen associated with aristocratic kin groups. There were also village councils and ritual officers. Sometimes chiefs arose

Michael C. Howard

who were able to exert influence over groups of villages. The realms of these chiefs, however, were highly unstable (Lehman 1963: 89-90, 139-55). Some Northern Chin lacked hereditary headmen and instead had elected village headmen or councils. Leadership among the Northern Chin was associated with Feasts of Merit (Lehman 1962: 182-85). The Southern Chin had localized patrilineal clans that tended to occupy a single village. Within these clans were unranked lineages. The Southern Chin had no distinct political offices, and in fact had no words for chief or headman, but there were informal leaders recognized as lineage heads.

Initially, Chin relations with the British mainly took the form of raids by Chins on areas under British control in Bengal. Following the annexation of Burma in 1885, the British mounted military expeditions against the Chin dwelling in the Chin Hills, such as the Chin-Lushai Expedition of 1888-89. Hostilities continued for the next few years and British military forces were not withdrawn until 1896, when civil administration in the area was established. Even then, much of the area occupied by the various Chin groups remained outside of British control for the next couple of decades. However, resistance to the British persisted, culminating in the Haka Rebellion of 1918. The central and adjoining Chin areas were brought under British control in the early 1920s. The town of Falam served as headquarters for the British administration in the Chin Hills. The southern Lushai Hills came under British control only just before the outbreak of the Second World War.

In the Southern Chin area the British designated an officer for the Arakan Hill Tracts in the 1860s, but relatively little progress was made in establishing administrative control over the area beyond its southern limits until after the First World War. The first Europeans did not enter the Matupi area until 1923. Even around the administrative center of Kanpetlet, little control was exerted beyond the immediate vicinity of the town itself. British administrative influence was never firmly established over much of the Southern Chin area. The Kanpetlet sub-division under the British was divided into *chaungs* (valleys) that were administered by a *chaung ok* (ruler of the valley) who was chosen by the government. Stevensen (1944: 7) comments that the hill-dwelling Southern Chin are "the wildest of the Chin tribes, some of whom have come under British administration only within the past twenty years, and are among the least known sections of the whole of the Burma Hills." Despite this, they were sometimes referred to as "Tame" Chin while the Northern Chin were sometimes referred to as "Wild" (Scott 1911: 107). After Burma became independent the new government formed the Chin Special Division out of the Chin Hills District and the Arakan and Pakokku Hill Tracts. Incorporation of the Southern Chin into the Burmese state progressed slowly. Lehmen (1962: 42) comments that even in the late 1950s blood feuds were still in evidence around Kanpetlet.

Most of the hill-dwelling Chin of Burma traditionally practiced slash-and-burn agriculture. The primary traditional subsistence crops of the more northerly groups of Chin were maize and millet, although they sometimes grew rice as well. In contrast, rice was traditionally the main subsistence crop of the Southern Chin. The lowlands Chin tended to practice irrigated paddy rice farming. Many Chin traditionally also grew some cotton and indigo. Irrigated paddy rice production has become increasingly widespread among upland Chin over the past few decades. The Chin have been dependent for centuries on external trade for a variety of prestige goods (including silk) as well as other important items such as iron and salt. Prestige goods among the Northern Chin included jewelry, brass gongs, brass pots, firearms, as well as certain types of locally produced blankets. The Chin exported only a few items such as beeswax and stick-lac. In the past, they also acquired many goods through raids.

Protestant missionaries began working in the Chin area in the late nineteenth century. By the 1950s, however, Lehman (1963: 186, 219-20) estimated that only about 20% of the Chin in Burma had converted to Christianity, the majority continuing to adhere to their traditional animistic religion. The Chin in the hills of Burma have their own shamans, mostly female, who seek to determine the causes of and to cure illnesses. Chiefs may also perform curing ceremonies.

The general differences in material culture between Northern and Southern Chin are reflected in their clothing. By and large, the Northern Chin produce more complicated textiles than the Southern

4.1. Siyin Chin chiefs [Scott and Hardiman 1900, I/II: plate 11, f.pg. 441]

4.2. Group of Siyin Chin men and women, including a woman in a dress made
from grass [Scott and Hardiman 1900, I/II: plate 19, f.pg. 104]

Michael C. Howard

Chin. Stevenson (1944: 7) comments in regard to the dress of the Chin of different regions that "the clothing of the Chin women differs little in its modesty from north to south except in the length of the skirt; but even the shortest skirt is never immodest, so expert are the wearers. The dress of the men can be said to dwindle from little in the north to still less in the south, and the sex exhibits a magnificent resistance to the wide climatic variations to which it is exposed." The immodesty of the Southern Chin men is also commented on by Spearman (1880, I: 67) when he remarks that "the waist cloth is, in these hill tracts, reduced to the smallest possible dimensions; in fact it can hardly be said to have the slightest pretensions to decency."

Northern Chin

The Northern Chin are subdivided into a number of ethnolinguistic groups and there is some confusion among writers as to the identity of many of these groups. There are three main subdivisions occupied by the Northern Chin: Tiddim, Falam, and Haka. In addition there are the Thado who live to the north of the Chin Special Division and the Zotung who are the southernmost Northern Chin. There are several ethnolinguistic groups within each of the three subdivisions. The Tiddim Subdivision includes the Siyin, Zome, and Tedim. The Falam Subdivison includes the Lushai, the Falam (who themselves can be further divided into six groups), Bawm, and Ngawn. Within Haka Subdivision are found the Haka (who can be divided into five groups), Tawr, Senthang, and Mara. One other small Northern Chin ethnolinguistic group is the *Yos,* who number around 3,000.

Stevenson (1944: 6) comments in regard to dress of Northern Chin males that "there is a sharp division between the northern groups and their Lushai cousins on the one hand, and the Falam and Haka Chins on the other. The northerners ... wear a broad cloth round the waist, and are known as *Mar,* while the Falam and Haka Chins wear a long narrow loincloth ... and are called *Pawi.*"

The different Chin groups share a common origin and this is, to some extent, reflected in the similarity of designs and motifs of Northern Chin textiles. Further, because descriptions of Northern Chin textiles in the literature are rather limited, and

data lacking in respect of textiles in museum collections, it is often difficult to attribute these textiles to specific groups. The situation is also complicated because of widespread trading in textiles, with individuals in one group wearing textiles produced by another.

Thado. The Thado, also known as Kuki-Thado, are the northernmost group of Chin-speakers in Burma. They live in the Somra tract and the northern part of the Kamhau Tribal Area east of Manipur. There are about 30,000 in Burma and some 125,000 in India.

Siyin. There were about 10,000 Siyin in Burma in 1991, living in the Tiddim Sub-division. They were called Tautes or Tauktes in early Manipur records. They had a reputation as slave hunters in the past.

4.3. Contemporary Tedim Chin woman
[photo by Laura Kan]

Zome. The Zome are sometimes called Kuki Chin. There were 30,000 in Burma in 1991, living in the Tiddim area of Chin Hills, and some 12,000 in India.

Tedim. The Tedim are the largest group of Northern Chin in Burma. In 1990, there were 190,000, living in the Tiddim District of the Chin Hills. Another 32,000 live in India. Two subgroups are the Sokte and Kamhau. Other nearby languages are Saizang, Teizang, and Zo.

Lushai The Lushai are also known as Hualngo. They live west of the Tedim in Falam Subdivision on the western slopes of the Inbuk Range. In 1983 there were 12,500 Lushai in Burma, 330,000 in India in 1991 (where sub-groups include Fannai, Mizo, Ngente, and Pang), and about 1,000 in Bangladesh.

4.4. Lushai chiefs [R. Reid, *The Geographical Journal,* vol. 103, nos. 1/2, 1944: f.pg. 21]

Relatively detailed descriptions of Lushai type dress based on observations from India are provided by Shakespear (1912). He notes that Lushai textiles are made of cotton that is grown locally and spun into yarn by women for domestic use. He remarks (1912: 10) that "the cloths in general are white, but every man likes to have two or three blue cloths ornamented with stripes of various colours." He reports (1912: 31) that the ornamentation of cloths consists primarily of "lines of different colours." In this regard, he notes that "white cloths have blue and red stripes down the centre and some times one traversely about a foot from either end" while "coloured cloths are mainly blue, with stripes of red, yellow, and green" and that "zigzags are not uncommon, and short lengths of this pattern are placed haphazard on cloths and coats."

Shakespear describes men's clothing and the manner of its wearing as follows (1912: 8-9):

> The men's dress could not well be simpler, consisting as it does of a single cloth about 7 feet long and 5 feet wide. It is worn as follows: One corner is grasped in the left hand, and the cloth is passed over the left shoulder, behind the back, under the right arm across the chest and the end thrown over the left shoulder.... In cold weather, one or more cloths are worn, one over the other, and also a white coat, reaching well down to the thigh but only fastened at the throat. These coats are ornamented on the sleeves with bands of red and white of various patterns. When at work, in hot weather, the Lushai wraps his cloth round his waist, letting the ends hang down in front.

To this description of men's clothing he adds that "when the Lushais were fighting us in 1892 I was struck by the whiteness of their garments. The men … were always dressed in nice clean coats and cloths.…I was told that it was considered the correct thing to come properly dressed when there was fighting on hand, but a raiding party I once came across was dressed far more suitably. A single cloth wrapped tightly round the waist, a haversack protected by a bear or tiger skin guard over the shoulder.…" (1912: 10).

Shakespear also draws attention to cloth that distinguishes the status of the wearer. Thus, "the dress of the chiefs is the same as that of the common people, except on occasions of ceremony, when they wear dark blue cloths with red lines of a particular pattern, and plumes, made of the tail feathers of the king crow, in their hair knots…. The cloth referred to above can also be worn by anyone who has given certain feasts" (1912: 10). Also "a man who has earned the title of 'Thangchhuah' … is allowed to wear a cloth of a certain pattern and those who have killed men in war have special headdresses, known as 'chhawndawl' and 'arkeziak'" (1912: 11).

Shakespear (1912: 11) describes women's clothing as follows: "all women wear the same costume; a dark-blue cotton cloth, just long enough to go round the wearer's waist with a slight over-lap, and held up by a girdle of brass wire or string, serves as a petticoat which only reaches to the knee, the only other garments being a short white jacket and a cloth which is worn in the same manner as the men."

Finally, he also describes making a quilt (1912: 30): "A very serviceable form of quilt called a *puanpui* is made by passing round ever fourth or fifth thread of the warp a small roll of raw cotton and drawing both ends up. A row of these cotton rolls is put in after every fourth or fifth thread of the woof, so that on one side the quilt is composed of closely placed tufts of cotton."

Falam. Some 100,000 Falam live in the Falam Subdistrict of the Chin Hills. There are a number of subgroups among the Falam, from around 4,000 to 20,000 in size. These include, from largest to smallest, Laizao, Zanniat, Zahao, Tashon, Khualshim, and Lente. The Laizao and Zahao belong to what is sometimes referred to as the *"Shimhrim"* tribe" (Stevenson 1944: 5). The Bawm, Ngawn, and Tawr may be included as Falam although their speech is distinctive enough to be classified as different languages. There are about 9,000 Bawm, around 15,000 Ngawn, and only some 700 Tawr. The Bawm and Ngawn live in Falam Subdivision and the Tawr live in Haka Subdivision. Their culture is more closely related to the Haka. Laizao serves as a *lingua franca* among the Falam Chin.

Traditionally the Falam divided their tribal groups into two categories according to how the men wore their hair and by the color of their loincloths: Biar Dum and Biar Rang (Stevenson 1943: 13). The Zanniat, Tashon, Lente, and Hualngo belong to the Biar Rang group and wore a white loincloth, while the Laizao, Zahao, Ngawn, Bawm, and Tawr belong to the Biar Dum group and wore a black loincloth.

Prior to British rule, Tashon village was an important center of trade between the east and west. Its economic importance was mirrored in political power, the Tashon also being the most powerful tribe in the Falam area. Items traded included slaves, salt, mats, blankets, cotton, lac, iron, and grain. The Tashon collected a tax on all goods. The heyday of this pattern of trade was the late nineteenth century. By the 1930s trade in the area had become much more free and Tashon power was reduced.

There was some craft specialization among the Falam. The Laizao specialized in making cotton blankets. Cotton thread came from the east, primarily to the seven Laizao villages who used the thread to make blankets, mainly of a type known as *puanpi*, which were in turn traded back east (Stevenson

4.5. Zanniat Chin (a Falam sub-group) in ceremonial dress [Stevenson 1943: f.pg. 137]

1943: 104). Tashon and Lente villages were known for making earthenware pots. Other villages made mats and metal implements. Stevenson (1943: 115) associated this specialization with environmental conditions: "…where plots are large and fertile they receive the bulk of the effort; where land shortage or sterility pinches the family budget, the alternative sources of income are exploited more fully. Thus one finds the Laizo seven villages spend more time on their blanket weaving." In the case of the Laizao then, blanket weaving serves to make up for their agricultural deficit. Other villages did weave for domestic use, but the Laizao alone appear to have produced woven goods for the market.

Textiles were also associated with various rites of passage among the Falam. This can be seen in the case of marriage among the Zahao (Stevenson 1943: 122-129). The Zahao bride must wear a *sawilukhum* headdress and *rangkha* and *elkiim* waist belts. These types of cloth are heirlooms passed from mother to daughter. If the bride's family does not possess them, then they must be bor-

4.6. Contemporary Haka Chin woman in traditional ceremonial dress
[photo by Laura Kan]

rowed and their cash value given to the groom. Stevenson notes that the production of such cloths had almost ceased at the time of his residence, resulting in fewer being owned and a rise in cash transactions. Zahao weddings also entail the presentation of cloth gifts. Among the obligatory gifts are at least ten cord belts to be presented by the bride to the groom's classificatory sisters. The groom's family also gives cloth to the bride. These pieces of cloth are laid along the path the bride walks on to the groom's house (which is referred to as the *puan pah*). (Stevenson 1943: 126). This type of blanket is woven by the Lushai, who live to the west, and is obtained through trade. Stevenson (1943: 122) remarks that "the most obvious way of gauging the social importance of a Zahau wedding is by these cloths, which are often very valuable." The brideprice includes blankets. Among the transactions in the brideprice settlement is the *puan pi* or "big blanket" price. This refers to the presentation of a thick cotton blanket "with threads looped on one side like a turkish towel."

After the marriage there are post-marriage reciprocities. Thus, if a pig has been killed at the wedding, then the wife's father must give a new skirt to his daughter and a new blanket to her husband. The quality of this blanket reflects the social standing of the father. If he is a poor man of low status, then he will give a relatively simply blanket known as a *zaudi puan.* If he has given a feast of merit and is therefore of higher standing, he will give a more prestigious type of blanket known as a *vai puan.*

Upon a man's death in a Zahao family, his sisters or closest female cousins are expected to provide a shroud, or *puan fun,* to cover the body. Again, if the man is of lower status, the shroud will be a *zaudi puan;* if he has given a feast of merit, then it would be a *vai puan.*

As noted above, in Falam society, types of blankets are associated with the social standing of a man. This status is linked to giving so-called feasts of merit. There are nine types of these feasts. Upon giving a *sia thum thah* feast, a man gains the right to wear a *vai puan* blanket and becomes eligible to be a member of the community council. Giving the higher status *khuang tsawi* feast gains a man the right to wear a *khuang puan* blanket, become a member of the council, and make a window in his house (another mark of status).

Michael C. Howard

Unfortunately, Stevenson provides relatively little information on what the various textiles that he mentions actually look like. He mentions four types of blankets among the Zahao. From lowest to highest ranked they are: *puan nang, puan dum, vai puan,* and *khuang puan.* The first of these is plain white and the second plain black. The latter two are decorated, but the nature of their decoration is not described.

Haka. Some 100,000 Haka occupy most of the Haka Subdivision. Subgroups of the Haka Chin include the Lai, Klangklang, Zokhua, and Shonshe. Among the textiles woven by the Haka is a silk blanket, known as a *cawng-nak,* that is worn by both men and women during ceremonies. The silk is imported from the lowlands so the blankets are extremely expensive by local standards. Lehman (1962: 165) refers to these as "among the most elaborate products of the Northern Hills Chin." As with other Haka Chin weaving these blankets feature very fine diamond and zig-zag supplementary weft patterns. Such patterns are woven in stripes running in one direction while plain twill weave stripes are woven in the other direction. Lehman (1962: 165) discusses the production, sale, and use of these silk blankets:

The market for such expensive goods is too irregular to permit professionalization, yet these women are in many respects the most skilled artisans in all the Chin Hills. Certain of the best weavers in Haka town have considerable reputations and their products are sold widely. Good blankets are used in marriage payments and other formal presentations in the culture, but weaving remains a purely domestic industry.

In the southern part of the Haka Subdivision women weave coarse plain white blankets for domestic use and for sale. These are known as *zo puan rang* and serve as general purpose blankets. Lehman (1962: 165) notes that "these blankets are cheap, wear out rapidly, and are in constant demand, hence there is always a market for additional supplies."

Senthang. There were 18,000 Senthang in 1983 living in the Haka Subdivision of the Chin Hills. Descriptions of their dress are hitherto not available.

Mara. The Mara are also known as Maram or Lakher (by the Lushai). In 1989 there were 14,000 Mara in Burma, living in the far west of the Haka Subdivision along the border with India. In India

4.7. Group of contemporary Haka Chin women dressed for a dance performance
[photo by Laura Kan]

40

they live in the Lushai Hills of Assam. Subgroups include the Tlongsai, Hlawthai, and Sabeu. The Tlongsai are furthest to the west and the Hlawthai and Sabeu are found to the east with Hlawthai to the north of the Sabeu. The Hlawthai and Sabeu live to the southwest of Haka along the Kolodyne River.

The Mara had a reputation for raiding other peoples. On such raids they would kill the men and seize the women and children along with goods. The British encountered them during the 1888-89 Chin-Lushai Expedition but the Mara did not come completely under British administration until 1924. British rule, however, was largely indirect and many practices were allowed to continue—although slavery and raiding were stopped.

Lewin (1870: 306) and Shakespear (1912: 213) mention an embassy being sent by a Thongsai Mara chief to the Chittagong area bearing ivory and home-spun cloth as gifts. The members of the party were murdered. The cloth is not described.

A Christian mission was established at Saiko around the turn of the century, but according to Parry (1932: 19) during his time "it has made little headway." While on the whole Parry approved of the activities of the mission, he did criticize it for making the boys at school "wear shorts and cut off their top-knots" and commented that "there is no virtue in cotton drawers or in short hair" (p. 20). He goes on to defend the traditional dress of the Mara: "the Lakher's dress is suited to his surroundings and his needs, his cloths are woven and decorated in the most artistic patterns; surely it is better to encourage the people to weave and wear their own beautiful cloths than to impose upon them the drab uniform of khaki drawers and cotton shirt…. When a primitive people have beautiful things they should be encouraged to wear them; far from inducing them to adopt a debased form of Western dress, we should endeavour to preserve all that is beautiful in their own costume. By so doing we shall increase their self-respect and encourage them to develop their own art on their own lines" (Parry 1932: 20-21).

Parry provides a relatively detailed description of Mara dress and, while his work deals with the Mara in Assam, their culture was much the same as the Mara in Burma. The primary item of Mara male clothing is the loincloth. Parry (1932: 29) re-

fers to two types of loincloth: "the *dua kalapa* for everyday wear, and the *dua ah* for more ceremonial occasions." Both loincloths are described as being of about the same dimensions: 3 1/2 yards long and 1 1/2 feet wide. While the *dua kalapa* is plain, the *dua ah* is ornamented and is "worn at beer parties, feasts, marriages and other ceremonies" (Parry 1932: 30). The body of the *dua ah* consists of a plain white cloth, "but at each end there is sewn on a 2 1/2-foot length of dark blue cloth, richly embroidered with patterns of different coloured silks" (Parry 1932: 30). The ends are "displayed in front and behind" when worn. In the past when at work a man wore only a loincloth, but Parry notes that during his time men also sometimes wore "a plain cotton coat called *viapako*" (1932: 31).

Parry mentions several types of shoulder-cloth (1932: 31). These are worn by both men and women and measure about seven feet by five feet. The finest of these is called a *cheulopang* and is worn only by those of the chief's family. It has a dark indigo ground with two white stripes in the middle, "heavily embroidered with patterns in silk, said to represent the eyes of different birds and beasts." A second fine shoulder-cloth worn by those of the chief's family as well as other "well-to-do people" is the *cheunapang*. This one has a red ground and is decorated with red and yellow silk. A third type of shoulder cloth is the *viapang*. It is a plain dark indigo cloth with a red stripe down the center. Another type is a *zeupang*. It is described as a "thin cloth with white stripes on a black ground" (Parry 1932: 31). The most common type of shoulder-cloth is the *chiaraku*. It is white with two broad black stripes. There is also a plain white shoulder-cloth known as a *pangzapa* and a heavy, coarse cloth used as a blanket known as a *siahriapang*.

Mara women wear an indigo cotton under skirt called a *cheinahnang*. The lower portion of this skirt is decorated with silk threads. A shorter skirt is worn over this. If this over-skirt is plain indigo it is known as a *hnangra* and if it is decorated it is called a *viahnang*. Parry (1932: 38) notes that the "women of Iana village are famed for the beauty of their embroidered skirts, which command a ready sale." He also describes a special skirt worn only by women of aristocratic families known as a *sisai a hnang*. These skirts are decorated with cowries and beads, and the patterns varies in different villages. Parry (1932: 38) describes one of these skirts from the village of Savang:

> The cloth itself is dark blue, and the top quarter of the cloth, which is tied round the waist, is left plain. About three quarters of the way up are places three rows of cowries, one below the other, running the whole width of the cloth; below these comes a row of small, round, green, beads called *chhihrang*, followed successively by a row of wild coix seeds called *sachipa,* another row of *chhihrang,* a row of red beads called *sisai,* another row of *chhihrang,* a row of *sachipa* and a row of brass beads, of the size and shape of a match, called *dawchakopa.* Below the brass beads follow successively a row each of *sachipa, chhihrang, sisai, chhihrang, sachipa,* finished off at the bottom with tassels of red silk. The cloth is sometimes finished off with a row of the wings of a brilliant green beetle (*Chrysochroa bivittala*) instead of with the red silk tassels. The upper row of beads is sewn firmly on to the cloth, the lower rows are strung on to cotton thread, and hang down in a fringe below the bottom of the cloth.

Such cloths are made by aristocratic women and form part of their dowry. Mara women also wear a short sleeveless blouse called a *kohrei.*

The Sabeu of Khihlong and Heima were reported in 1901 to wear far simpler clothing than other Mara (Parry 1932: 31-32). The men "strap their penis to their stomach in a vertical position, holding it there by means of a little strip of cloth, from the ends of which strings go and fasten round the waist and at the centre of the cloth." The women wear only a small pieces of bark in front held on by a waist string.

Anal. The Anal are also known as Namfau. There are over 5,000 Anal living in Burma, another 7,000 in India (in southeast Manipur), and possibly a few in Bangladesh. Dialects of Anal include: Laizo, Mulsom, and Moyon-Monshang. Their language and culture is similar to that of the Lamkang (or Lamgang), who live in Manipur and Nagaland. Culturally the Anal are also close to the Mara. In India in 1963 they decared themselves to be ethnically Naga. They are sometimes referred to as Naga-

Chin. There are no descriptions of their dress.

Zotung. The Zotung (also called Banjogi or Bandzhogi) are the southernmost Northern Chin. They numbered about 40,000 in 1990.

Southern Chin

The Southern Chin occupy the Kanpetlet Subdivision at the southern end of the Chin Hills district and a portion of the Arakan Hill Tracts. There are six main ethnolinguistic groups among the Southern Chin, but each of these groups includes a diverse number of subgroups. Unlike some of the Northern Chin groups for whom we have at least adequate descriptions of their textiles, the textiles of the Southern Chin are poorly described—beyond constant references to the scantiness of the loincloths worn by the men.

Writing in the late nineteenth century, Spearman reports that the Chin of the Arakan Hill Tracts cultivated cotton that was "much sought after by Arakanese" (1880, II: 73). The exception to this are the Asho (or Khyeng) who he reports did not cultivate cotton for sale (1880, II: 67).

4.8. Chin from unidentified group, probably Southern Chin [Scott 1911: f.pg. 154]

Daai. There are about 10,000 Daai (sometimes referred to as Mün, Utbu or Khyo) who live in and around Kanpetlet, Matupi, and Paletwa townships, on mountain slopes at altitudes of around 900 to 1,800 meters. They are swidden farmers whose main crop is rice. Lehman (1962: 86) comments that they are "very heterogeneous, culturally and linguistically."

Lehman (1962: 86) briefly describes the men's clothing of one group of Daai: "some *'Dai* men wear red cane belts; others, to the east, wear a short, brilliantly striped kilt." Another group of Daai-speakers are known as M'Kang (or M'Kaang). The M'Kang are sometimes referred to as the Cane-bellied Chin in reference to the red cane girdles worn by M'Kang men and boys, although both 'Dai and Matu also are known to wear similar cane girdles. Lehman (1962: 86) comments that M'Kang men "also wear indigo-dyed loincloths so narrow as to leave the testicles fully exposed on either side." He has little to say about M'Kang women's costumes except that "a few women today wear the *Ng'men* sleeveless shirt" (Lehman 1962: 85).

Matu. The Matu number about 40,000 and linguistically are sometimes classified as Khumi. They

4.9. Southern Chin husband and wife
[Stevenson 1943: f.pg. 7]

live near the town of Matupi and were the most isolated of the Southern Chin. This remoteness is reflected in the fact that they are poorer than other Southern Chin and have the simplest material culture. Significantly, unlike other Chin, they lack any form of bridewealth payments (Lehman 1962: 87). The Matu were pacified in the 1920s and had schools built for them in the 1930s. Regular colonial administration, however, was not established until the mid-1940s.

Lehman (1962: 44) notes that until recently (i.e., the late 1950s) the Matu wove much of their cloth of wild flax. The use of such fibers for weaving is rare among other Chin. Matu clothing included men's loincloths ("two fingers' width") and women's skirts.

Mun. The Mun (also known as Chinbok) number some 50,000, living in the hills from the Maw River down to the Sawchaung. Burmese live to their east and Arakanese to their west. They include the group described by Lehman (1962: 83-84) as the Ng'men, also referred to sometimes as Northern Chinbok. The Ng'men live around the settlement of Mindat and claim to have migrated to their present homeland from the lowlands to the east. They had a reputation for being warlike.

Lehman (1962: 84) remarks that the Ng'men "have a fairly elaborate material culture" and describes their dress as including: "multicolored striped blankets, men's sitting cloths, men's loincloths in the form of a genital sheath, women's sleeveless shirts, and other items not found west of there."

Chinbon. About 20,000 Chinbon live in and around Kanpetlet, Saw, and the upper reaches of the Yaw River.

Lowis (1911: 22) comments that the dress of Chinbon women leaves little doubt that they are Southern Chin rather than Central Chin, though no description of their dress is provided.

Khumi. There are about 40,000 Khumi, also known as Khami (although Khami can refer to a subgroup of Khumi). The Khumi are called Hkwemis ("the dogs' tails") by Burmese. They live along the Kaladan River in the Arakan Hills in Burma, some also live in Bangladesh's Chittagong Hill Tract and a few in India. A group known as the Khumi Awa or Southern Khumi live in the coastal areas of the Arakan Hills and speak a dialect that differs from the inland Khumi or Northern

Khumi. Formerly the Khumi lived in the Chin Hills, but moved to the present area in the middle of the nineteenth century. Khumi was the main language of the Arakan Hills at the turn of the century—the 1901 census listed 24,389 Khumi speakers. Lewis (1911: 22) notes that the Khumi and Mro are generally categorized separately from other Southern Chin in part because of a few distinctive characteristics, "including the fact that the women do not have their faces tattooed" like most Southern Chin women.

Spearman (1880, I: 153; II: 253-254) provides an early, albeit limited, description of the Khumi, estimating their population to be 7,000 and dividing them into two divisions, the Khumie and Khamie. He describes them as "the most warlike tribe living within the tribute-paying limits" (1880, II: 253), having been driven down out of the hills by the "more warlike and stronger Shandoo." He recorded them as being divided into a number of clans, each having its own chief. They are reported to practice slash-and-burn rice cultivation and to move their villages when nearby plots are exhausted about every three years: "Wandering thus every

4.10. Mun Chin women (also known as Chinbok) [Scott and Hardiman 1900, I/II: plate 27, f.pg. 324]

three years and in continual dread of being massacred by their relentless foes" (1880, II: 254).

Spearman describes their dress as follows (1880, II: 254): "the women wear short petticoats kept on by numerous brass rings round the waist; the men are almost naked, but have a small cloth round the loins the ends hanging in front and behind, whence the Burmese corruption of the name into Khwe-myee or 'dog's tail.'" He elaborates on the loin-cloth elsewhere (1880, II: 66): "the dress of the male Khamie is a long home-spun cotton cloth about one foot in width which is passed several times round the waist and once between the legs, the coloured ends hanging down in front and behind." He further describes the woman's petticoat as being "a short dark blue cloth reaching to the knee and open at the side" and which is "fastened round the waist with a belt of cords covered either with large beads or copper rings" and notes that they also wear "a small strip of cloth" to cover their breasts (1880, II: 66). Spearman also describes their blankets: these "are, generally speaking, white and have thick ribs of cotton run in to make them warm; some are large like Turkish towels" (1880, II: 76). A similar type of blanket, also described as being "like a turkish towel," is reported by Stevenson (1968: 126) as being made by the Lushai.

Asho. An estimated 10,000 Asho (also known as the Khyeng or Khyang) live in the lowlands of Burma near the Irrawaddy River, with a small number in Bangladesh. There are four dialects: Thayetmyo, Minbu, Lemyo, and Khyang. Spearman refers to the Asho as Khyeng. The Laytoo may be another subgroup of Asho or a separate group.

Spearman describes women's clothing as consisting "of a short waist cloth open on both sides and a smock frock like that worn by the Karen but very short; the clans further south wear it long" (1880, II: 67). Quoting from a report by R.F. St.John's ("Report on the Hill Tracts of Northern Arakan, 1870-71," p.27) he notes that they wear a loincloth "reduced to the smallest possible dimensions in fact it can hardly be said to have the slightest pretentions to decency" (1880, I: 184-85). He reports that men who have come into contact with the Burmese on the plains usually adopt "the Burmese kilt or waistcloth" while women "are naturally pretty and far less willing than the men to adopt the Burmese costume, generally wearing a dark blouse ornamented with red and white thread" (1880, II: 265). He notes that their blankets have "broad stripes of bright colours like those worn by the Toungthoo" (1880, II: 76).

Spearman also mentions the use of cloth in the payment of fines for breaking betrothals. Should a man to whom a woman is betrothed break the engagement, the fine paid to the woman is: "five pots of Khoung, a bullock with Rs. 30, a pig three feet in girth, a spear, a fork, a bag and a piece of ornamental cloth." If the woman breaks off the engagement she must pay the man: "a brass dish worth about Rs. 15, a silk cloth and a silk belt each worth about Rs. 5 and a silk turban worth about eight annas" (1880, II: 263). For adultery a woman apparently "forfeits the whole of her property to her husband and has also to give two gongs, a bullock, a brass dish, a dha-lway or sword and a piece of blue cloth" (1880, II: 264).

The Naga

The majority of Naga live in northeastern India with a smaller number living just across the Burmese border. In Burma the Naga live in western Sagaing Division within a territory that extends from the Patkoi range in the north to around Thaungdyat in the south and from the border with India in the west to the Chindwin River in the east (see Stevenson 1944: 15-18).

Ethnolinguistic identities or categories among the Naga are complex and often ambiguous and sources vary a good deal in identifying Naga groups living in Burma. The southern portion of Naga territory in Burma is occupied by *Tangkhul Naga*. There were over 70,000 Tangkhul Naga in India in 1990 living in northern Manipur and southern Nagaland. To their north are the *Yimchungru Naga*. They numbered some 40,000 in India in 1990 living in Nagaland. Next, further to the north, are the *Khiamnungan Naga* (also known as the Kalyo-Kengyu Naga. There were 20,000 Khiamnungan in India in 1987 living in Nagaland. Sardeshpande (1987: 179) provides a list of Khiamnungan villages in Burma. East of the Khiamnungans in Burma are a group of Naga known as the Heimei. This group is closely linked to the Khiannungans and will be treated as part of the same group here. According to tribal history (Sardeshpande 1987:

8), there were originally four Khiamnungan settlements that included the settlement of Thang or Noklak. The people of Noklak migrated to various locations, including eastward into what is now Burma. This group of Khiamnungans from Noklak eventually became the Heimei. To the far north are *Konyak Naga*. There are around 100,000 Konyak Naga in India living in eastern Assam and northern Nagaland. The majority of the Konyak living in Burma belong to a subgroup called Rangpan Naga who linguistically are known as Tase Naga. Around 1990 there were an estimated 10,000 Tase/Rangpan Naga in Burma and about 7,000 in India. The *Wancho Naga* live to the north of the Konyak in India (their population is estimated to be around 30,000), and some live across the border in Burma as well.

To the west of these Naga groups in India other Naga groups include Rengma, Sangtam, Chang, and Phom.

Slash-and-burn agriculture is widely practiced among the Naga. Their crops include rice, millet, maize, taro, and cotton. In some areas there is also terraced wet-rice cultivation and terraced taro cultivation. Important social units among the Naga include clans, lineages, and age-groups. In the past most Naga lived in relatively permanent, often fortified, villages. Their villages are usually divided into distinct geographical units, known as *khels*, that are relatively autonomous, but cooperate with each other on certain occasions. Each *khel* contains at least one young men's house, or *morung*. The *morung* plays a number of important social roles in Naga society and is a place for holding major rituals. Prestige is acquired through offering sacrifices and sponsoring feasts of merit (much like the Northern Chin).

While Naga villages were relatively self-sufficient, trade was important and the Naga maintained friendly, if limited, relations with the Ahom and Manipuri monarchies. Especially important was trade between the hill-dwelling Naga and lowland peoples. Among the items traded by the Naga were locally grown cotton, palm-leaf mats, ivory, and a variety of agricultural and forest products. From the lowlands the Naga obtained salt, dried fish, china, and a variety of items used for decorative purposes such as cowrie shells, beads, brass wire, and some ornaments produced specifically for the Naga market.

Michael C. Howard

The earliest European contact with the Naga was made in the 1830s. They found a linguistically diverse peoples living in numerous small villages. Beyond the village there was little in the way of political organization except for temporary alliances. A sense of tribal identity was poorly developed. The Europeans set out to understand and categorize what they perceived as somewhat chaotic conditions. The result of British efforts to create order was the gradual emergence in the Naga hills of tribal names and identities, in which styles of clothing were often used to identify the various tribes.

British colonial intervention from India was a piecemeal affair. The British sent ten military expeditions to the Naga territory between 1835 and 1851. In 1851 British forces withdrew from Naga territory and more or less left the Naga alone until 1866, when the Naga Hills District was formed in what was largely Angami territory with its headquarters at Samagudting. The British began developing tea plantations in the hills and established a new administrative center at Kohima in 1876. As a result, hostilities between the British and certain groups of Naga increased. These culminated in an attack by a group of Angami on the British base at Kohima in 1879 and British military retaliation in response. Rowney (1882: 169) comments that as a result of this military action by the British "peace was ostensibly restored; but it is hardly to be supposed that it will be long preserved." Gradually, however, nominal British rule did spread at last and the boundary of the scheduled district, which remained mostly outside British rule, was pushed progressively eastward.

British authorities banned headhunting, although this ban was not adhered to in isolated areas, and also sought to secure peaceful relations among the Naga. Some remote areas to the east remained subject to military pacification up to 1946. Colonial rule was largely indirect through government appointed chiefs. The British tried to limit Naga contact with the rest of India by making the Naga hills an excluded area. Gradual assimilation into the world beyond was encouraged, however, through the work of the American Baptist Missionary Society and by encouraging trade. The missionaries built schools and hospitals and educated an increasing number of Nagas.

In 1916 some 17,000 Nagas from India were recruited by the British to fight as soldiers in France. This had an important impact helping to unite Nagas within British India who eventually sought independence as a Naga nation. A politico-religious movement known as the Haraka Cult began to spread among the Naga in 1929. It was led by a man named Jadunang, who had served in the British army in Mesopotamia. Jadunang called for independence from the British and led a revolt against British rule. The movement spread among the Burmese Naga, led by a man known as Saya San, who also attacked the British. Jadunang was captured and executed in 1931, but the revolt continued under the leadership of a woman named Rani Gaidiliu, who was arrested and imprisoned in 1933 (see Yunuo 1974 and Das 1982 on Naga nationalism).

The British established a loose structure of indirect rule over the Naga in Burma only in 1940. Even then, many Naga remained outside even minimal colonial administration. Immediately prior to the Japanese invasion, the British were still engaged in mapping and exploring parts of Naga territory and there continued to be reports of large headhunting raids. At that time there were an estimated 75,000 Naga within the colony's boundaries. Portions of Naga territory became the scene of intense fighting between British and Japanese forces during the Second World War. The more isolated Naga areas in Burma were not occupied by the Japanese, but many Naga actively supported the Allied forces. Moreover, especially on the Indian side of the border, the presence of large military forces in the region resulted in reduced isolation for the Naga and greatly improved infrastructure.

Although during the war the British had briefly considered creating a separate colony made up of the various Naga territories, by the end of the war it was decided to divide the area between an independent India and an independent Burma. A group of Naga drawn from a cross section of Naga tribes from India responded in 1946 by forming the Naga National Council (NNC) that called for the creation of an independent Naga nation. Led by an Angami Naga named Zapho Phizo, the NNC pressed for independence and in 1956 proclaimed the creation of a federal Naga government (NFG) and began organizing an army. Hostilities broke out between Indian and Naga forces that resulted in widespread destruction and disruption of Naga villages.

The Indian government created the state of Nagaland in 1963. A cease-fire was agreed to the following year and a peace accord signed in 1975. Naga political forces split in the mid-1960s between those wishing to continue to press for independence and a Sema-led group seeking accommodation. Continued armed opposition to Indian rule was led by a group aligned with the Chinese communists calling itself the National Socialist Council of Nagaland (NSCN). The NSCN established a base across the border in Burma from which it launched raids into India. Naga associated with the NSCN converted many local Naga, who until then had remained largely outside missionary influence, to Christianity. Some Naga in Burma became involved in the on-going ethnic insurgency against the Burmese-dominated central government, though as minor participants. As part of a general offensive, in 1984 the Burmese army launched attacks on the NSCN.

Rowney (1882: 170) provides an early description of Naga clothing that is fairly typical of the accounts of missionaries, soldiers, and others from the late nineteenth century:

> There is no clothing for either sex in the higher elevations, and hence some imagine that the name Nágá may, perhaps, have been derived from the word 'Lungá,' or naked. At the foot of the hills the limbs are usually covered with a small piece of cloth dyed with indigo, a larger piece of coarse cloth being also used for covering the body when needed; while nearer the tea gardens the men wear kilts of different patterns and colours, and the women picturesque petticoats, and a cotton *chádur* thrown across the back and chest.

Rowney (1882: 173) adds that Naga women weave "both with cotton and with nettle fibres."

The quality of ethnographic observation of Naga life improved markedly during the early twentieth century as the result of the work of two government administrators: J.H. Hutton and James P. Mills. Hutton was the Deputy Commissioner of the Naga Hills and later served as Honorary Director of Ethnography for Assam. He conducted research in particular on the Angami and Sema and published important monographs on them in 1921 (Hutton 1921a, Hutton 1921b). Later he became Professor of Anthropology at Cambridge University. James P. Mills joined the Indian Civil service in 1913 and went to the Naga Hills in 1916 as an assistant to Hutton. In 1930 he replaced Hutton as Honorary Director of Ethnography for Assam. He published important monographs on the Lhota, Ao, and Rengma (Mills 1922, 1926, 1937). In 1947 he became Reader in Anthropology at London University's School of Oriental and Asian Studies. Hutton and Mills provided far more detailed information than previous observers about Naga textiles and the role of textiles in Naga societies. See Hutton (1921a: 22-33, 60-63) on the Angami and (1921b: 10-18, 48-51) on the Sema, Mills (1922: 8-11, 36-40) on the Lhota and (1937: 20-26, 67-68) on the Rengma (also see Kauffmann 1938). Unfortunately, little of this research is of direct relevance to the textiles of the Naga living further to the east in Burma.

Research on the Naga was also conducted prior to the Second World War by Austrian born anthropologist Christoph von Fürer-Haimendorf. Fürer-Haimendorf studied anthropology at the University of Vienna and the London School of Economics and Political Science. In 1936-37 he conducted fieldwork among Konyak Naga, who had recently come under British administration. While headhunting had been suppressed in the village of Wakching where he resided, it was still practiced in surrounding areas. He wrote a narrative of his life among the Konyak Naga (Fürer-Haimendorf 1939; also see Fürer-Haimendorf 1969) that included graphic accounts of an expedition into the little known territory to the east: "the unexplored mountains of the Kalyo Kengyus and the Patkoi Range" (1939: 130). The expedition also encountered the Yimchungru, a "scarcely known tribe" (1939: 131) that, like the Kalyo Kengyu (Khiamnungan), was still very warlike and practiced headhunting. Fürer-Haimendorf was to spend around fifteen years in India and Nepal, returning to the Naga only briefly in 1962, when he visited the Konyak Naga of the Tirop District of Assam (Fürer-Haimendorf 1976). He retired from the chair of Asian anthropology at the University of London in 1976. Since Konyak Naga live in Burma, his descriptions of their textiles will be referred to below.

Michael C. Howard

Unsettled conditions in Nagaland after the Second World War hampered further ethnographic research. At the time when Fürer-Haimendorf revisited the Naga in 1962 little research had been conducted since his pre-war study. The most important work during this period was that by Verrier Elwin (see Elwin 1959, 1964). During the following decades only a few other publications devoted much attention to Naga textiles in India (see Naga Institute of Culture 1968, Shirali 1983, Jacobs 1990, Sardeshpande 1987).

Very little has been written about the Naga textiles of Burma. Stevenson (1944: 18) describes the dress of Naga men as consisting of a "small girdle, from which a flap about 6" wide is looped to cover the genitals, and a cotton blanket which is loosely thrown over the shoulders" and the dress of the women as comprised "of a narrow skirt, extending to the waist to about 8" above the knee cap, and a cotton blanket thrown over the shoulders." For further information we must rely largely on material focusing on India. Of the works on Indian Naga, Sardeshpande (1987) is the most relevant for Burma as although his concern is primarily with the Khiamnungan and Konyak Naga of India, he makes some comments about those living across the border in Burma.

A few general points can be made about Naga textiles. Rowney's notion that the more isolated Naga were naked has been borne out by subsequent observation and research. Fürer-Haimendorf, writing about the Konyak Naga among whom he worked in the late 1930s comments about males (1969: 12):

Men and half-grown boys seldom wore more than a tight belt and a small apron, but at the time the custom of covering the private parts was probably of comparatively recent introduction.... many middle-aged men worked naked in house and field [and] were in the habit of performing their ritual duties naked.

They were rarely completely naked, of course, for they would usually wear some kind of decoration and often had a thin waist band of bamboo or fiber. During the 1930s he found that young girls often went about naked and as they matured wore skirts which sometimes barely covered the pubic areas. He notes that even in 1962 some young men went about naked.

Textile production among all Naga is the domain of women. Cotton is grown below elevations of about 1,000 meters, above which people obtain cotton through trade or formerly they used bark or leaf fibers. Cotton is spun onto a spindle that is weighted with a stone or wooden spindle-whorl. Weaving is done on a backstrap loom that is tied to a tree or a wall. Natural plant dyes were exclusively used until the 1920s, when aniline dyes were introduced and soon came into common use among the more westerly Naga. Embroidered patterns are sometimes added using a porcupine quill and dog's hair. The only time that men become involved in the production of textiles is for painting figures on the white cotton band found on *tsunkotepsu* cloths made by the Ao and Rengma (Jacobs 1990: 44).

The discussion below of textiles of the Naga groups in Burma, are based primarily on material from India.

Tangkhul

Mr. Porter, who led a punitive expedition against the Tangkhul in 1894, reported that although the people possessed clothing, they preferred to go about completely naked (Grant Brown 1911: 27). Mr. Porter did note that "when visiting riverine villages the men wear a sash tied round the waist with a loose end hanging down in front—a device which, even with the addition of a ring, hardly meets the demands of decency" (Grant Brown 1911: 28).

T.C. Hodson (1911: 21-22) provides a much more detailed description of the dress of the Tangkhul Naga living in Manipur:

The dress of the Tangkkhul men consists of a simple cloth worn round the waist and tied in a knot in front leaving the ends hanging down. These ends are fringed with straw pendants. The waist cloths are made of stout cotton woven in red and blue stripes two inches wide and horizontal. Over the body they wear in cold weather a long cloth in red and blue stripes to which in the case of chiefs custom permits the addition of a handsome border. Another pattern is in white stripes with terra cotta stripes and a black and white checker pattern, the plain variety being worn by the common people and the variety with the fringed border twelve to eighteen inches deep with white, orange, green and red stripes being restricted to chiefs. They often dispense with the not very ample clothing above described....

On high days and holidays the men wear a much more elaborate costume than that described above. It consists of a handsome kilt embroidered with ornaments like sequins and the headdress is the *luhup* with decorations of toucan feathers and tresses of hair.

The women wear small caps of blue cloth when working in the fields. Their petticoats reach from the waist to the knee and are made of cotton cloth manufactured in the weaving villages with red and white or black and white stripes two inches in width. Occasionally those who have some pretence to wealth or position wear petticoats of red with small stripes of white and black. A small jacket of the style worn by Manipuri women or a single cloth of the kind worn by the men completes the costume.

The particular patterns employed are described as follows (1911: 46):

Lozenge-shaped patterns are woven into the borders of the cloths and serve as trade-marks, possible as "luck" marks, and therefore possessing a magical value, and as ornaments, their presence adding to the price.

The following ten patterns of cloth are manufactured:

1. *Pakhon phi*, worn by men, white center with black or blue and red lines on the border.
2. *Leirum phi*, red and white with black marks.
3. *Kairao phi*, red and black or blue stripes.
4. *Lai phi*, worn by women, black and white stripes.
5. *Longkhum kasum*, women's cloth, red and white stripes.
6. *Sukham phi,* white ground with red or black border.
7. *Pordesum phi*, red with black or blue and white cross markings.
8. *Langoudesum phi*, women's cloth, black and red stripes.
9. *Kasendesum phi*, broad red and narrow black stripes, worn by women.
10. *Melao phi*, the waist-cloth worn by men, blue and red stripes.

There are no variations from the "sealed patterns" except in the case of the cloths worn by the *khullakpas* or headmen of a clan or village, who are by custom permitted to decorate their cloths with a handsome fringe with the loose ends of the threads tied into tassels, and a pattern of orange, red and white colours with occasionally a little green, diamond pattern on the edge. The stripes of the decorative border are pointed like the pattern of a backgammon board....

Hodson provides additional information about cloth production in his discussion of manufacturers (1911: 45-47). Here he notes that there are six Tangkhul villages that specialize in weaving. Women of these villages generally do not marry men from non-weaving villages and when they do are forbidden to weave. Weaving is done exclusively by women using a backstrap loom made of two pieces of bamboo and a leather strap. The raw cotton is produced by Kukis living west of the Manipuri capital, and the Tangkhul obtain this cotton from the royal bazaar in the capital. Hodson describes several dye sources (1911: 45): black or dark blue from the juice of the wild indigo (sometimes lampblack is used for black); red or terracotta from a bark purchased from the plains; and green, yellow, and orange from the barks of jungle trees. In reference to the dyeing process, however, he remarks that "it is not at all easy to get the people to talk about the details of their industry, because they suspect an inquirer of ulterior motives and cannot understand his curiosity."

Roy (1979) provides a brief survey of the Tangkhul of Manipur and their dress, but his book contains more information on other ethnolinguistic groups in Manipur. His book includes a few photos of Tangkhul women wearing traditional costumes and weaving. In his list of various local names for weaving implements, he mentions (1979: 18) that the Tangkhul name for spinning wheel is *tareng*. His work includes a survey of types of cloth and motifs which mentions several Tangkhul cloth types (1979: 49-50) and differs from Hodson's earlier list:

> *phangvai kashan (phanek):* a cloth used only by wealthy women, this cloth features spear motifs near the ends of the center piece, alternative red and black patches in between which are wavy white lines on a red and green background on the side pieces.
>
> *changkham:* a body cloth used by both sexes, with alternating red and black stripes in the center and spear motifs near the borders.
>
> *seiyang kashan:* a skirt (*phanek*) made of three pieces sewn together.
>
> *shankhan:* a skirt with black and white stripes and a red background.
>
> *kongla kashan:* a skirt with red, black, and white stripes decorated with cross-hatching.
>
> *kashang kashan:* a skirt with white stripes on a red background.
>
> *khoran phi:* a body cloth used by both sexes featuring three motifs: *Phungyai* (goddess of wealth), *seihatphei* (leg of an insect), and *siras* (representing the prime of life and youth).
>
> *thang-gang:* a special cloth used by a person who has demonstrated bravery by killing enemies, who has a good house, and who has had a particularly good harvest.
>
> *phalengchi:* a mill made red blanket presented by the Manipuri rajah to Tangkhul chiefs and their assistants.

Shirali (1983: 67-68, 79), in a survey of textiles and bamboo crafts in northeastern India conducted in late 1976, sponsored by the Indian government's Ministry of Industry, describes two contemporary Tangkhul textiles (a tubeskirt and a shawl) made in Ukhrul, northeastern Manipur. The two textiles are woven out of commercial rayon, and the author comments that women are learning to weave on frame looms, although more traditional textiles are still woven on backstrap looms. The tubeskirt (106cm x 185cm) is mainly red with black stripes bordered by thin yellow lines. Geometric motifs in white, pink, green, and red are distributed within the rows. They are woven out of thicker yarn than the rest of the cloth and in an extra weft so that the weft is visible only on the front of the textile. The shawl (89cm x 190cm) is relatively plain, consisting of two panels stitched together and a black band in the center with the rest of the shawl featuring thinner stripes in dark red, light red, and white. The border is green and white. There is also a photograph (1983: 60 fig.66) of three Tangkhul women in Ukhrul wearing tubeskirts.

Jacobs (1990) has color photographs of four Tangkhul shawls and three skirts that are probably Tangkhul. Unfortunately, no information beyond the ethnic group of origin is provided. Three of the shawls (top right p. 282, bottom right p. 282, and p. 283) are red with four to five broad black bands and a few narrow white and black stripes. They are relatively plain with bands of spear patterns in contrasting colors (green, red, black, and white) near the ends. The fourth shawl (p. 284) is white with two plain indigo bands and four smaller bands made up of white and indigo square and some thin red lines. Two of the women's skirts are red with black or black, red, and white stripes with no additional patterning or black with four white stripes and no other patterning (top left p. 304, bottom right p. 304).

Yimchungru

The Yimchungru (also known as Yimchunger) were outside of British colonial administration prior to the Second World War and early ethnographic material on them is limited. Their textiles in India are described in some detail (along with drawings of details) in the Naga Institute of Culture's *The Arts and Crafts of Nagaland* (1968: 34-40). The Yimchungru have ten types of shawl:

> *aneak khim:* worn by men and women without restrictions; plain black.
>
> *mokhok:* worn by a common person who is neither wealthy or a warrior; plain white.
>
> *amurk khim:* worn by any man or a woman; middle black panel with five rows of twelve evenly spaced relatively small red rectangular designs for a total of sixty;

the panels on the sides have alternating red, black, and blue bands.

sangkonglim khim: the log drum shawl, worn by a man or woman without restriction; black, narrow white band in each of the three panels; a "w"-shaped red design in the band is said to resemble the design on log drums.

tsungrem khim: worn only by rich women; similar to the *amurthe khim*; the shawl gets its name from a story about a beautiful woman named Tsungrem who descended from heaven and was captured by a young man while picking flowers from his garden, the man then married her and soon became very wealthy.

rong khim: worn only by a warrior; if a non-warrior were to wear this type of shawl it was believed that he would die of leprosy; eight lines with eight or twelve larger and more prominent red designs for a total of sixty-four or ninety-six; the designs are found on all three panels; the shawl featuring ninety-six designs is reserved for warriors of particular repute, the red being said to symbolize the blood of enemies.

kechinger rong khim: a second order warrior's shawl worn by a man who has taken the right hand of a slain enemy; black with narrow gray stripes at the edges; seven rows of eight relatively small red rectangular designs for a total of fifty-six; the designs are found on all three panels.

amurthre khim: worn by a man who has killed a tiger (the pattern of the shawl is said to resemble the stripes of a tiger skin); when the owner of the shawl dies a tiger figure made of bamboo and covered in the shawl is placed on his grave; blue background, eight lines of red designs spread over four patches in the middle panel; the spaces between the patches have other designs; the side panels have alternating blue, black, and red bands.

rehuke khim: the cowrie shawl, worn by wealthy men; black background, small cowrie shells are stitched on to the cloth to form rows of circles, there can be up to eight rows of with sixty-four circles for the shawl of an exceptionally wealthy man; a human figure of cowrie shells is added if the owner is also a warrior.

lungtungshe khim: worn only by a warrior who has offered a feast of merit and referred to as a "complete" shawl; similar to the Ao *tsunkotepsu* shawl, but without paintings on the white band.

Among the skirts commonly worn by Yimchungru females are two types. One is called a *kechingperu khim.* It is the type of skirt first given to a girl when she is required to wear a skirt. It is white with narrow black and white bands and red "w" and "v" designs in the center. The second is called a *alongza khim* or *langa imjung.* It is worn by rich women only. It is black with two wide red bands in the center and very narrow red and blue bands on the sides. The black portion in the center between the two wide red bands has red lozenge and zigzag designs.

Elwin (1959: 45) shows drawings of Yimchungru textiles woven at the Tuensang Cottage Industries Centre (located in northeast Nagaland). Jacobs (1990) also has photos of two Yimchungru shawls and one woman's skirt (again, with virtually no additional information on the pieces). The first shawl (top right p. 293) is described as being for a man who has completed the full series of feasts of merit. The description, thus, implies that it is a *lungtungshe khim* shawl. In fact, it appears to be an example of a *rong khim* shawl with twelve rows of red designs and, therefore, to have belonged to a warrior of high repute assuming the account in the Naga Institute of Culture's *The Arts and Crafts of Nagaland* (1968) is accurate. The second shawl (bottom right p. 293) is almost identical to the first one, but is described as a shawl for a man who has taken heads and is likely to be another example of a *rong khim* shawl. Both shawls have alternating white, blue, and red stripes of equal width. The skirt (bottom right p. 301) is black with red stripes and red supplementary patterning and is likely an example of a *alongza khim* or *langa imjung* skirt.

Michael C. Howard

Khiamnungan

The Khiamnungan (also known as Kalyo-Kengyo) were also beyond British colonial administration prior to the Second World War and, thus, are poorly described in the older ethnographic literature. As mentioned above, the group in Burma known as Heimei have been included as a subgroup of Khiamnungan.

Elwin (1959: 31) notes that they "embroider their blue fabrics with red squares of dog's hair" and that the "Khienmungans and Changs have a broad cowrie belt, with a brass disk in front" (1959: 31, 33). Their shawls are described in *The Arts and Crafts of Nagaland* (Naga Institute of Culture 1968: 40):

> The Khienmunghans also have a number of shawls, designs of which indicate the status of the owner. The general pattern of design is black on which rectangular or square red designs are embroidered. One of the commonest shawls is 1.5 meters long and 1.2 meters wide. It is a black cloth with narrow white bands at each of the two ends at an interval of 2 cms. In the black portion of it are embroidered fifty six red rectangular designs each measuring 4 cms long and 3.5 cms wide arranged equally in seven rows. The same kind of shawl are worn by upper Konyak and Eastern Sangtam groups.

It is also mentioned that they have a cowrie shawl that is worn by warriors (1968: 44).

Jacobs (1990) has photographs of two Khiamnungan (Kalyo-Kengyo) textiles and one cowrie shell shawl of the type used by the Khiamnungan and others, but that is not identified as to specific group (p. 297). The first of the Khiamnungan textiles is a shag carpet-like shawl that has a white base consisting of three joined panels with indigo yarn forming the shag part (p. 289). The second piece is a woman's skirt worn by the Sangtam but bought from the Khiamnungan (bottom right p. 303). It is black with a variety of thin white stripes. As with most other pieces in the Jacobs volume, no additional information is provided.

Sardeshpande (1987) provides the most detailed information on Khiamnungan textiles and dress. While he focuses on Khiamnungans living in India he also makes occasional reference to those across the border in Burma. At the time of his writing, Sardeshpande (1987: 56) reports that Khiamnungan weavers tended to get their yarn and thread from commercial centers rather than making their own from locally grown cotton or other fibers. In addition to cotton, in the past the Khiamnungans also made yarn from bark and dog hair. This yarn has since been replaced by wool. He also notes (1987: 55) that commercial dyes are rapidly replacing natural ones, but remarks that "everyone without exception is agreed on the fact that the local dyes were better and fast as compared to the market commodity which fades fast and spreads when wet."

The primary item of Khiamnungan male attire is a cotton loincloth. Sardeshpande (1987: 68) describes this as consisting of "a cuplike inner cloth pouch covering the genitals and a short 6 inch wide and about 16 inch long outer flap hanging in front from the string belt." The loincloth of a boy under the age of twelve, known as a *khepla,* is white with four thin horizontal red stripes on the outer flap. Males over the age of twelve wear a loincloth, known as a *sangpo,* shaped as above, that is black with three white vertical double lines down the sides and two thick red vertical lines in the center. Sardeshpande (1987: 69) notes that this pattern is identical for Khiamnungan in India and Burma.

Men also wear a cotton shawl, known as a *nyethailon.* This shawl is plain white, measuring about six feet by three and a half feet, and made of three pieces of cloth stitched together. Traditionally, those who have taken heads during special ceremonial occasions wore a shawl known as a *nyechet* instead of a *nyethailon.* This shawl measures about six feet by four feet which is also black, but features special decorations. There are four pairs of white stripes on the top and bottom and a series of red rectangles placed in seven horizontal rows about six inches apart. Two rows are placed near the top and bottom and three in the center. The three center rows are joined by stitching. The *nyechet* has lost much of its traditional meaning in recent years and Sardeshpande (1987: 71) comments that "these days Nyecet has become the popular and common shawl worn by most. Even guests are presented with Nyecet irrespective of their head-taking propensity or capability."

Men wear fancier shawls on ceremonial occasions. Sardeshpande (1987: 71) describes the ceremonial shawl known as *shetneh* or *nein*. This shawl is the ceremonial version of the *nyechet* and features circles of small cowrie shells sewn in six inch diameter circles around every other red rectangle. Other special ceremonial items of dress include the *nyekha* and *phacham*. The *nyekha* is worn by warriors when performing ceremonial dances (1987: 71). It is a thick piece of cotton cloth measuring about sixty centimeters in length and twenty-five centimeters in width. It is covered with small cowries which along the sides are patterned to look like flowers. The *phacham* is also worn by warriors during ceremonial dances as well as being carried into battle, where it is used to bandage wounds, and placed by the body of a dead warrior to honor him until the body is removed for burial (1987: 72). Phacham made of a white piece of cotton cloth measuring about 2.5 meters in length by eight centimeters in width. These are decorated with black and red crosses and parellel lines. Older *phacham* had black stips of cloth with gibbon hair attached.

Sardeshpande (1987: 69) reports that "these days trousers, shirts, vests, jackets, cowboy hats and shorts" are rapidly replacing more traditional items of male dress.

Until recently, Khiamnungan females "wrapped a narrow loin cloth called Nyecho round lower hips and just about covering frontal privacy" (Sardeshpande 1987: 69). These are made of cotton. Young girls under the age of twelve wore a white *nyecho* that was one meter long andfifteen centimeters wide, decorated with "squares marked in black double vertical and single horizontal lines, the horizontal end lines also being double, and additional single vertical red lines a foot apart." Upon reaching puberty, females begin wearing a black *nyecho*. This cloth is about one meter long and twenty centimeters wide. Adult women also wore a black *nyethailon*. On ceremonial occasions and during festivals the plain black *nyethailon* was replaced with another type of black shawl known as a *khowneh*. This shawl is decorated with groups of seven white lines at the top and bottom and four white stripes in the middle (Sardeshpande 1987: 70).

Women now wear non-traditional skirts of various designs and a wide range of clothing over their upper bodies, include "a bush shirt erasing any difference between male and female insofar as the upper body is concerned (1987: 69-70). Sardeshpande (1987: 70) also remarks that in one village across the border in Burma he saw "some housewifes in midis and maxis picked up from a Noklak fancy shop."

Konyak

Konyak Naga living in Burma are primarily of the Rangpan or Tase subgroup. Sardeshpande (1987: 111) refers to the Konyak living in the India-Burma border area as Upper Konyak. These are the Konyak who live among the hills astride the Patkoi range. He says that their northern limit in Burma is around Mawhpun near Hkamla and to the south towards Lasan (Lachen). Hkamla and Lasan roughly demarcate their eastern boundaries.

There is no material describing the textiles or costumes of the Konyak in Burma or of the Rangpan-Tase in particular, but there is a good deal of material on other Konyak groups in India. Fürer-Haimendorf (1969) provides especially good information on the dress of the Konyak Naga as of the late 1930s. Men wore a loincloth that was tucked into a belt made of bark. The width and length of the loincloth varied. Middle-aged and older men generally wore plain blue loincloths, but boys and young men "favoured aprons embroidered in red and yellow wool, which was obtained in the markets of the plains" (1969: 12). These embroidered loincloths were usually gifts from girlfriends. Elwin (1959: 48) provides an illustration of such a sash dating from after the war colored red, green, blue, and yellow. Fürer-Haimendorf (1976: 31) notes that when he revisited the Konyak Naga in 1962 old men in the hills still wore only a belt with no loincloth and comments that men began to wear loincloths "only as trade with the inhabitants of the plains increased." Sardeshpande (1987: 147) refers to the male's loincloth as a *mai* and gives the dimensions of the outer flap as about two feet long by nine to ten inches wide. The cane and leather belt he refers to as a *singphiang*. He describes the loincloth as being made of black cotton with twin red lines in the center and thin green vertical lines on the outer edge.

53

Fürer-Haimendorf (1969: 12) reports that "women and girls of Thenkoh villages wore narrow, oblong pieces of cloth wrapped round the waist, with one corner tucked in over the left hip. The skirts were about 10 inches wide and provided the cover required by Konyak standards of decency." The skirts of girls and unmarried women usually were plain white or blue, while married women preferred "skirts with patterns of narrow stripes in red and white" (1969: 12). The dress of women in Thendu villages was somewhat different. Young girls sometimes went nude, and adult women "put on a narrow skirt, usually not more than 6 inches wide" (1969: 12). Sardeshpande (1987: 147-148) refers to the female skirt as a *shingkai* and says that it is eighteen inches broad.

Fürer-Haimendorf (1969: 13) mentions that women sometimes wore skirts at ceremonies that indicated status differences. Those of "pure chiefly blood" wore "red and white striped skirts decorated with embroidery, glass beads, and tassels dyed of goat's hair." Women from "minor chiefly clans" wore similar skirts, but without the goat's hair tassels. Commoners tended to wear dark blue skirts with no ornamentation. Sardeshpande (1987: 150) describes women's ceremonial attire as including a knee-length skirt called a *shingluk.* This skirt is described as having a black background and being made of two pieces of cloth that are stitched together. The upper piece has three equidistant half inch green stipes and the lower piece features nine stripes in the middle (blue-red-black-white, blue-red-black-white, and blue) and a thin green line at the bottom. This skirt is also sometimes worn as a shawl.

During the rainy season, Thendu girls and women sometimes also wore a rain cloak made of shredded palm leaves (Elwin 1959: 13). When it was not raining, this cloak might be worn round the hips. Elwin (1959: 9) provides a photograph of a Konyak girl in such a "grass skirt."

According to Fürer-Haimendorf (1969: 13), the Thendu people made cloth only from the bark-fiber of the *Urticacaea Debregasia velutina* shrub. They had to obtain cotton cloths from the Thenkoh people, who themselves produced relatively little cotton and made some of their cloth also out of bark-fiber. Fürer-Haimendorf (1969: 20) regards weaving such bark-fiber cloth as an older weaving tradition preceding weaving cotton cloth. He describes (1969: 20) the processing of bark-fiber as follows:

> The bark had first to be torn to shreds, teased out, and dried. From this a coarse thread was spun on an ordinary spindle, which was weighted by a stone or hardwood spindle whorl. But the yarn was, in this state, too rough to be used for weaving, and long hours of boiling in water were necessary before it became sufficiently pliable and could be woven into cloth.

In some interior villages cotton seeds were removed "with the help of pebbles" (1969: 20). Elsewhere the wooden machine commonly found throughout much of mainland Southeast Asia was used for this purpose. In this instance, it was probably introduced from Assam. Weaving was done on a backstrap loom. Pieces of cloth initially were sewn together with needles made of bone, but by the time of Fürer-Haimendorf's research steel needles were widely used.

Cloth made from bark was usually left uncolored, a dull off-white. Some cotton cloth was also left undyed. If dyed, the most common colors were shades of blue produced from indigo. A red color was made by soaking the thread for two to three days in a solution made from the roots of the *Rubia sikkimensis.* Women of child-bearing age were not permitted to dye cloth, the activity being reserved for older women. Fürer-Haimendorf was unable, however, to discover a reason for this.

While the Konyak Naga studied by Fürer-Haimendorf do not appear to have developed as wide a range of textiles associated with status as did many other Naga groups, there are several shawls and other items of clothing among the Naga as a whole that are associated with status. These shawls are usually made out of cotton, although there are also shawls made of bark-fiber. Fürer-Haimendorf (1969: 13) does mention one status-related shawl which is a "richly embroidered cloth with red and white stripes" that is worn only by men who have taken heads. He may be referring here to a type of shawl similar, or the same as, two shawls illustrated in Jacobs (1990: 292, top left 293) that are described as belonging to a man who has completed the full series of feasts of merit. *The Arts and Crafts of Nagaland* (Naga Institute of Culture 1968: 51, 55) describes six different types of shawl worn by the Konyak (there are also plain blue shawls):

> *meyni:* worn by chiefs and elders only; broad dark blue and red bands with four lines of cowries in circles and red-colored fringe (about ten centimeters in length) tied at intervals along the lines formed by the cowries; the cowries are a sign of achievement (in the past this meant head-taking), and the fringes indicate the wealth and popularity of the owner; cowrie shell shawls are mentioned by Fürer-Haimendorf (1976: 120) and Elwin (1959: 31, 33).
>
> *hompani:* worn by village elders; same as *meyni* but without the cowries or fringes.
>
> *nye-myon:* worn only by elders at important meetings; red with narrow black lines about three to four centimeters apart; a diamond pattern is woven at intervals in the red band.
>
> *nyauni:* worn by wealthy men; a red base with three narrow black lines near the edges and groups of four narrow black lines at regular intervals towards the center; a broad band in the center with lozenge patterns in white
>
> *shatni:* worn by wealthy women; one of these is given to a woman by her parents when she marries, which she does not wear, but puts away to be used to wrap her body when she dies; red base two narrow white lines and two narrow black lines near the edges; five black bands in the center with a white curved design; crossed at regular intervals by three narrow red lines
>
> *nikola:* worn by women; white with a dark blue stripes and red lozenge designs in the center

Sardeshapnde offers descriptions and names for Konyak shawls that differ from the above. These may reflect differences among Konyak groups with the Naga Institute of Culture's descriptions being for Lower Konyak and Sardeshpande's for Upper Konyak. It is likely that Sardeshpande's descriptions best reflect the shawls of Konyak living in Burma. Sardeshpande (1987: 147) describes the common man's shawl that he says is referred to as a *inkyakyoubu* or *mupaningkhyak.* He describes it as being black "with six lines of red rectangles two to three inches by one to two inches in the middle portion and four half inch strips of green on either edge, with one more thick green line outside each group of strips." He refers to the ceremonial shawl as a *olengkhyak* and describes it as follows (1987: 149-150):

> The basic background colour of the Olengkhak is red, with black and white, in that order, added on. The basic design is short lateral double strips of reclining V lines opposing each other.... There are three pieces in each shawl, which are then stitched together. The two outer ones are identical, red background with one half inch black strip at either end and two half inch black strips in the centre. The middle piece has three strips of twin V lines with two black and red strips separating the former three. At the broad end the twin V shape strips are left as six inch white strips.

Interestingly, Sardeshpande makes no mention of status-related shawls, cowrie decorations, or special women's ceremonial shawls.

Ceremonial male attire also includes a cloth sash attached to a basket worn astride one hip. This belt is referred to as a *saopak.* It is three to four inches wide and made of white cotton with thick red lines of diamond shape along its length.

Fürer-Haimendorf's books on the Naga contain a variety of photos depicting the dress of the Konyak Naga among whom he worked. Elwin (1959) also provides a number of useful illustrations, including a young man's colorful sash (1959: 48), details of six designs used in women's skirts (1959: 51) and a photo of a Konyak girl making a skirt at the Cottage Industries Training and Production Centre at Mon that is located in the far north of Nagaland (1959: 189). Sardeshpande (1987) includes colored drawings of three Konyak shawls among the plates at the end of his book. Finally, Jacobs (1990: 175) has two 1985 color photographs of Konyak Nagas from Burma. The women in one photograph are topless with plain white long skirts. The man in the other is dressed in modified European-style clothes. Jacobs also has photographs of three Konyak textiles. The first (top left p. 274) is described as a youth's painted bark belt with human and animal figures with tassels that are worn at the back. Then there are two almost identical shawls (p. 292, top left p. 293) that, as mentioned above, are described as belonging to a man who has completed the full series of feasts of merit.

Wancho

Wancho dress appears to be similar to that of the Konyak. Descriptions of their dress is limited. The two main published sources on the Wancho in India are Elwin (1964) and Barua (1991). Elwin (1964: 279-280) provides illustrations of two Wancho bags. Barua (1991: 226) mentions "shoulder bags of various designs" alone among their textiles and provides five rather grainy black and white photographs: four of Wancho women wearing plain short skirts and one of a Wancho chief wearing a plain white loincloth. There are no descriptions of Wancho dress in Burma.

The Mru

Mru is spoken by over 35,000 people in the Arakan Hills of Burma, by another 15,000 to 20,000 across the border in the Chittagong Hills of Bangladesh, and by some 15,000 in neighboring parts of India. The Mru (also known as Mro or Mroo) live in close proximity to many Chin speakers. According to Brauns and Löffler (1990: 34) the Mru are divided into five groups: Anok, Tshungma, Domnong, Dopreng, and Rumma. The southern Tsungma (who go by the name Longhu) live in close proximity to the Khumi and have adopted many aspects of Khumi culture. The Dopreng and Rumma are the southernmost groups, living in Bangladesh and across the border in Burma's Rakhine State. The Mru appear to have been displaced from their home in the Arakan Hills into the Chittagong Hills by the Khami.

Mru society is divided into patriclans. Spearman (1880, II: 424-425) names fifteen Mru clans and states that each is under a chief, meaning clan leader. Such leaders generally have little power in what is basically an egalitarian society. Links with outside hierarchical societies in the past created

positions of village headmen, known as *karbari* (in Bangladesh) or *ruatsa* (in Burma, meaning "village eater"), but these headmen exerted little more power than any household head. There is also a tradition of "big-men" or *tshai-ria*. These are clan heads who were able to exert influence over a group of clans. The Mru also have feasts of merit which bestow prestige but no power. Such feasts of merit had become rare by the 1950s.

The dress of the Mru is relatively simple. Men's dress consists of a thin loincloth and a headcloth. They also sometimes wear a sleeveless jacket. Women's dress is equally simple, consisting of a short skirt and various items of jewelry. Their clothing is all made of cotton.

Spearman provides an early account of Mru costume. He describes the dress of the men as consisting of "a strip of cloth round their loins and between their legs" (1880, II: 425) which he describes as blue and "about four inches wide" (1880, II: 66). He also comments that they "are not particular as to their head dress or personal appearance" (1880, II: 66). He reports that the women wear essentially the same clothing as Khami women: "a short petticoat" (1880, II: 425) which he further describes as "a short blue cloth reaching to the knee and open at the side" which is "fastened round the waist with a belt of cords covered either with large beads or copper rings" and that "over their breast is worn a small strip of cloth" (1880, II: 66). Spearman describes Mru blankets as usually having "a black and white pattern, shewing only on one side" (1880, II: 76).

A more contemporary and comprehensive description of Mru textiles and dress is provided by Brauns and Löffler (1990: see p. 133-137), based on fieldwork in the 1960s. The Mru grow cotton which is harvested in October and made into thread, spindles being used rather than a spinning wheel. Their cotton gins are usually made by Bengali carpenters, it is "the only machine utilized by the Mru" (Brauns and Löffler 1990: 133). Backstrap looms are used for weaving, the men making the loom parts (the authors provide drawings of a loom and spindle on p. 135). Plant dyes are still used for red and indigo, otherwise commercial dyes and colored yarns are purchased. Though most cotton is grown for domestic use, raw cotton and thread are sold at nearby markets to Bengali traders. Ceremonially, young women are given richly decorated looms before marriage, as a wedding gift from their future husband.

By the 1960s men's loincloths were usually made of commercial cotton. The cloth is undecorated and commonly colored red, white, or indigo. Previously loincloths were made of locally produced cloth, employing natural dyes, and with some embroidered decoration. The "work jacket" is still made of local cotton. It is sleeveless, made from a single piece of cloth, white with red and black stripes.

The woman's skirt, *wan-klai,* is an indigo strip of cotton cloth measuring about 150cm x 25cm. The ends of the cloth are sewn together and worn so that the skirt consists of two layers of cloth that are wrapped round the hips. There is an embroidered strip measuring between 10cm and 30cm on the outer backside of the skirt. The patterns are left up to the individual and are embroidered with a needle. While old pieces used natural dyes, newer ones employ commercial dyes. For everyday wear the pattern is worn inside out, and it is shown only during festivals. The edge of the skirt is trimmed with white or red ringlets. In the past, small shells from a fruit were also used.

A few other types of textile are used. Mru men sometimes use a shoulder bag, white with brown stripes, which were still being made in the 1960s, though rarely. Blankets are made from three stips of cloth. These may be plain or feature broad white and red stripes and thin black stripes. They are about two meters long and woven with especially thick thread. At the ends the warp threads are twisted. Single pieces of cloth are also used as coverlets for children. Finally, Mru sometimes wear cloaks, but these are always of imported cloth. In the 1960s green or blue cloaks were popular. Previously, red and yellow were popular colors.

Textiles feature in marriage exchanges, but are less prominent than is the case with some the materially richer and more hierarchical Chin societies to the north. The Mru divide wedding goods into male and female. Male goods include weapons (mainly spears) and chickens. Female goods include lengths of cloth and fish. There are supposed to be balanced exchanges of spears and cloth. Blankets are not particularly associated with hosting of feasts of merit. When a person dies, the corpse is on display for two to three days, dressed in fresh clothing. When the body is placed in the coffin, it is covered with a piece of cloth.

5

The Kachin

As Leach (1954: 41) notes, the Burmese originally used the category Kachin to refer loosely to "the barbarians of the north-east frontiers" and did not use it as an ethnolinguistic category. The term Kachin subsequently has come to be used commonly as a cultural category for Jingpho-speakers, but also includes speakers of Taman, which is a closely related Kachinic language. Within Burma the Jingpho are usually known as Jinghpaw. In addition to standard Jingpho there are a number of dialects. These include: Hkanu (or Hkahku), Kauri (or Gauri), Tsasen, Duleng, and Htingnai. There are around 600,000 Jingpho speakers in Burma, living mainly in Kachin State as well as in northern Shan State, in a very mountainous region with narrow valleys. Those Jingpho living closest to the Shan have assimilated aspects of Shan culture.

There are about 10,000 Taman in Burma's Kachin State. There is little information on them, but their culture seems to be similar to that of the Jingpho (see Lowis 1911: 27-27).

The Jingpho

Jingpho is recognized as an official nationality in China. There are some 100,000 Jingpho-speakers living in a compact area in the mountains of southwestern Yunnan. There are also around 7,000 Jingpho-speakers in Assam and Arunchal Pradesh States in India, where they are known as Singpo. Rowney, writing in the late nineteenth century, describes the Singpos as being divided into twelve relatively autonomous clans, each with its own chief (1882: 166-167). They are Buddhists who also believe in malignant spirits.

Prior to the coming of state control to the Jingpho there were two different forms of Jingpho socio-political organization, *gumsa* and *gumlao*. The *gumsa* system was aristocratic and hierarchical and the *gumlao* system democratic and egalitarian. Those adhering to the *gumsa* system were organized into chieftanships of varying size. The office of chief was hereditary, passed on from father to youngest son, and chiefs came from chiefly kin groups. The chief's power, however, depended largely on personal initiative. There was also a council of elders. In addition to aristocrats and commoners, the *gumsa* system also included slaves. Slavery, however, was gradually eliminated under British rule, although it appears to have survived in some areas into the 1920s.

The Jingpho recognize a common ancestry and are subdivided on the basis of family or clan names. According to Hanson (1913: 13), they are said to be descended from a semi-mythical ancestor called "Wahkyet wa". His five eldest sons were the founders of five clans associated with hereditary chieftanships. There were also three younger sons whose clans became associated with three of the senior clans. Members of these clans could become chiefs, but were not afforded the same status as the hereditary chiefs of the senior clans. The ancestral home of these clans appears to be in the region of the borders of Burma, China, and Assam. From this area they moved south into Assam and Burma, settling around the present town of Putao in Burma. They then spread out, exterminating, driving out or conquering those in their path. Gilhodes (1996: 107) provides an apt dictate from the Kachin's great spirit concerning their raiding activities: "Rob your neighbors, but don't allow yourself to be caught." Palaungs and Chin were driven south and the

Khamti Tai were cut off from other Tais of the Shan states. Many valley dwelling Shans in the north were forced to pay tribute to the Jingpho chiefs.

The Kachin built their villages on top of ridges and before the advent of British rule, warfare and raiding were common among them. Since then settlement in valleys has become more usual. They are swidden farmers and agriculture is household based. Rice is their main crop. Among their other crops are maize, millet, and cotton. There is also a tradition of growing opium poppies.

Some Jingpho-speakers moved into Assam in the early nineteenth century (where they are known as Singpo) and in the mid-nineteenth century began moving into the northern Shan states and neighboring areas. Scott (1911: 93) comments that their movement to the south and west is due to a combination of factors: (1) over population, (2) their practice of slash-and-burn agriculture, and (3) an inheritance pattern whereby land is inherited by the youngest son and older brothers are often forced

to move in search of new land. They were feared by their neighbors. Thus, Scott and Hardiman (1900, I/II: 332) report:

> The Burmans and Shans stood in great awe of the Kachins. For some years before the annexation, it was a common thing for villagers in the Bhamo district to sleep in boats on the river, so that they might have some chance of escape from a sudden raid. Bhamo itself had been attacked in 1884 by a combination of Chinese and Kachins and was almost completely destroyed.

Reverend Hanson (1913: 12) paints a similar picture of the Jingpho:

> The Kachin chief lived in his mountain "fortress," from which he sent subordinates to collect taxes or levy blackmail on the Shans and Burmans in the lowlands. If there was any delay in payment, or if they showed any spirit of insubordination, the robber-chief took quick vengeance, raiding their villages or imposing a heavy fine in grain, cattle and money.

The British first encountered Jingpho-speakers in Assam around 1824 and over the next ten to fifteen years British military intelligence collected a good deal of information on them and other Jingpho-speakers to the east. Early British writers, much like the Burmese, tended to lump various hill-dwelling peoples under the category of Kachin or an equivalent name. These people lived in what came to be known as the Kachin Hills Area. Some early twentieth century observers, however, used Kachin as a linguistic category, and in this regard the categories Kachin and Jingpho came to be used somewhat interchangeably. In terms of identification of dress this has tended to be the case.

British military and administrative control was established among the southern Jingpho towards the end of the nineteenth century, while other areas were not brought under control until near the outbreak of the Second World War. The 1901 census enumerated 67,340 Jingpho/Kachin, but an equal number was estimated to be living beyond British administration. By the early twentieth century, British administration extended only a little beyond the

5.1. Two Taman girls from the Upper Chindwin River area. [Stevenson 1943: f.pg. 42]

railhead town of Myitkyina. Following a Chinese visit to Hkamti Long in 1906 and a raid on the village of Hpimaw, the British took greater interest in this northern area. They established a new district headquarters at Hkamti Long (renamed Putao) in 1914. Ward (1921: 282) writes that a group of Jingpho living in unadministered territory raided tribes under British juridiction in 1915 and resisted a British puntative expedition sent in response. British rule, once established, was largely indirect. Kachin State was created in newly independent Burma in 1947.

American Baptist and European Catholic missionaries began work among the Jingpho in the Bhamo area in the late nineteenth century. During the early twentieth century missionaries became active in other areas as well. Most Kachin, however, continued to adhere to their traditional religious beliefs and practices that focused on worship of a variety of ancestral spirits and numerous other spirits that function mainly to frustrate people. Their religious specialists included non-hereditary shamans and diviners.

Leach (1954: 55) remarks that "apart from speech, the most obvious cultural variable in different parts of the Kachin Hills is dress"—a much stronger assertion than that of Gilhodes, who contends that "the costume varies a little according to the tribes" (1910: 619; 1996: 111). Most of the people living in the Kachin Hills (including speakers of several different languages) "live in much the same sort of houses, they cultivate land in much the same sort of way, they adhere to much the same sort of religious practices, to a substantial extent they share a common body of myth and tradition, but costume and the details of material culture show wide variation." He continues by noting that the variations in dress "are more or less regional and have only a low correlation with language differences." Unfortunately, Leach does not elaborate this theme beyond noting that "there is certainly plenty of scope here for a student of material culture" (1954: 55) and mentioning that some Jingpho decorate their cloth with brocade weave and others with plain stripes and that Hkahku (Hkanu) Jingpho in the north wear tubeskirts while southern Jingpho wear rectangular skirts.

Reverend Hanson (1913: 46-47) describes men's dress as follows:

5.2. Two Jingpho women [Scott and Hardiman 1900, I/II: plate 24, f.pg. 276]

> …there is no uniformity as to material worn, or the particular cut of coat and trousers. Nearly everything they wear is bought in the Shan, Chinese and Burman bazaars, and styles and shades vary accordingly…. The Hkahku me probably kept closest to the ancestral way of dressing. They wear a long, narrow, variegated turban, leaving the high top-not in view, a blue coat with long, wide sleeves, and a towel-like loin-cloth coming down to the knees. Among the southern Kachins, especially east of the Irrawaddy, the loin-cloth has given place to Shan or Chinese trousers…. The only articles common to the men of today is the long, useful sword and the equally indispensable bag or haversack…. The bags are elaborately embroidered, and the different patterns indicate the taste and fancies of different communities…. They often display a considerable amount of ornament,

and young men carry a richly embroidered "towel" tied to the shoulder strap, always a gift of some young women, and worn for her sake.

While he mentions that different groups have distinctive bags, he does not elaborate as to how they differ.

Hanson (1913: 47-48) offers the following description of women's dress:

> They still make by hand nearly everything they wear. The only difference in style as such is necessitated by climate. The women of the Hukong valley and generally on the west side of the Irrawaddy, wear a simpler and more comfortable dress than their sisters living at higher altitudes. The dress of the genuine hill woman is quite elaborate, picturesque and expensive. The married women put on a tall, folded *head-dress* of blue cloth; unmarried women and young girls go bare-headed.... The *jackets* are short, with or without sleeves. The regulation jacket with long sleeves is generally elaborately decorated with embroidery, porcelain buttons, silver clasps and cloth of bright red or green. A row of silver disks or buttons go around the neck; a cross of porcelain buttons ornaments the back, and bands of red or green finish off the cuffs.... The *skirt* is short, barely reaching below the knees. It is skillfully embroidered, many of the patterns being both artistic and effective.... The skirt is put on so as to be folded at the right side, and is held in place by a large number of cane rings. The wearing of these rings, sometimes over a hundred, together with narrow bands of cowries, and lacquered bands of various designs, is peculiar to the Kachin women.... The Hkahku women and those that live on and near the plains, find such an abundance of finery too heavy and cumbersome, and prefer a few simple rings or a sash or a band. During the cold weather leggings are worn held on by a number of fine rattan rings.

Hanson (1913: 48) also notes that on very special occasions, such as dances or important weddings, "the more wealthy women and the young girls of the leading families will appear in beautifully embroidered skirts not otherwise worn."

Gilhodes (1910: 619) notes that on festive occasions women wear a red waistcloth or belt that her refers to as a *shinggyit*. He also (1996: 112) uses the term *labu* for a man's trousers.

Ward (1921: 217) provides a description of one group of Jingpho known as the Duleng, who live near to the Tai-speaking Khamti and are widely known as blacksmiths. He states that both men and women wear a "coloured handkerchief" over their hair and that the only other garment worn by Duleng women is a skirt that is "usually dark blue striped with dull red, and fastened rather above the waist." The most distinctive item of women's dress are black rattan coils that they wrap round their breasts rather than wearing a jacket: "drawing attention to rather than modestly concealing" their breasts. However, he also provides a photograph of a Duleng woman (facing page 224) wearing a long-sleeved white cotton blouse.

5.3. Group of Jingpho [Scott and Hardiman 1900, I/II, plate 30, f.pg. 390]

Although not referred to in the discussion of clothing, in a discussion of funeral preparations, Hanson mentions blankets (1913:199). Unfortunately no description is given of the blankets.

Leslie Milne (1910: 81) comments that the skirts of Jingpho women are "bright in colour when new, but dingy when old, owing to the dirt with which they become ingrained" since "Kachins seldom wash themselves; they work and sleep in garments which are rarely removed until they become so ragged that new ones are necessary."

In an account of the markets in the Northern Shan states, Leslie Milne (1910: 137) describes some of the imported materials from Germany that the Jingpho use to make their clothing: "Kachins can buy the cheap red German flannel which ornament their jackets, also the scarlet braid which, when cut into lengths of a few inches, is made into fringe to decorate their bags."

Carrapiett (1929: 16) comments that by the 1920s women rarely wove cloth at home for men's clothing any more. Instead men had come to dress, more or less, in Burmese fashion with their clothing made from commercial cloth purchased at local markets. Likewise, Gilhodes (1996: 112) remarks that Jingpho men often wear Burmese, Chinese, or European clothing.

Men did, however, continue to carry locally made bags known as *n'hpye*. These bags were usually presented as a gift to a man by the woman who wove it. Carrapiet (1929: 16-17) describes it as being black or red, "decorated with beads, shells, and silver coins" and "profusely embroidered in red, green, and black." The strap is usually "about two inches wide" and is "sometimes embroidered." In addition, "hanging to the bags are numerous red, black, and green tassels." Carrapiett (1929: 18) cites T.F.G. Wilson, who notes that the style of these bags "differs according to locality" and provides additional information about the bags:

> Those worn by soldiers or military policemen are elaborately woven with coloured thread with swastika, key, diamond and square designs. The outerside of a haversack is adorned with a red braid and silver bosses. The sling is a strip of cloth of the same material as the haversack, usually minus the embroidery. The haversack is slung on the left side across the right shoulder, and several lover's knots or streamers (*Hpajet-pan-byao*) are attached to the sling and hang behind over the left hip. The haversacks and streamers are generally gifts from a man's female friends. The Hukawng [the Hukawng Valley is the northeast of Kachin country towards the Naga Hills and west of the Hkanu] and Kha Khu [Hkanu] Kachins wear smaller sized N'hpye than those worn by the sepoys. It is woven from silk, or silk and cotton mixed, and of very pretty designs. No red braid is used. The sling is in the form of a rope and is made of different coloured yarns— black and white, dark blue and red, black, brown, and yellow, etc. Lover's knots are seldom attached to Kha Khu bags. They are occasionally studded with a line of silver bosses.

Unlike the men, in Carrapiett's time, the women continued to wear more traditional clothing made of domestically produced cloth. He describes the women's costume (1929: 15-16) as consisting of a skirt that "is about two yards long and about a span in width" and that is commonly decorated with "broad bands (about six inches broad) of black and red alternatively relieved by narrow white lines where they join." He notes that "a purple band sometimes takes the place of black and green lines those of white." This piece of "cloth is worn round the waist in two folds" with a portion of it "hitched upwards into a belt on the left side so that it falls over the hip partly in front and partly at the back down to about the knee." The lower part of this portion "is very prettily embroidered in silk cotton of various colours" and in patterns such as "flowers, stars, swastikas, and circles." Another pieces of embroidered cloth "hangs from the waist on the right side, either as a single strip or double according to the fancy of the wearer." There is also a belt, "usually of white cotton." Women wear a black coat, usually with full-length sleeves but sometimes with shorter ones. These coats are "highly decorated with beads, silver buttons, four-anna and eight-anna pieces, and red, black, and green embroidery." Either a white or black cotton "bodice" or a dark colored cotton cloth wrapped around the breasts is worn under the coat. A black turban covers a woman's hair. This turban is sometimes decorated with "a fringe of red Turkey cloth" (1929: 16). Women also wear cane rings around their waist and on their legs between the knee and calf.

Gilhodes (1996: 114) provides information on Jingpho customs of dressing children:

> ...children are clad from a pretty early age. A boy first puts on his wallet; a little girl, the pearl necklaces, bracelets of bulrushes and afterwards a vest. Gradually the costume completes itself, and, between five and seven years, is becoming for all, and it is decent before that age in well-to-do families which like to supply their children with clothes from an early age.

Carrapiett (1929: 18) cites a couple of sources who mention regional differences in costumes (in addition to Wilson mentioned above). Thus, J.T.O. Barnard notes that Hkanu women "always wear the skirt down to the ankles; her sisters in the south up to the knees" and that Hkanu women wear a cloth across their chests known as *"ning-wawt."* P.M.R. Leonard discusses dress among the Jingpho of the Sinlum Hills that lie just to the east of Bhamo. He comments that the type of skirt known as *pukhang* "is seldom or never seen in the Sinlum Kachin hills." Instead, women in this area wear skirts that are "(1) dark blue with thin white and red lines running diagonally across at intervals of three or four inches; (2) the same pattern as above but embroidered at both ends for nine or ten inches; (3) the same as (2) above but the lower edge is embroidered." Mr Leonard also comments that "Burmese lôngyis are seldom worn in the Sinlum hills, but at festivals silk Burmese patsos are always worn."

Clothing plays a role in important Jingpho rites of passage. Cloth is included among the item comprising the brideprice. Dead men and women are dressed in their finest clothing after the body is washed. Among the other items placed with the dead are a man's shoulder bag and a woman's weaving implements. The body thus adorned is placed on a stool for presentation to the ancestors and later placed in a shrine room.

5.4. Jingpho woman, Myitkyina, Kachin State (1997) [photo by Laura Kan]

There is little mention of specialized costumes in the existing literature on the Jingpho. The nat priest or *tumsa* wore a special costume at important festivals. It is described by Carrapiett (1929: 17) as consisting of a yellow silk robe and leather hat made in China.

Ethnic Costumes and Clothing Decorations from China, (Shanghai Theatrical College 1986: 190-197) provides recent descriptions of Jingpho costumes of relevance to the Jingpho of Burma. Thus, it is noted (1986: 190) that "the sub-branches of the Jingphos wear more or less that same kind of costumes, except the people of Cha-shan sub-branch, who wear a kind of long garment similar to the outer garments of the Lisus in Yunnan." It is also mentioned that their costumes do not indicate social position. The description of women's clothing mentions that women's wrap-around skirts may have up to three hundred kinds of decorative patterns. The other items of women's dress described include a collarless short jacket made of black cloth or velvet that opens from the front and has buttons, a close-fitting white waistcoat worn under the jacket, red sashes worn around the waist, red brocade scarves worn on the head. It is also mentioned (1986: 191) that "in regions bordering Burma, many young women wear red or purplish tubular skirts or skirts of print cotton cloth." A man's costume is described as comprising narrow usually short-sleeved jackets that reach just above the waist, loose-fitting black trousers often with patterned bottoms, decorated waist belts, and decorated shoulder-bags. Older men are said to wear black turbans and younger ones white turbans with decorated ends.

Elwin (1959) provides some information on the textiles of the Singpho of India. There are drawings of motifs found on their textiles on p.41 of his book.

6

The Karen

There are over four million Karen living in Burma in three areas: (1) the plains of the Irrawaddy, Sittang, and Salween deltas and the coast of Tenasserim; (2) the Pegu hills between the Irrawaddy and Sittang Rivers, which is a region of steep hills and narrow valleys; and (3) the Shan highlands from the plateau of southern Shan State to the narrow valleys and hills of Kayah and Karen states to the south.

The sixteen Karen languages spoken in Burma are divided into the Sgaw-Bghai and Pho groups. Sgaw is the most widely spoken language of the Sgaw-Bghai group and Pwo of the Pho group. The Karen are sometimes also divided into the categories of Northern Karen and Southern Karen. The Northern Karen include the Kayah while the Southern Karen include the Sgaw and the Pwo. This division manifests itself in different external cultural influences. The Northern Karen are closest to and have been most influenced by the Tai speaking Shan whereas the Southern Karen have been most influenced by the Mon and Burmese peoples. There are also differences between those Karen who live on the plains and those who live at higher altitudes. The Pwo, in particular, are mainly lowlanders. Pwo legends claim that they were driven into the lowlands by the Sgaw. Those Karen living on the plains such as the Pwo generally grow wet rice and those in the hills are usually swidden farmers. In relation to textile production, the highlanders tend to weave with backstrap looms while the lowlanders use fixed frame looms like the Burmese. The highlanders also have a tradition of growing cotton and of selling cotton cloth to lowland Burmese and Mon.

Karen are further divided on the basis of religion. The indigenous religion of the Karen centers on beliefs in spirits and impersonal power. Among the indigenous religious practitioners were the male village chiefs and the eldest female heads of matrilineal kin groups. The former was responsible for a variety of rites propitiating village and nature spirits and the latter for rituals relating to ancestor spirits as well as divination and curing. Mon, Burmese, and Shan influence resulted in many Karen becoming Buddhists, although this tended to be a syncretic mixture of indigenous beliefs and Buddhism. Their situation was complicated further by the arrival of European Christian missionaries in the nineteenth century, the first started to work among the Karen in Tenasserim in 1825. A particularly important early Baptist mission among the Karen was established at Bassein in the southwest of the Pegu division, in 1835. The influx of Christianity resulted in the emergence of several millenarian movements. The missionaries also opened schools, created written forms of several of the Karen languages, and trained a number of Karen as clergy, teachers, doctors, and administrators. According to the 1931 census the religious breakdown among the various Karen groups was as follows: Sgaw 67% Buddhist, 25% Christian (Baptist), 8% pagan; Pwo 93% Buddhist; Pao almost 100% Buddhist; Kayah mainly pagan; other smaller hill groups mainly Christian (Baptist, Catholic, and Anglican).

The Southern Karen traditionally had a village-based political organization that was relatively egalitarian in nature, the village headman having relatively little power. Shan influence among the Northern Karen, however, resulted in the emergence of a more hierarchical system with chiefs who were able to form confederations. The most important of these confederations were the small Karenni principalities of Kantarawady, Bawlakhé, Kyebogyi, and Nammekon in the present Kayah State.

After the 1824-26 Anglo-Burmese War the British gained control of parts of Lower Burma inhabited by large numbers of Sgaw and Pwo Karen. British rule, mainly indirect, was established over most other Karen during the latter part of the nineteenth century. The hill-dwelling Karen did relatively well under British indirect rule and missionary influence during the first decades of the twentieth century. Kayah State was created in 1948, after Burmese independence out of the former Karenni principalities. Agitation by Karen to the south led to the creation of Karen State in 1952. Since then many of the hill-dwelling Karen have engaged in a protracted war with the Burmese-dominated central government .

American Baptist missionary Rev. Harry Ignatius Marshall's 1922 monograph, *The Karen People of Burma: A Study in Anthropology and Ethnology,* provides the most detailed written description of Karen dress in Burma. While providing more detail than other accounts, Marshall's account is nev-

ertheless far from comprehensive. In an opening statement in his chapter on Karen dress Marshall comments that "to describe in detail the costume of every tribe of the Karen would be like going into all the minutiae of the tartans of the Scotch and would of itself fill a volume" (1922: 35). Unfortunately, Marshall's own work does not do justice to this complexity and a more comprehensive volume has never been produced for the Karen.

Traditional Karen dress has a number of common features. Among the items of dress worn by most Karen is the loose fitting blouse or tunic known as a *hse.* The length and decoration of the *hse,* however, varies considerably from group to group. Types of *hse* are worn by both men and women. Women also wear a skirt known as a *ni.* There is some variation in the patterns of the *ni* as well. In the past, men, especially in the more isolated areas, wore loincloths, but by the early part of this century various types of trouser were in common use. In addition, as noted by Spearman (1880, II: 228), trousers tended to be more common men's attire in the north, whereas long tunics were more common attire in the south. The other item of near universal use is a shoulder-bag or *hteu.* These are relatively plain. Most Karen also make some form of blanket.

Marshall makes a number of observations about changing dress patterns among the Karen in the early 1920s. He remarks (1922: 37) that Karen men living on the plains and delta region of Lower Burma generally dress like the Burmese and only wear traditional Karen clothing during the "Bgha" feast and that many Karen men to the north and east wear variations of Shan costumes. In contrast, he notes that women are far more conservative in retaining their traditional dress than men and comments that "long after every man in a village has taken on the Burmese costume, the women continue to wear their characteristic black smock over their Burmese jacket and 'longyi' (skirt)" (1922: 38).

6.1. Graduates of the Bassein Karen Girl's School, 1872 [Carpenter 1883: f.pg. 299]

While research on Karen dress in Burma in recent years has not been possible, relevant comparative data is available on the Karen living across the border in Thailand, of whom the two major groups are Sgaw and Pwo. There are also smaller groups of Pao, Kayah, and Bwe, but those writing on the Karen in Thailand have generally ignored them. The two most relevant works are a chapter by Paul and Elaine Lewis, who spent years as missionaries among the hill tribes of Burma and northern Thailand, in *Peoples of the Golden Triangle* (1984: 68-99), and an article in the *Journal of the Siam Society* by E.M. Hinton (1974). The Lewis's chapter, which describes Sgaw and Pwo Karen dress, remarks at the outset that "the name 'Karen' has become almost synonymous with 'Weaver,' so outstanding are the products of the Karen looms" (1984: 72). Hinton's chapter is based on research in a Pwo village near the Burmese border in 1968-69. Both works include a number of illustrations.

The Sgaw-Bghai Karen

The Sgaw-Bghai subgroup of languages can be further divided into Sgaw, Bghai, Kayah, and Brek. The Sgaw languages include both Sgaw and Paku. The Bghai languages include Bwe (also sometimes called Bghai Karen), Geba, Geko (sometimes called Gai-kho), Lahta, and Padaung. The Kayah languages include Kayah (also called Karennyi or

6.2. Karen schoolgirl (sub-group not identified)
[Stevenson 1943: f.pg. 33]

Red Karen) and Yinbaw. The Brek languages include only the Brek.

Sgaw

There are around two million Sgaw living in Burma and some 300,000 in Thailand. Many live in the Irrawaddy delta area, also in the Pegu hills between the Irrawaddy and Sittang Rivers. Spearman (1880, II: 628) characterized them as "the most peaceful of the Kareng tribes," although he concedes that they had a history of hostility towards the Pwo "whom they have partially exterminated in the Mergui district and against whom they were preparing a raid when Tenasserim was ceded to the British."

Spearman (1880, II: 628) briefly describes their dress as consisting of "a white tunic or smock with several parallel narrow bars of red round the bottom." Marshall provides a far more thorough description of their dress. He describes (1922: 35) men's dress in different areas:

> [Those] living back in the hills [wear only a tunic that] reaches from the shoulders to the calves.... in the Pegu Hills the Sgaw wear a garment that is white above, except for red selvedge lines along the seams, and has the lower third woven with red. The border between the two colors may be more or less variegated and embroidered. In the Moulmein and Papon districts and the eastward the garment is made of alternating wide strips of white and red running its whole length.

Small girls are described as wearing a tunic that reaches to their ankles. After puberty women wear a tunic and a skirt (1922: 38). He continues (1922: 38) about women:

> In some villages they wear a white 'hse,' without any ornament or color, but in other places they wear a black garment ornamented with colored yarns at the neck and around the armholes. In some localities the maidens wear the long white 'hse,' reaching to their ankles, until they are married; but it is more common for them to put on the skirt and wear

6.3. Group of Karen
(sub-group not identified
but probably Sgaw)
[Marshall 1922: 80]

6.4. Sgaw Karen women,
Tavoy District
[Marshall 1922: 52]

6.5. Paku Karen women [Marshall 1922: 272]

a shorter 'hse' at about the time they arrive at maturity.

The design and the dress of the Sgaw Karen woman, Marshall reports (1922: 38) is

supposed to be derived from the python. The story is that 'Naw Mu E,' one of the mythical characters of ancient times, was kidnapped by a fabulous White Python and carried off to his den. Later, her husband, hearing of her plight, came and rescued her by sacrificing himself at the mouth of the den, whereupon the woman was released and enabled to return to the upper earth again.

Among the versions of this story is one in which the woman is "compelled by the python to weave patterns on its skin that still remain, but on being released" the woman showed her contempt for the python "by weaving skirts for herself of the same pattern" (1922: 38).

The collection of the Ethnographical Museum, Göteborg, includes three Sgaw tubeskirts (Hanson 1960): (1) bright red cotton cloth with vertical stripes in green and lilac (Ac#35.39.715); (2) upper portion striped red cotton, lower portion bright red cotton (Ac#35.39.801); and (3) black, white, and red plaid cotton, described as for a man (Ac#35.39.710). The collection also includes a Sgaw man's headcloth (Ac#25.39.711) made of white cotton cloth with yellow and green horizontal stripes and bright red vertical stripes.

Paku

Around 5,000 Paku live in Kayah State in the hills east of Taungoo. Spearman (1880, II: 471) comments that "they have suffered considerably from the inroads of the Red Karen whose forays were rendered the easier in that no one Pa-koo village would help any other." At the time of his writing an estimated 2,000 Paku had converted to Christianity.

Spearman (1880, I: 167) describes Paku dress: "White tunic or blouse without stripes and with a narrow border of embroidery at the bottom, with the patterns differing in every village." Marshall (1922: 35) comments likewise that Paku men "wear

a white tunic with a narrow red border around the bottom. In each village this border has a distinctive form."

Bwe

The Bwe are also known as the Bghai Karen. Some 16,000 Bwe live in the hills around Toungoo and in the Kyebogi region in southwestern Kayah State. A small number also live in Thailand.

A.R. McMahon, chief administrator in the Toungoo district in the 1860s, offers one of the earliest accounts of Bwe dress. He notes (1876: 300-301) that the Bwe "located on the affluents of the river [the Sittang] wear short drawers like the Gaykhos [Geko], with radiating red lines near the bottom, while those to the south of them wear a white armless sack-like garment, with perpendicular bands fashioned like those patronized by many other tribes." He then remarks (1876: 301) that "the missionaries have accordingly distinguished them by the names of Pant Bghai (Bwé) and Tunic Bghai (Bwé) on account of these peculiarities in their dress." Spearman (1880, I, 167), drawing on the writings of the missionary Dr. Mason, describes the dress of the Mopgha, who were one of the early groups to convert to Christianity and one of the Tunic Bghai, as comprised of a "white blouse with red perpendicular lines."

Marshall (1922: 35) states that Bwe men at the time of his stay in Burma wore a tunic that was shorter and more close fitting than that of the Sgaw and Pwo. He also notes (1922: 36) that "in the early days" Bwe men "wore scant loin-cloths, but nowadays they wear longer cloths or Shan trousers, like many other hill tribes." The loincloth may also be replaced by short trousers. Marshall (1922: 36) also describes the variations among different groups of Bwe: "The Bwe tribes usually wear tunics of vertically striped weaves, some of them, e.g., the Mopgha, with narrow red lines" and that "the so-called 'Pant Bwes' ornament their breeches with radiating lines at the bottom." He (1922: 38-39) mentions a pattern of the Mopgha women consisting of "a variety of figures in magenta, yellow, and green, on a black ground," but remarks that at the time of writing "younger women no longer knew how to make the pattern." Instead, Bwe women usually would wear "a black 'ni' or skirt with a few horizontal stripes of white and red running through the middle."

Spearman discusses various aspects of clothing in relation to funerary activities. Thus, he describes annual feasts for the dead held for three years after the death at the new moon in late August or early September in which a piece of bamboo is laid across a corner of the house "and on it are hung up new tunics, new turbans, new patticoats, beads and bangles which are presented to the deceased" (1880, II: 114). He also notes that priests at funerary ceremonies "have embroidered tunics given to them by the people" and that "sometimes these are embroidered with silk and often with red silk, and are made much longer than ordinary garments" (1880, II: 120).

Geba

The Geba are also known as the Mepu, Karenbyu, or White Karen. There are over 40,000 of them and they live in the northern part of Kayah State and Mobye State which is a Southern Shan State. They are mostly Christian.

Geko

There are around 10,000 Geko (also called Gai-Kho) living in the Yamethin and Toungoo Districts of Mobye State, a Southern Shan State. They are described by Spearman (1880, II: 149) as a "fierce and savage" tribe, many of whom fell under the influence of Baptist missionaries, as a result of which most Geko became Christian, and came under British influence in the late nineteenth century. .

McMahon (1876: 360), who calls them Gaykhos, reports that Geko "men wear short drawers with red embroidery, similar to those worn by the Bwés," while "the women wear the ordinary petticoat, supplemented by a red and white jacket." Spearman describes Geko dress as follows: "trousers of silk and often handsomely embroidered; red lines at the bottom radiating like the rays of the rising sun" (1880, II: 149). He also notes that they raise silk worms and produce their own silk (1880, II: 149). Marshall (1922: 35) reports that Geko men (he refers to the Geko as Kerhker or Gai-hko) wear "a

6.6. Group of Padaung women [Scott 1911: frontispiece]

tunic embroidered with vertical figures like towers, from the top of which lines radiate like the rays of the rising sun."

Lahta

This is a small subgroup found in Mobye State, a Southern Shan State. There do not appear to be any published descriptions of their specific dress.

Padaung

There are over 40,000 Padaung in Burma and a small number in Thailand. They live in Kayah State as well as in Mobye State. Spearman (1880, I: 167) refers to them as the Ta-roo, but lists "Padoung" as one of their other names. According to Scott and Hardiman (1900, I/II: 536), they refer to themselves as Kekaawngdu and the authors describe them as "most zealous agriculturalists." Scott and Hardiman also note that the Padaung are active traders who exchange rice and cotton for salt and betel from Toungoo and host large markets in their chief towns. They obtain black cloth from the Kayah.

Spearman (1880, I: 167) describes the men's dress as comprised of "very short trousers" and that of the women as consisting of "short togas besides the brass coils round the neck and below the knee which distinguishes them from some of their neighbours as they wear brass coils above the knee also." Scott (1921: 126) provides a more detailed description of a Padaung woman's costume: "the women wear a coloured scarf twisted into the hair; a coat which is slipped over the head has a V neck and very short arms, is usually black, and is ornamented by a coloured border and sometimes by embroidery. The skirt, or kilt, is striped red and blue, and stops short above the knee." The most distinguishing feature of Padaung women's costume is a coiled brass neck band, as described by Scott and Hardiman (1900, I/II: 537):

They wear a neck band of brass rod, which varies from five to twenty-five coils according to the age of the woman. The rod is about one-third of an inch in diameter and the object is to lengthen the neck as much as possible, this being considered a mark of beauty. The appearance of a Padaung

woman, with her small head, long brass bound neck, sloping shoulders, and the sack-like folds of her smock-frock, inevitably suggests a champagne bottle....The brass used for these coil necklaces is obtained from the Shan States. The girl begins to wear them as early as possible, and fresh coils are added as she grows.

Scott and Hardiman (1900, I/II: 536) describe the dress of Padaung men as "the same as that of the Western Shans—loose trousers and short coats, which may be of any colour, but are generally blue or white," but notes that "the villages situated at a distance from the trade routes and trade centres ... have retained the more primitive short breeches."

The collection of Göteborg Ethnographical Museum, includes three Padaung textiles (Hansen 1960): (1) a woman's blouse of plain white cotton with reddish brown line along the edges (Ac#35.39.624); (2) a woman's tubeskirt, the upper part of undyed white cotton, the lower half of black cotton, with two stripes in a reddish lilac color running horizontally on the lower portion, 64cm wide x 124cm long (Ac# 35.39.625); and (3) a man's trousers made of yellow-brown cotton cloth (Ac# 35.39.628).

Kayah

The Kayah are also known as Karenni, Karennyi, or Red Karen. In Burma they speak Western Kayah. There are over 200,000 Western Kayah speakers in Burma and a few in Thailand. In Burma they live west of the Salween River in Kayah and Karen states.

Spearman (1880, II: 243), citing a report by Dr. Mason, describes Kayah dress as follows:

The men wear short red pants with perpendicular, very narrow, black or white stripes. Sometimes the pants have a black ground and the stripes are red or white. Below the knee are black bands formed of twisted thread and varnished with the black varnish that abounds in this country obtained from the *Melannorrhaea usitatissima*. A wrapper of white with a few red or black stripes is wrapped around the body, and many wear Shan jackets which seem to be an addition to the Kareng dress. A bright red turban is worn on the head and an ornamented bag is hung across the shoulder.... The female dress is peculiarly picturesque, though every garment is only a rectangular piece of cloth. The head dress is a large red or black turban, wound up to form a small tower on top of the head. There is no gown but a cloth like the Roman toga, tied by two corners on the right shoulder, and the left arm is sometimes kept covered, but more often it is drawn out above the garment. A second piece of cloth, like the first, is kept on the hand like a loose shawl or tied round the waist. One of these garments is usually red and the other black, though occasionally both are red. For a petticoat another rectangular piece of cloth is wrapped two or three times around the person, and is kept in its place by a wampum belt, some half a dozen inches in diameter.

6.7. Two Kayah women (also known as Karenni or Red Karen) [Scott and Hardiman 1900, I/I: plate 14, f.pg. 529]

Lowis (1919: 45) did not seem to think too highly of the female costume, commenting "their skirts are short, and the leg immediately below the knee is swathed in an uncouth gathering of cane bands and beads." Scott (1921: 121-22) provides a more sympathetic description:

> The Red Karen women wear a short skirt reaching to the knee. Usually it is dark coloured, but sometimes it is red. A broad piece of black cloth passes over the back across the right shoulder, and is then draped over the bosom, and confined at the waist by a white girdle tied in front.... A piece of black cloth is thrown jauntily over the head, sometimes with red tassels, like those of the Taungthu. The general effect is striking, and when things are new, not by any means unattractive.

Scott, however, does describe the Kayah as being "conspicuous even among hill races for his dirtiness" (Scott and Hardiman 1900, I/II: 524) This theme continues in his description of the Kayah male's dress (1900, I/II: 524):

> The men wear short breeches reaching to just below the knee. These are red when new, but speedily turn to a dirty black. They are fastened by a leather belt. Some wear a small, open, sleeveless dark-coloured coat, but the greater number perhaps wear instead a cotton blanket stripped red and white, thrown round the shoulders. In the hot weather both coat and blanket are discarded. Some sort of handkerchief is generally twisted round the hair....

Marshall (1922: 37) provides a similar description of Kayah male dress, while paying closer attention to the fabrics used:

> The Red Karen, who take their name from their red garments, wear short breeches of red cotton and a short close-fitting tunic of the same color.... These people use a blanket, which is red and white striped when new. They discard both the tunic and blanket in warm weather. Cotton is the most common

material used, but in Toungoo silk is often used, either alone or with cotton.

Scott and Hardiman's (1900, I/II: 525) description of Kayah female dress differs somewhat from that given by Mason, but in general terms is in agreement:

> The women wear a short skirt, reaching to the knee. Usually it is dark coloured, but sometimes it is red. A broad piece of black cloth passes over the back across the right shoulder and is then draped over the bosom and confined at the waist by a white girdle tied in front, the ends hanging down with more or less grace according to the newness of the article. Round the waist and neck are ropes of barbaric beads, and a profusion of these also decorate the leg, just above the calf, which also is encircled by innumerable garters of black cord or rattan... A piece of

black cloth is thrown jauntily over the head, sometimes with red tassels like those of the Taungthus.

Scott and Hardiman also present (1900, I/II: 396-399) an account by T.H. Giles on Kayah dyes. Giles lists the following colors used by the Kayah in dying cotton: crimson, yellow, green, dark blue, light blue, and black. The Kayah alone among the people in the Shan states artificially stimulate the production of lac for red dye. It is reported that while natural dyes are still widely used, the use of aniline dyes and pre-dyed thread was spreading rapidly. By way of example, Giles comments that "even of the two blankets, the red and the yellow, used by the Talai, the ruling race in Eastern Karenni and Bawlake, the red is entirely made of cotton bought ready dyed in Taungu. The yellow, however, still continues to be made of cotton dyed with the simple materials at their disposal" (Scott and Hardiman 1900, I/II: 396). Giles also notes that the Kayah use, but do not cultivate, indigo. The indigo dye or

6.8. Group of Kayah women [Scott and Hardiman 1911: f.pg. 155]

dye-stuffs are obtained from bazaars at Loikaw and Loi Ngun. They do, however, make black cloth from a tree leaf and this cloth is sold to the Brè and Padaung.

Kayah textiles are not well represented in museum collections. Hansen (1960) mentions two pieces in the collection of Göteborg's Ethnographical Museum: (1) a tubeskirt made of bright red cotton cloth with black and brown stipes (Ac# 35.39.622); and (2) trousers made of coarse, bright red cotton cloth (Ac# 33.39.623). The Pitt Rivers Museum has a pair of Kayah men's trousers in its collection (Ac# 1893.44.2). The trousers were donated by a H.G. Leveson in 1893. Their length is 61cm and the waist measures 51cm.

Yinbaw

Around 7,000 Yinbaw living on the Shan Plateau of eastern Mobye State and in southwestern Kayah State. There do not appear to be any written descriptions of Yinbaw dress, but Scott and Hardiman (1900) do include two photographs on

6.9. Two Yinbaw Karen men [Scott and Hardiman 1900, I/II: plate 20, f.pg. 134]

"Yimbao Karen," who can probably be identified as Yinbaw. In the photographs, the men wear short trousers and jackets, the women's dresses, do not cover the shoulders,and one woman wears a shoulder-cloth.

Brek

There are about 17,000 Brek (or Bre and called Laku by themselves) living in the mountains of the Kantarawady and Kyebogyi districts of Kayah State. They are mostly Christian.

Spearman (1880, I: 168: 168) comments that "they go about almost naked." Marshall notes that "the Brecs are the poorest tribe of Karen and wear the scantiest clothing, consisting of short trousers" (1922: 42). He describes these short trousers as being "belted in at the waist with a string" and as "white with narrow stripes" (1922: 36). Marshall also mentions (1922: 42) that they "have rough small blankets, which they throw around themselves in cold weather," although "more often they appear without them." Both of these accounts overlook significant differences among different groups of Brek.

Scott and Hardiman (1900, I/II: 531-532) reprint a description of the Brek by a W.H.L. Campbell who notes that the Brek are commonly divided into three distinct groups: northern, southern, and Mano who live to the east. Campbell describes Mano dress as follows (Scott and Hardiman, I/II: 532):

> The wilder men have exactly the same type of features as the Brè and wear a pair of short red and white striped trousers tied at the waist with a bit of string, a blanket for a coat.... Their legs are ornamented with cotton stained black and coiled below the knee with brass rings to keep the coils separate.... The dress of the women is usually the same as that of the Karenni [Kayah] women, only instead of black cotton coils round the legs they wear white; but the dress of those in the southern villages is different. There they wear a short red Burmese *lungyi* and a coat of the same pattern as is worn by the Burmans. This is probably due to intermarriage with the Yangtalsi of the Bawlake State, who affect this costume.

Campbell describes the southern Brek as being extremely poor, much more so than other Brek. He notes that the men wear the same costume as northern Brek, but that women have a different style of dress. Southern Brek women "wear a long blue *thindaing* or gabardine with a blue petticoat, striped horizontally with pale red. No brass ornaments are worn and no head-dress…" (Scott and Hardiman 1900, I/II: 532). Campbell indicates that the northern Brek are much more active and well-to-do agriculturists than the southern Brek. The following is his description of northern Brek dress (Scott and Hardiman 1900, I/II: 533):

> The dress of the men is similar to that of the Mano and Southern Bre, but that of the women is more like that of the Padaungs. They wear a white and pink striped *thindaing* with a narrow pink border and under this a short deep blue and red petticoat. Brass tubing is coiled round the leg from the ankle to the knee and from above the knee to half-way up the thigh. Large brass hoops are worn

round the neck and ear-plugs in the ears. There is no head dress…

The Pho Karen

The Pho subgroup includes the Pao and Pwo languages in Burma and several other languages in Thailand. Both Pao and Pwo are categorized as Southern Karen.

Pao

The Pao are also called Taungthu or Black Karen, and some 600,000 Pao live in Burma, in the southwest of Shan State and Tenasserim. Within Shan State they are associated especially with the state of Hsa-htung (or Thaton).

Spearman (1880, I: 187) describes the "Toung-thoo" as "short of stature, strongly built and swarthy, wearing a dress, consisting of trousers, jacket and turban, almost invariably of dark royal blue very like that worn by the northern Shan." He does not describe the dress of women. Scott (1921: 127) provides a much better description:

> The Taungthu men dress exactly like the Shan. The women wear the Karen poncho, or camisole. It is black, adorned with embroidery, much or little, according to the position of the wearer. Under the sack-jacket is worn a petticoat which neglects to go below the knees. Below the knee are garters of black thread, worn in a band rather than in a bunch.… Leggings black or white are also worn occasionally. The forearm also is covered with strips of various-coloured velvet. Green and purple are the favourite colours. The head-dress is very elaborate. The basis is a black cloth, or *tabet,* wound round the head turban fashion and ornamented with a variety of coloured tassels.

Scott and Hardiman (1900, I/II: 554) note that the Pao women's *thindaing* is similar to that of the neighboring Burman-speaking Taungyo, with the chief difference being color: that of the Pao being black and that of the Taungyo being red. Marshall (1922: 40) adds that the women's *hse* or blouse is decorated with "fern-like figures."

6.10. Two Yinbaw Karen women [Scott and Hardiman 1900, I/II: plate 22, f.pg. 197]

The collection of the Göteborg Ethnographical Museum, includes (Hansen 1960): (1) a Pao skirt made of black cotton sateen (Ac# 35.39.404); and (2) a pair of leggings made of plain indigo dyed cotton with a cord attached for tying the leggings on (Ac# 35.39.405).

Pwo

The Pwo are also sometimes called Pho, Mepu, or White Karen. There are over 1.2 million Pwo Karen living mainly in the Irrawaddy delta. Some also live in the hills of what was formerly Upper Burma, in Loi-long state. The Pwo Karen known as Mepu are found especially in the Pyinmana District of Loi-lông state. They are called Talaing Kayen by the Burmese, as a result of their living alongside the Talaing or Mons who live in the same general area.

Scott and Hardiman (1900, I/II: 551-552), relying on information provided by F.H. Giles, provide a description of the dress of the White Karen or Mepu living in the Paunglaung valley of Loi-long state:

The women of the race wear a *thindaing,* a sort of blouse, or tight fitting smock with short sleeves, often made of silk in the Paunglaung valley. It is half white, half red, the white half being the upper. Beneath this is worn a skirt, or petticoat, reaching to within six inches or so of the knees. It is made of cotton and the pattern is usually red and deep blue stripes. The head-dress is called *tabet* and is of a chequered material, much like that worn by the Taungyo.... Broad ribbons of cotton, dyed black with *thit-si,* are also twisted round the arm to make up for the want of sleeves to the *thindaing....* On festival occasions the women add to the beauties of the *tabet* by adorning that head-dress with feathers and pieces of coloured glass.

The men also wear a short *thindaing* reaching to the hips and a pair of trousers about the length of running, or boating shorts. They have cane rings twisted round the waist like the Palaung women, but not so many of them.

6.11. Group of Pao Karen women [Scott 1911: f.pg. 126]

The turban is of cotton and is tied up in a ball in front.

Hinton (1974: 27), writing on Pwo Karen in Thailand, points to differences in dress among women, depending on their marital status: "single girls wear a long white dress, richly decorated with red… while married women wear a red skirt and blouse." He comments in regard to women's clothing in the community he studied that "colours are bright—red, green or black for preference—and accessories are as elaborate as the Pwo can make them."

Other Karen

There are four groups of Karen whose languages are not classified as belonging to either of the above subgroups. These include the Manumanaw, Wewaw, Yintale, and Zayein.

Manumanaw

Approximately 3,000 Christian Manumanaw live in the western part of Kyebogyi in Kayah State. Their dress does not appear to have been described.

Wewaw

A very brief description of the Wewaw is to be found in Spearman (1880, I: 166), who considered them to be "in a very low stage of civilization" and lists them under Saw Karen. He (1880, I: 166) describes their dress as "of all kinds" and states that "until latterly the women did not know how to weave, whence their nondescript dress."

Yintale

The Yintale are a very small group of Buddhist Karen living in the southern part of Bawlakhe in Kayah State. Their dress does not appear to have been described.

Zayein

Around 10,000 Zayein (also known as Sawng-tung or Gaung-to Karens) live in southern Shan State. Apparently, the latter name, Gaung-to, refers to the men's practice of shavin their head except for a small patch over the ear. Scott and Hardiman (1900,

I/II: 539) cite F.H. Giles who says that the Zayein originally come from the Amherst district of Lower Burma and moved to Loi-long and Mong Pai States in Upper Burma.

This same Mr. Giles describes Zayein dress (Scott and Hardiman 1900, I/II: 543):

The dress of the men consists of a short pair of trousers about fifteen inches long, tied round the waist by a string, and a long coat reaching as far as the knees. This is tied at the neck, but otherwise open in front. both trousers and coat are white.… The women wear a short white *thindaing* or smock. This is turned up with black round the neck, arms, sides, and down the back and front; round the bottom there is a pink border about three inches wide. This blouse or smock reaches half-way between the hips and the knees. Some of them are ornamented with shells. Below this is worn a skirt, reaching not quite to the knee. It is white with a black, red and black border, the first line an inch wide, the

6.12. Group of Zayein Karen women
[Scott 1911: f.pg. 120]

second one and a half inches, and the third three inches.... Cotton dyed black is worn round the leg below the knee; below this a strip of blue or red cloth is wrapped round the calf, and brass rings are coiled round from the ankle up to within four inches of the knee on both legs.

The hair is combed and as much as possible is forced into a silver receptacle, like a dome, about five inches high by two inches in diameter. The head-dress is worn round this, the dome appearing above it. The head-dress itself is very elaborate and striking. It consists of eight pieces of red and white cloth, about twenty inches long and six inches broad, pleated together so as to show a narrow red and white stripe. On this a piece of black cloth is sewn and upon this is worked with *kaleik* seeds a red and yellow lace or net pattern. This appears only in front. The whole is kept in place by a narrow band of silver worn like a tiara. The effect is very becoming.

Lowis (1919: 45) provides a much briefer description of Zayein dress: "smocks and leg rings are the ordinary features of the women's dress in all the clans, and short trousers those of the men's attire.... in some cases the women's head dresses are peculiar."

Göteborg's Ethnographical Museum (Hansen 1960) has three Zayein textiles in its collection. These include: (1) a short, sleeveless woman's blouse made of coarse undyed white cotton with no decorations (Ac#35.39.740); (2) a man's short-sleeved jacket also made of undyed white cotton (Ac# 35.37.738); and (3) a man's short trousers made of undyed white cotton cloth with brown thread stitching (Ac# 35.37.739). They were all collected at Watha. There are drawings of the men's clothing, but no photographs.

Scott and Hardiman (1900, I/II: 544) also describe a group of Karen known as the Sinsin, who they say "are of the same race" as the Zayein "but have left their villages and live intermingled with Shans and Taungthu." While they are said at the time to have retained their own language, otherwise they had adopted many Taungthu customs. The men are described by Scott and Hardiman (1900, I/II: 545) as dressing like Taungthu or Danu, while the women retained a distinctive dress:

> The women wear a long *thindaing* which reaches down to the knee. This is white with a blue line round the neck, the sides, and down the front and back. The sleeves are bordered with narrow blue and red stripes. Cotton dyed black is coiled round the waist over this. No petticoat is worn.... The hair is worn like the Taungthu women and the head-dress is the same.

Other Karen groups have been named in the literature, who appear to have been subsumed into one or other of the groups listed above or assimilated into other groups.

7

The Akha, Lahu, Lisu, and Pyen

There are seven peoples speaking Lolo languages in Burma: Akha, Hani, Lahu, Lahu Shi, Lisu, Pyen, and Sansu. The Hani and Sansu may be subsumed under the Akha and Lahu Shi placed along with the Lahu.

The Akha

The Akha are recognized as part of the Hani nationality in China, where they live between the Yuanjiang and Lancang Rivers in southern Yunnan. There are over one million in China divided into more than twenty subgroups. Most of the Akha in Burma (often referred to as Kaw or Ekaw) live in the Shan State hills east of the Salween River, primarily in eastern Kengtung State. In 1931 there were estimated to be over 40,000 Akha in Kengtung State. At present there are perhaps 200,000 Akha in Burma.

There are eight major groups of Akha living in adjacent areas of southern China, northeastern Burma, and northern Thailand, with distinctive styles of dress: the Meu-i, Adzho, Musa, Ulo, Lomi, Parnee, Makha, and Patch. The Meu-i, Adzho, and Musa are found in China and Burma. The Ulo were the first group of Akha to move into Thailand from Burma and are found in both countries. They comprise the largest group of Akha in Thailand. The Lomi are named after Loi Mi (Bear) Mountain in Shan State. Some of the Lomi fled the violence in Shan State and moved across the border to Thailand. The majority of Lomi still live in Burma. The Parnee are named after a village near Mai Sai in Thailand. They fled the communists in Yunnan and stopped briefly in Burma on their way to Thailand. The Makha and Patch Akha are found in Shan State.

Akha villages are located generally at relatively high elevations. The Akha practice slash-and-burn agriculture and grow rice along with a variety of other crops. Opium poppies are also grown and selling opium is a source of income for some Akha villages. Political organization in the past centered around autonomous villages with chiefs who possessed limited powers and councils of village elders. The Akha were not known to be especially aggressive and often found themselves in a subordinate position to neighboring peoples. Debt slavery with neighboring dominant groups was relatively common and sometimes Akha were drafted into military service or as laborers. Akha religion is essentially animistic with a pantheon of spirits and a central role assigned to ancestor worship. There are male and female village priests and shamans. In many ways the priest is the most important political figure in the village.

The Akha are descendants of the Yi nationality (also known as Lolos) of southern China, from whom they split over one thousand years ago. From the Yi homeland in southwestern Sichuan, the ancestors of the Akha and Hani moved south towards Vietnam and Laos. Jim Goodman (1996: 25-26) speculates that the Akha may originally have been disaffected Yi commoners, known as White Bone Yi. The Akha first appear in recorded history in the twelfth century, with mention of a small city-state of the Adzho Akha named Tumlah located near the China-Laos-Vietnam border area. This appears to be the only time that any group of Akha were organized beyond the village level. The history of Tumlah is not an especially happy one. Warfare in the late twelfth century led the Adzho Akha to flee into the mountain forests and the Akha then more or less disappear from recorded history until the nineteenth century. Political turmoil in Yunnan starting in the mid-nineteenth century seems to have led some Akha to move further south into regions that included northern Burma.

Following annexation of Upper Burma in 1886, the British occasionally sent various agents into the areas occupied by the Akha, including Christian missionaries. For the most part, however, the Akha remained relatively isolated from British colonial administration. Lowis (1919: 36) commented that "missionary work has extended of late years into the Akha country, but apparently, the Akhas are not as ready to embrace the Christian faith as the Lahus." The Akha largely avoided the conflict of the Second World War, but in 1951 they and the Lisu and Lahu were caught in the crossfire between communist and KMT forces in Yunnan and many moved to Burma and Thailand in an effort to escape the fighting. Then in the 1960s, as the Shan State area became the scene of fighting between the Burmese and various other ethnic minorities and communists, the Akha in Burma found themselves once again caught between combatants. Akha living near the Laos border fell under control of the Communist Party of Burma and Akha men were recruited into the communist and other armies in the region. Over the past few decades the Akha have been caught up in the fighting and drug trade that has dominated their Shan State homeland. Such conflict has resulted in several thousand Akha migrating to Thailand.

Akha textiles are generally made of handspun cotton. The Akha grow cotton and Akha women spend much of their time spinning and weaving cotton cloth and making clothing. The Akha are also known to trade and sell cotton to other hill dwelling peoples (Adams 1974). Bernatzik (1947: 418) mentions Akha making barkcloth, but this does not appear to have been a widespread practice.

There are a variety of rather brief descriptions of Akha clothing from the early twentieth century. Scott and Hardiman (1900: I/II: 589590) includes the following description:

> The men's dress is practically that of the Shan or the Chinaman; coats and trousers dark blue or black, turbans black, dark blue, or occasionally red, the only relief to the general somberness. Some of the wealthier men on market days appear in elaborately braided coats, with a considerable quantity of silver ornaments, coat-buckles, buttons, necklaces, and earrings.
>
> The dress of the women is much more distinctive, as always with hill tribes, and varies according to different clans. As a general thing it consists of a short coat which stops a long way short of the next garment, a sort of kilt, rather than a petticoat, which reaches from the waist half way down to the knee and has a singular aptitude for getting unfastened. The head-dress varies with the clans and with most is rather striking ... the calves are covered with cloth leggings as a protection against leeches rather than as a covering or as an adornment, which they certainly are not.

Scott and Hardiman include a description of some of the headdresses, but do not specify with which group they are associated. Davies (1909: 395)

7.1. Group of Akha men [Scott 1911: f.pg. 100]

reports that "the women wear a very short coat not reaching nearly down to the waist, and an equally short skirt which does not reach down to the knees." Lowis (1919: 36) describes the women's dress, consisting of "its abbreviated skirt, leggings and bamboo head-dress," as being "very distinctive."

More recent writing on the Akha of Thailand by Paul and Elaine Lewis (1984) and Jim Goodman (1996) provide considerably more detailed descriptions that are of relevance to the Akha of Burma. Goodman (1996: 71) comments that "in the traditional Akha view art is something one wears" and "the most outstanding examples of this are the traditional cotton jackets."

Goodman (1996: 72-73) provides a very thorough description of the production of Akha cloth. The Akha spin with a drop spindle, and Goodman notes that spinning is the first skill taught to young girls, since the mother usually cannot spin enough thread

to meet her family's requirements. The thread produced is tightly spun with considerable tensile strength. Akha women weave outside, usually setting up their loom after the rice harvest. The loom comprises "two pairs of erect bamboo poles about six meters apart, connected by bamboo rails, with perhaps a roof overhead.... The weaver stands in the middle, operating two treadles to shift the string heddles, weaving cloth at about waist high level." The cloth made on this loom is between seventeen and twenty centimeters wide. While some of the cloth is left white, most of it is dyed dark blue with indigo. Unlike the Tai, Karen, and Lawa, who use the common *Indigofera tinctoria,* the Akha cultivate *Polygonum tinctorium* in their gardens for indigo dye. Goodman considers this to be the most difficult of their natural dyes to process. The shredded leaves are soaked for a few days in water that has been poured through ashes. The solids are then removed and powdered lime is added to the water, which is allowed to ferment. A froth appears and is removed. The dye bath is now ready. The cloth is placed in the bath for half an hour or so and is then removed and placed on a line. The cloth is a yellowish color, but as it is exposed to the air it gradually turns green and then blue. To get a deep blue-black requires a number of dippings and takes up to a month of daily baths. In making a jacket, a woman starts with two strips of blue cloth and stitches them together half way. She then begins to embroider the cloth and to add appliqué patterns. Such items as the sleeves, front flap, and collar are added later.

Goodman's descriptions of Akha clothing focuses on their jackets. Ulo jackets features rows of small running stitch lines covering most of the lower half of the jackets on both sides. The patterns consist of lines, zig-zags, and various named motifs. Women's jackets usually reach to mid-hip, while men's jackets tend to be shorter. Women's jackets are also often ornamented with cowries and buttons and usually have no collar. The sleeves of women's jackets have rows of contrasting colors. The strips of colored cloth on the sleeves have been made from commercial cloth for many decades. Men's jackets have a collar, a single band of color on the sleeves, and are embellished with small silver half-spheres.

Lomi jackets feature appliqué comprised of rows of contrasting triangles or diamonds which are placed on a strip of colored cloth and outlined with three to four twined threads. The assembled piece

7.2. Group of Akha women
[Scott 1911: f.pg. 101]

is attached to the jacket. Such a jacket usually has two or more rows of appliqué with bands of embroidery in between. Each of the stitched pattern has a name. Appliqué patterns generically are referred to as butterfly tongue or *alumela*. The jackets of younger women tend to feature more color and be embellished with rows of beads and coins, as well as cowries, beads, Job's tears, and horsehair. There is a special jacket worn mainly at funerals; the entire back is covered in patterns, and it may take a year to make. Lomi men wear a shorter jacket with a collar and rectangular fastening flap on the front. The man's jacket has less color on the sleeves, but the front flap is heavily embroidered

Ulo and Lomi clothing is the most commonly encountered. Less commonly seen or described is the clothing of the other Akha groups in Burma. The Makha jacket has embroidery similar to the Lomi jacket, but does not have any appliqué. Instead, the Makha cover the area with lines of tiny stitches around a space left blank in a diamond or triangle shape. The front of the jacket has very little embroidery and mostly has straight vertical lines. Makha men's jackets have a front fastening flap. The woman's jacket of the Patch Akha has little decoration. The front and sleeves of the jacket appears to be relatively plain. Decoration consists of a thin multicolored stripe where the sleeve joins the jacket body and a few other colored stripes.

Paul and Elaine Lewis (1984: 230-232) provide information on social aspects of Akha dress. Women's dress changes with age. Teenagers wear more decorative clothing when in search of a mate, sometimes including elaborate hats. Also, between the age of eleven and seventeen, young women wear short skirts above the knee. When they reach fifteen they begin wearing a pieces of black cloth around their chest for support, decorated with beads and appliqué. Women start wearing waist cloths at age seventeen, which serves as a sign of being grown up. An Akha bride wears a white skirt and cap. After a woman reaches menopause she can assume the status of a white skirted woman. To do so she needs the permission of her husband and eldest son. This gives her equal status with a man and allows her to perform many rituals and ceremonies. Young men travel away from their home village to look for a bride, specially dressed for the occasion: "their mothers will have made beautiful jackets and shoulder bags for them, and they will wear silver ornaments in their carefully wrapped turbans" (1984: 230). When a person dies, special clothes are prepared to be worn by the deceased; and the body is then wrapped in a black shroud that is covered with a red cloth. Prior to burial the shroud and red cloth are temporarily removed so the body can be dressed in additional clothing when placed in the coffin.

The Lahu

It is estimated that between 90,000 and 150,000 Lahu (or Muhso) speakers live in Burma, mainly in Kengtung state. There are also over 300,000 in Xishuangbanna in China (where they are an official nationality) and some in Thailand (around 40,000), Laos (around 10,000) and Vietnam (over 5,000). Among the dialects of Lahu are: Na (Black Lahu), Nyi (Red Lahu), and Shehleh. Lahu Shi or Yellow

7.3. Lahu woman [Scott 1911: f.pg. 94]

Lahu is a distinct language. There are about 10,000 Lahu Shi speakers in Burma in the Kengtung district as well as some in China and Thailand.

The Lahu Na appear to have lived for some time in southwestern Yunnan and northeastern Burma. From here some of them migrated to northern Thailand and northwestern Laos. The Lahu Nyi are an offshoot of the Lahu Na. They live in Burma and are the largest group of La'hu in Thailand. The Lahu Shi live in Yunnan and Burma and a few live in Thailand. The Lahu Sheleh migrated from Yunnan to northern Thailand in the early twentieth century. They have frequent contact with Lisu, Akha, and Yao, but there is little intermarriage. The Lahu Nyi and Lahu Na in Thailand maintained close ties with Lahu in Burma and some returned to Burma in the 1950s under the influence of a religious leader. The Lahu in Kengtung are Lahu Na and Lahu Shi.

Traditionally, Lahu agriculture differed according to locality, although most practiced some form of slash-and-burn agriculture and relied to some extent on forest products. Lahu living to the north grew buckwheat and maize, not rice, their chief crop being opium. To the south, the Lahu grew rice.

The Lahu initially lived independently under the rule of thirty-six theocratic chiefs of *fu*. Outward migration occasionally brought them into conflict with neighboring Burmese, Shan, and Chinese. The Chinese initiated the conquest of the Lahu in 1887, but, as noted by Davies (1909: 393), the Lahu are "a warlike race" who gave "the Chinese much trouble in conquering them." Lowis (1911: 35-36) comments that "the Lahus are best known for the resistance they have offered to the Chinese along the border" as well as remarking on their "readiness to adopt Christianity." After a great deal of resistance, the majority of Lahu were brought under administrative control by the Chinese. Those living further to the south were gradually came under indirect rule by the British. Also, although their religion initially combined elements of Buddhism and spirit worship, in Upper Burma, as noted by Lowis, many converted to Christianity.

In the past, the Lahu grew their own cotton and spun and wove cotton cloth (see Telford 1937: 113). Most weaving is done on foot-treadle looms, although backstrap looms are also used for bags, straps, and other small items. Lewis and Lewis (1984: 174) comment that most of the Lahu in

Thailand at the time of their writing no longer wove their own cloth on the larger looms, with the exception of a few Lahu Na women, many of whom still produced bags on backstrap looms. Most of the Lahu in Thailand have used commercial cloth for some time now to make their traditional costumes. All of the groups continue to embroider their traditional costumes and the Lahu Na and Lahu Shi still do patchwork and appliqué to decorate their costumes.

Each of the different Lahu groups in Burma (Nyi, Shi, and Na) possessed similar, but distinctive, dress. Lahu Na or Black Lahu dress is described by Mr. Warry in Scott and Hardiman (1900, I/II: 580) as follows:

> The Black La'hu men wear coats and trousers of black or very dark blue cloth of the ordinary Shan cut, and their turbans are of the same material. They make a very sombre crowd. The women wear a long coat of similar material reaching nearly to the ankles and slit up at the sides to the hips. It is not unlike a dressing gown, or an Annamese woman's coat, except that the later is not divided at the sides. This robe is fastened at the throat and over the bosom by a large silver boss or clasp; below this it falls away and exposes a triangular portion of the person there, and shows part of an under-garment which looks like a skirt, but may be trousers, as Captain H.R. Davies declares it is. Bead patterns and embroidery ornament the upper part, but there are no bright colours, and the turban, which is much the shape of a curling stone, is also black.

Next, Warry (Scott and Hardiman 1900, I/II: 581) describes the dress of the Lahu Nyi or Red Lahu:

> The Red La'hus do not differ in cut of dress [from the Black Lahu], and ordinarily the dress of the men does not differ at all. Now and then, however, they have strips of red and white round the sleeves of their coats and the legs of their trousers, like the Lü Shans, and sometimes they have white or yellow turbans.... The women's fashion of dress is the same [as the Black Lahu], but instead of being all black the outer long coat

is ornamented with red and white stripes, arranged like the frogs on a tunic. The under-garment is also frequently brown or some other colour than black. The ornaments do not appear to differ in any way, but the turban is narrower and higher, something like a chimney-pot. It is black.

An interesting question that arises from these descriptions concerns the traditional style of the woman's under-garment. Did it consist of trousers or a skirt? Either in fact is possible. Davies (1909: 393) remarks that in China Lahu men have adopted Chinese dress, but the women still retained a distinctive traditional dress comprised of: "a long coat reaching nearly down to the knees, trousers down to just below the knees, and gaiters, the whole very dark blue or black" and a turban "of the same colour" that is "put on so as to leave a long piece hanging down behind." Thus, he is quite clear in his reference to women wearing trousers. Moreover, *Ethnic Costumes and Clothing Decorations from China* (Shanghai Theatrical College 1986: 183) reports that Lahu women in the Lancang area "wear long black trousers of black cloth." However, the latter description is accompanied by a drawing of a Lancang Lahu women in fact wearing a skirt. A photograph of a Lahu woman a couple of pages later (1986: 185) also shows her wearing a skirt. In addition, the various Lahu groups in Thailand have worn skirts in recent decades as part of their traditional costumes. There is also a Lahu Nyi skirt from Burma in the collection of Denison University (but no trousers). It is, however, a relatively recent piece. Unfortunately, museum collections do not contain older Lahu skirts or women's trousers to help settle the matter. It could be that at one time Lahu women in Burma wore trousers, but subsequently adopted skirts. Meanwhile, as Davies described Lahu in Yunnan only, and with evidence from Thailand, it seems reasonable to conclude that Scott and Hardiman were correct in thinking the garment was indeed a skirt.

Lewis and Lewis (1984) provide relatively recent detailed descriptions of Lahu dress in Thailand for the Lahu Nyi (Red Lahu), Lahu Shehleh, Lahu Na (Black Lahu), and Lahu Shi (Yellow Lahu) that assist in providing a better understanding of Lahu textiles in Burma. The costume of Lahu Nyi women that they describe and illustrate (pages 176-177) differs significantly from that described by Mr. Warry in that the women's outer garment consists of a short jacket rather than the longer tunic. The jackets described by Lewis and Lewis are made of velvet or satin for festive wear and the body of the jacket may be black, blue, or green. They are edged all around with additional strips of predominantly red cloth with a variety of stitched designs. In addition, the women wear a tubeskirt made up of three panels. The top panel is mainly red with woven stripes of other colors. The central, and widest, panel may be plain (usually black or blue), but may include horizontal red stripes embellished with couched thread. The bottom panel may be a piece of plain white cloth on everyday skirts, but on festive skirts is usually made from a piece of red cloth with a great deal of couched thread of different colors attached. Lahu Nyi women also wear black or blue leggings with red and white trim.

Lahu Na women's dress, as described by Lewis and Lewis (1984: 180-181), is similar to that described in Scott and Hardiman, except that more decoration appears to have been added to the long outer tunic. Lewis and Lewis describe such clothing as still being made from homespun cloth dyed with indigo until very dark. They note that the tunics open on the right or down the front. This seems to differ from the more somber style described above, the addition of "bands of predominantly red and white appliqué which consists of triangles, squares, and strips with a double row of scallops in red and white" along the split side and bands of blue and red cloth with embellishments across the back and on the sleeves (p. 180). The black tubeskirt is also decorated with strips of colorful cloth. The turban, however, remains plain black. The addition of such bright colors to these costumes is likely a recent innovation and more contemporary costumes from Burma apparently made by the Lahu Na are as equally colorful as those described by Lewis and Lewis.

The costume of the Lahu Shi is not described in Scott and Hardiman. Lewis and Lewis note that Christian Lahu Shi women in Thailand "dress like Shan or Northern Thai, while men wear ready-made clothing, usually in Western style" (1984: 182). The traditional women's costumes that Lewis and Lewis describe are those of Lahu Shi from Laos. These are made of commercial cotton dyed black. The costume consists of a short jacket with sleeves, a tubeskirt, and a headcloth. Costumes differ depending on the marital status of the woman. The jacket of an unmarried woman is decorated with bands of red cloth, embroidered patterns, and rows of metal buttons and cowrie shells. The skirt consists of three panels. The top panel is made of a piece of handwoven Shan or Laotian striped cloth, the middle panel is black with splice strips in red and other colors, and the bottom panel is black with a red hem line. The headcloth is black with a great deal of ornamentation at the ends of brightly colored cloth, such as buttons, beads, and coins. The costume of a married woman is more somber. The jacket has fewer red strips and no embroidery, although it can be heavily decorated with metal buttons and balls. The skirt also may have a top panel of striped handwoven cloth, but contains less decoration in the two other panels. The headcloth is also less decorated and may be plain black.

7.4. Group of Lisu (sub-group not identified)
[Scott 1911: f.pg. 93]

The Lisu

As many as 250,000 Lisu-speakers scattered across northern Burma. Another 500,000 Lisu in China where they are an official nationality. There are also over 20,000 Lisu in northern Thailand. Dialects of Lisu include Hwa or Hua (Flowery or Variegated) Lisu, He (Black) Lisu, Pai or Pe (White) Lisu, and Lu Shi Lisu. The first three refer to differences in dress. Early writers on Burma frequently use Kachin terms for the Lisu such as Yawin, Yaw-yen, or Ywoyen. These essentially mean "wild people." Some writers on Burma also treat the Lisu as a subgroup of Karen. The Lisu are also called Yawyin. The 1901 census of Burma enumerated only 1,427 Lisu (or Lisaws) and most Lisu at that time lived outside areas administered by the British.

Davies (1909: 392) describes the Lisu in Burma as living "in very out of the way places right on the tops of the ranges, among the dwarf bamboos and the very sources of the hill-streams—ideal spots for a quiet life where scarcely even a wandering Kachin ever intrudes." The Lisu believe that they originated near the headwaters of the Salween River, from where they have migrated south. As late as the 1960s, Lisu were still migrating into Burma from China. They first arrived in northern Thailand during the early twentieth century. Lewis and Lewis (1984: 242) comment that the "Lisu in Thailand tend to be quite different from those in northern Burma … partly due to their isolation from the main population further north for several generations."

The Upper Salween region occupied by the Lisu in China was effectively outside of Chinese control prior to the Second World War. The Black Lisu in particular were noted for their independence and as being warlike. Rose and Coggin Brown (1911), who spent some time among the Hua or Flowery Lisu in Burma to the south of the Black Lisu, describe the latter as being independent of Chinese authority and having a reputation for attacking their neighbors and travelers passing through their territory, using crossbows with poisoned arrows. They report that the Black Lisu killed two German explorers passing through their territory in 1911. The Black Lisu tended to wear clothing made of hemp. The Flowery Lisu live south of the Black Lisu in northern Shan State and were considered to be more tame. Flowery Lisu women wore colorful multilayered clothes made of cotton.

Lisu live in scattered communities in the Shan states of Burma. In Burma (see Leach 1954: 59) they have intermarried with neighbouring Jingpho, hence many Lisu live in ethnically mixed communities. The Lisu may work as laborers on Palaung tea plantations.

The Lisu are slash-and-burn agriculturists in some areas and have irrigated terraces in others. Their chief crops are maize, millet, and buckwheat. They also grow hemp in the north and cotton further south. In addition, the Lisu grow opium, which traditionally was sold to Chinese traders.

Lisu society is stratified with hereditary chiefs who in the past exercised control over several villages. Some of these more isolated Lisu villages were reported to have lacked chiefs. During the late nineteenth and early twentieth centuries the Pai or White Lisu were subject to hereditary *sawbwas* or chieftains who were often Chinese or of mixed descent, recognized Chinese authorities and paid

taxes to them. Davies (1909: 37-38) describes the Lisu of the Mong Ka plain as follows: their chief was "an ancestor of someone or other who conquered the original inhabitants for the Chinese Government and as a reward he and his men settled down there as soldier colonists and the government of the place was given to him and his descendants. The Lisus and Chinese now live together quite amicably and no doubt the original settlers took Lisu wives so that their descendants are as much Lisu by race as Chinese." Lewis and Lewis (1984: 257) discuss village headmen who are chosen by village elders and are "more of an arbiter and judge than a ruler." They also describe Lisu communities comprised of patrilineal clans with no formal headmen or chiefs.

The Lisu are animists with an emphasis on ancestor worship and exorcism, with few Buddhist elements. Lisu villages choose a village priest to act as a go-between in dealings with the village's guardian spirit, affording very high status. Male shamans also have a role.

John Anderson, the Medical and Scientific Officer for two British expeditions in 1868 and 1875 that encountered Lisu while traveling in northern Burma and Yunnan, provides an early, though brief, account of Lisu dress (Anderson 1871, 1876). Archibald Rose and J. Coggin Brown provide a more comprehensive description of Lisu dress from the early twentieth century. They describe (1911: 258-259) the dress of men as comprised of

7.5. Lisu woman, Myitkyina (1997): Everyday wear [photo by Laura Kan]

...a long, undyed hempen coat reaching to the knees and open in the front, short breeches and a pair of leggings hanging loosely at the ankles without shoes or socks. A broad hempen turban usually covers the head, though a Tam-o-Shanter is occasionally seen, also of hemp.... Among those who have been affected by Chinese influence and who attend the Chinese markets, the hem is commonly with the Chinese cut. Even these men, however, will generally wear their buttonless gown below their Chinese outer coat, whilst all retain the leggings and make a profuse use of cowries, discs of bone, white buttons and seeds for decoration, chiefly in the form of necklaces, bracelets and bands for their hempen bags and dâhs.

And they describe women's dress as follows (1911: 259-260):

> The original costume of the Lisu woman appears to have been a short coat and skirt of hemp with leggings, and a fillet across the hair studded with silver or cowrie ornaments, and this is still retained in the Upper Salween district. Nearly every community and clan, however, appears to have its distinctive dress; at Lotsolo (Salween about Lat.26 degrees- 15') Prince Henry found them "In a dress with parti-coloured sleeves, an armless blue waist-coat with miniature white checks and a brown border, and an apron and broad sash. Their costume was completed by a turban of, in some cases, a blue and red scarf fringed with cowries. Almost all had small coral earrings said to be peculiar to these 'Hua' or 'Flowery' Lissous." The most elaborate dress appears to be one used in the Kuyung

7.6 Lisu woman, Myitkyina (1997): Festive wear [photo by Laura Kan]

Kai district and we, therefore, give a detailed description.

Head-dress: about 5 ft. long and 1 1/2 feet broad; the central breadth a long piece of blue cloth, 5 times as long as each of the ends; the ends are made of pieces of cloth, sewn in strips of maroon, white and deep yellow. The ends are about 2 inches broader than the blue cloth, which is fringed with blue where the ends join it. On the outside edges of the end pieces and at each junction of the strips are long, double tassels consisting of clear beads in the upper part, joined by a cowrie to a large tassel of maroon wool; there being seven tassels at each end. Four inches from one end of the blue there is a strip of cloth about 3 feet long and 1 1/2 inches broad, covered on one side with 42 white bone discs, varying in diameter from 1 1/2 inches near the blue cloth to 3/4 inch at the extremity, the cloth diminishing with them. This narrow strip is edged with red and yellow thread. To the 4th button are attached quadruple tassels of the same colour as the strips, and from the end of the button are suspended a series of eight tassels, consisting of beads and white seeds with fringes of maroon, buff and dark blue wool. The head-dress is worn like a puggaree, the blue part being twisted round the head and the stripes hanging in a double fold over the back, whilst the narrow, beaded strip is lopped over to keep it is place, the whole having the appearance of a striped and tasselled hood.

Costume. — The women wear breeches reaching to the knee, and over these a blue coat, which reaches to the waist in front and to below the knees at the back, and to which is attached a loose over-jacket in alternate buff and cream squares, whilst a strip of cream and buff stripes about a foot deep edges the tail of the coat. The long tail has two rows of ornaments, an edging of white seeds and a row of white cowries about four inches above. Attached to the waist by a belt, and hanging over the long-tailed coat, is a long folded strip of blue cloth, pointed at each end and edged and tasselled with chocolate and cream shades, and which forms a triangular lappet. In front is a double apron of blue cloth, edged with cream hemp and a row of cowries at the bottom, which, in combination with the tail of the coat, has the appearance of a skirt and is held by a broad belt, bossed with rosettes of red cloth and cowries. The bodice is finished by a collar of dark red cloth and cowries hanging over the breast, where it is finished by great square plaques of silver....

Lowis (1911: 34) describes their dress as consisting of "long tunics of blue hempen cloth, with occasionally red cuffs, and blue gaiters." He notes further that "on the borders of the Myitkyina District some local influence (possibly Lashi) has introduced a patch-work coat."

Ward (1924: 298) describes the clothing of some Lisu that he encountered at the market in Hkamti Long as follows:

The girls were dressed in the costume of the tribe, but the men were dressed anyhow, in odds and ends of Chinese attrire, with garments of their own. Only one man wore the long Lisu gown, slit up the sides and tied round the waist. Slung over the shoulder, they carried bags of grey monkey skin.... Not knowing the jargon for female attire, I can give only a rough description of their dress. A kilt or petticoat of white hemp cloth, thinly striped with pale blue, an a jacket to match—nothing else. The stripes run traversely. The ample kilt, tightly girdled at the waist, hangs in pleats; the long-sleeved jacket is low in the neck and loose in the waist.

The collection of Göteborg's Ethnographical Museum contains eighteen Lisu textiles (Hansen 1960). The men's garments include: (1) a jacket with sleeves made of cotton dyed indigo with collar and buttons (Ac# 35.39.219); (2) an under caftan with undyed white coton body and indigo-dyed stand-up collar (Ac# 35.39.96); (3) a waistcoat made of indigo-dyed cotton with four knot buttons (Ac#35.39.97); (4) a waistcoat made of indigo-dyed cotton, brought from China (Ac#35.39.220); (5) trousers made of indigo-dyed cotton, said to be of Chinese origin (Ac# 35.39.218); (6) trousers known as "mitzi" made of indigo-dyed cotton cloth (Ac# 35.39.628); and (7/8) two sets of tube leggings made of coarse, undyed white cotton cloth with blue stripes (Ac# 35.39.100; Ac# 35.39.789). The women's clothing includes: (9) a caftan of indigo-dyed cotton with appliqué (Ac#35.39.86); (10) trousers made of indigo-dyed cotton cloth (Ac#35.39.92); (11) an apron worn over a caftan, consisting of a small apron sewn over a larger one, made of indigo-dyed cotton cloth with appliqué cotton decoration in various colors, with a belt made of strips of cotton cloth (Ac# 35.39.87); (12) tube leggings made of indigo-dyed cotton cloth with brown and yellow appliqué (Ac# 35.39.90); (13/14) two breast covers made of indigo-dyed cotton with red flannel collar appliqué and small silver disks attached as decorations, these hang down from a collar that fastens around the neck and is worn under a caftan (Ac#35.39.93; Ac#35.39.94); (15) a sash made of indigo-dyed cotton with appliqué at ends (Ac# 35.39.88); (16) a headcloth made of indigo-dyed cotton with strips of white and yellow cotton and red flannel at ends as well as a row of metal bells, red glass beads, and white buttons, and tassels of beads and yarn (Ac# 35.39.89); (17) a headband made of bright red wollen cotton cloth with a band of coins sewn on one end (Ac# 35.39.95); and (18) a headloth made of indigo-dyed cotton cloth with variously colored stripes at the ends (Ac# 35.39.274). There are drawings of several of these pieces and photographs of one of the leggings (p. 39) and of a mannequin wearing a complete costume (p. 43).

Referring to recent developments, Lewis and Lewis (1984: 244) comment that the "Lisu style of dress, particularly for women, has changed dramatically through the generations. Originally they made their clothing of hand-woven hemp cloth, and indeed Lisu women in the northern tip of Burma and probably many parts of China still wear heavily pleated skirts of that material. Various styles of Lisu clothing are to be found in Burma, all differing from that worn in Thailand." On page 242 they have a photo of a Lisu woman from Burma. Lewis and Lewis (1984: 262) also remark that "many hours and considerable sums of money are devoted to the making of new outfits for the young people" in preparation for the Lisu New Year celebration.

The Pyen

There are two small groups of around 800 Pyen living near the Laos border. I have found no information on their clothing, but they appear to be closely related to the Pounoy (or Phunoi) who live just across the border in Laos. There are about 27,000 Pounoy and Chazee (1995: 199) says that only the very remote Pounoy villages still wear the traditional indigo clothes. Such traditional clothing for a woman consists of a long skirt, an apron and similar cloth in the back, a blue jacket, white leggings, and a blue turban with red pompoms. The traditional costume of a man is comprised of wide indigo pants, an indigo jacket, and a red turban. Unfortunately, Chazee gives no photograph to accompany his brief description.

8

The Wa and Other Upland Mon-Khmer Groups

The textiles covered in this chapter are those of the Upland Mon-Khmer peoples. The Mon-Khmer of Burma include the Mon, Wa (Perauk, Vo, or Lawa), Khmu, Palaung (Pale and Shwe), Rumai, Riang, Yinchia, Danau, Blang, Samtao, and Thai Loi.

The largest group among the Mon-Khmer-speaking peoples in Burma are the Mon, are also known as Talaing. The Mon are primarily lowland peoples who live in central and southern Burma, mainly in what were known as the Tenasserim and Pegu Divisions of Lower Burma. In 1901 there were 321,898 and only about half claimed to speak Burmese (Scott 1921: 131). Scott comments (1921: 131) that "in dress, manners, and ways the Môn and the Burman are now practically indistinguishable." Although the Mon now generally wear clothing similar to the Burmese, some distinctive cloth continues to be woven in Mudon, south of Moulmein. Most of the other Mon-Khmer-speaking peoples live in upland areas.

The Wa

The Wa live primarily east of the Upper Salween River in Burma and in nearby areas of China at altitudes often above 1,000 meters. In China, speakers of Waic languages are included in the Va nationality. The relative isolation of the Wa and political turmoil on the Burma side of Wa territory has meant that population figures are not overly accurate; it is estimated there are probably 300,000 or over.

There is relatively little ethnographic description of the Wa, and there has been no systematic research among them by anthropologists. The British generally considered them to be "the most primitive of all peoples of Burma" (Stevenson 1940: 14), in part because of their widespread practice of head-hunting. Smith (1991: 349) remarks that "virtually the only Wa custom to have been closely recorded was a predilection for taking human heads which, displayed on posts on the approach to each village, were believed to ward off evil spirits and ensure good crops." The British made a distinction between the "Wild Wa" who continued to resist colonial rule and practice head-hunting and the "Tame Wa" who settled in Kengtung and Manglun and abandoned head-hunting.

The Wa are primarily slash-and-burn agriculturists and extensive use of the hills over the years had resulted in their habitat being severely denuded by the twentieth century. For quite some time their primary crop has been the opium poppy. Main food crops are maize, beans, buckwheat, rice, and various vegetables. The rice is used to produce liquor. Cotton is also grown. Food is often in short supply and supplementary food is obtained by trading opium. Prior to the advent of the modern drug trade, external commercial relations were very limited. Scott and Hardiman (1900, I/II: 504) report that :

> A few Shans, tolerated as middlemen and resident in the Tame Wa country, and some sturdy Hui Hui, Chinese Mahomedans from the borders of Yünnan, come up yearly with salt and a little rice and perhaps a few cloths and go back again with loads of opium, but everything has to be carried on the backs of men, for no loaded animal can pass through the narrow village gates.

Traditional political organization of the Wa consisted of autonomous villages with headmen known as *kraw.* A few adjacent villages sometimes formed

8.1. Group of Wa headmen
[Scott 1911: f.pg. 133]

8.2. Group of Wa women
[Scott 1911: f.pg. 34]

8.3. Group of Wa women
[Scott and Hardiman 1900, I/II:
plate 28, fig. 2, f.pg. 337]

confederations with a common chief known as a *ramang*. The power of such chiefs, however, was relatively limited and villages retained their own headmen. Such chiefs and headmen had houses distinguished by extended forked rafters at the gable end that was often carved or painted. Scott and Hardiman (1900, I/II: 506) consider this one of the few examples of Wa art, remarking that "Wa art is not conspicuous, or rather is thoroughly inconspicuous."

Head-hunting played a central role in traditional Wa religion. It was associated with the founding ancestral deities, and skulls were viewed as serving a protective role for villages. The angry spirits of the deceased associated with the skulls were believed to keep away other spirits that might bring harm to villagers and their crops. While some heads were obtained locally, such as from recently deceased criminals, others were obtained by means of raids. These raids were carried out not only among other Wa, but also against more distant groups of Lahu or Shan. The so-called Tame Wa tended to become at least nominally Buddhist under Shan influence. Some also became Christian.

The British-Chinese Boundary Commission surveyed some of the Wa territory in 1893, but there was no immediate effort to establish a colonial presence. Minimal colonial administration was established in a few Wa areas between 1937 and 1942, and head-hunting was reported to be in decline. The Wa were by and large left out of the fighting during the Second World War and only very limited administrative control was established by the British after the war. The Wa were therefore still largely autonomous when Burma became independent in 1948. Chinese KMT forces in northern Burma pressed some Wa into service in the early 1950s, but the impact of external forces remained minimal until the 1960s, when the Chinese-backed Communist Party of Burma (CPB) became active in Wa territory. The Chinese initiated large-scale support for the CPB in 1967 and by 1973 the entire Wa region east of the Salween River was under its control.

Thousands of young Wa men were recruited into the CPB's army. Smaller numbers were also recruited into the Burmese army and into other insurgent forces. The CPB also undertook to improve the region's infrastructure. For example, an estimated 200,000 Wa were mobilized to work on road construction projects (Smith 1991: 256). While most of Wa territory remained securely under CPB control, fighting with Burmese and other insurgent forces was almost constant. The Wa suffered tremendous casualties—at least 30,000 Wa died fighting in the CPB's army and estimates of total deaths among the Wa between 1968 and 1989 are around 25% of the population (Smith 1991: 423). In addition, over 10,000 Wa fled as refugees to the Kengtung area in an effort to escape from conflict.

In April 1989 the Wa and other soldiers in the CPB's army rose up against their commanders and drove them across the border into China. Later in the year the Wa agreed to a cease-fire with the Burmese army that allowed them to keep their arms in return for a pledge to break ties with other ethnic rebels. The Wa were also promised development assistance and negotiations leading to creation of a separate Wa state. Since then relations between the government of Burma and the Wa have remained tense. The Wa do not yet have their state and remain a formidable military force. They also continue to play an important role in the regional opium industry.

Wa textiles are not well studied. Apparently not all Wa communities produced their own cloth (Lebar, *et al.*, 1964: 131), but I have been unable to find information about the distribution of weaving among the Wa or about how textiles were traded. Culturally, the Wa were closely related to the Lawa of northern Thailand, but their textiles differ. Lawa weaving is strongly influenced by the neighboring Karen.

James G. Scott (Scott and Hardiman 1900, I/II: 510, and Scott 1921: 136-137) is essentially the only published source on the clothing of the Wa in Burma. Scott makes a distinction between the dress of the Tame Wa and the Wild Wa. He comments that the Wild Wa wear "the most ornaments and the least clothes" while the Tame Wa "instead of ornaments wear clothes" (1921: 135-136). Along similar lines, but without much by way of descriptions, Lowis (1919: 39) wrote that "the Northern Was are at a very low stage of civilization and their dress is of the scantiest, whereas the women of many of the tame Was further south cover themselves fully."

Tame Wa men wear either Shan dress or loincloths and, sometimes, a blanket. Scott (1921: 135) mentions five different groups among the Tame Wa

(Hsin-lam, Hsin-leng, Hsin-lai, Hta-mo, and Mot-no) and notes that members of each of these groups wear a distinctive loincloth, "which is striped or chequered in various patterns, or in different colours, for the so-called clans." He describes the cloth itself (Scott 1921: 137) as being made of "string as sail-cloth, but reasonable soft and pliable." Wa blankets are said to be made of the same material, but "with more of a frieze character" than the loincloths and "some have really neat-woven border ornamentation" (Scott 1921: 137). Scott also comments that such clothing is quite filthy: "unfortunately, a man seems to wear only one loincloth and one blanket all his life" (Scott 1921: 137). His description of the dress of Tame Wa women is even less informative: "the women wear skirts and jackets, not always or often fastened up" (Scott 1921: 137).

During warm weather, Scott remarks that Wild Wa men and women go about naked, with the exception of a few ornaments (Scott and Hardiman 1900, I/II: 510; Scott 1921 136-37). In this regard, Seidenfaden (1967: 47) comments that "their lassies, who during the hot season go about stark naked, are well shaped and quite comely, when recently washed, says Sir George Scott." For ceremonies, Wild Wa men wear a very narrow loincloth consisting of "a strip of coarse cotton about three fingers broad" (Scott and Hardiman 1900, I/II: 510) with tassels at the end. In cold weather they may put a blanket over their shoulders. Unfortunately, Scott and Hardiman provide little description of the blanket: "a coarse home-woven coverlet—their bed in fact" (Scott and Hardiman 1900, I/II: 510). Wild Wa women wear a skirt in cold weather when outside the village grounds which, according to Scott, "is none too long if worn extended, but is usually worn doubled up, and is then all too short" (1921: 136). The skirt's short length led Scott and Hardiman (1900, I/II: 510) to remark that "as mere drapery it is ungraceful and as a covering for the body it can only be called shameless. But it is the shamelessness of the Garden of Eden." No mention is made as to patterns on these garments or of what they are made.

There is a brief description of contemporary Va dress in China in *Ethnic Costumes and Clothing Decorations from China* (Shanghai Theatrical College 1986: 178-181). The authors note that men's dress varies with locality. The men of Ximeng are described as wearing "collarless short jackets with an oblique neck-band … short, loose, dark-coloured trousers… and red or black head-bands" (p. 178). Women are described as wearing two types of blouse. One type is collarless and relatively plain with buttons down the front. The other has a collar, is fastened on the right side, and is ornamented in the middle and edges. Women also wear a striped tubeskirt.

Other Upland Mon-Khmer Groups

Several other groups of peoples speaking Mon-Khmer languages are included in this chapter.

Blang

There are only about 2,000 Blang in Burma. They live in the Mong Yawng area of eastern Shan State. Blang is also an official nationality in China and about 60,000 Blang live in southwestern Yunnan.

8.4. Palaung man and two women
[Scott 1911: f.pg. 132]

The dress of the Blang in China is described in *Ethnic Costumes and Clothing Decorations from China* (1986: 198-201). Blang men (p. 198) wear black long-sleeved, collarless jackets that open from the front, black loose trousers, and black or white cotton headcloths. Blang women (pp. 198-199) wear close-fitting, collarless jackets with long sleeves. They are closed to one side and have a bell-bottom lower hem with a patterned strip. Younger girls wear light pink or green jackets, while older women wear black ones. Women may also wear a close-fitting blouse under the jacket. The women wear two tubeskirts. The inner skirt is usually a light color and the outer features horizontal stripes in red, black, white, and occasionally other colors. The inner skirt alone is worn when at home or working in the fields. The outer skirt is added for special occasions. Leg wrappings are also worn sometimes. Adult women wear large turbans in black or blue-green that are decorated with tassels at the ends. Male and female clothing traditionally was made of homespun

8.5. Silver Palaung woman, Pong Dang, Chiang Mai Province, Thailand (1997). The Palaung of Pong Dang are originally from the Kengtung area in Burma and arrived in Thailand in the mid-1980s [photo by author]

cotton. Both men and women also carry shoulder bags that are predominately white with some ornamentation.

Khmu

Khmuic speakers live in adjacent areas of northwestern Vietnam, southern China, northern Thailand, and northeastern Burma. Scott and Hardiman (1900, I/II: 521) noted that at the time of their writing "so far as is known, there are no permanent settlements of them in British territory." Since then small numbers of Khmu do appear to have settled in Burma's northeastern border areas. Khmu is the most widely spoken Khmuic language. Most Khmu speakers live in northern Laos (over 500,000). Scott and Hardiman (1900, I/II: 521) mention three Khmuic-speaking groups apparently living around the border area (Hka Muk, Hka Met, and Hka Kwen) and comment that "these tribes have different dialects, just as the women have different fashions of dress, but the variations do not seem to be very great."

In regard to their dress, Scott and Hardiman (1900, I/II: 521) note that the men of these Khmu groups

> dress like the Shans in blue or white coats, buttoning on the right side, and blue trousers. Frequently there is a stripe of red, white, or yellow on the legs of the trousers, or the coat sleeves.... Occasionally they wear turbans, white, red, or yellow, worn level with the forehead; often they have Shan hats with no turban.

They describe the women as wearing "petticoats with horizontal stripes of colours differing with the tribes, and near the Mèkhong all have sleeveless coats of blue cloth which fail to reach the top of the petticoat." No information is provided as to specifically what these different colors are or with which specific group they are associated. There is very little more information available on weaving or clothing of the Khmu in Laos or adjacent areas and distinctive traditional dress appears largely to have disappeared.

Michael C. Howard

Palaung and Riang

The Palaung include the Ngwe Palaung or Silver Palaung (who speak Pale), the Ta-ang Palaung or Golden Palaung (who speak Shwe), and the Rumai. There are between 200,000 and 300,000 Silver Palaung, around 150,000 Golden Palaung, and 150,000 Rumai living in northern Burma. The Silver Palaung live in Shan State near Kalaw, the Golden Palaung in northern Shan State near Namhsan, and the Rumai in northwestern Shan State. Many of these people live in or adjacent to the former Shan state of Taungbaing (also known as Tawngpeng or Tawn-peng) which had its capital at Namhsan. This state had a largely Palaung population and a Palaung ruler. Within this and other states, the village was the primary political unit. At the village level were village headmen and clan chiefs. Taungbaing had tribute relations with the Burmese and Shan and the Shan exerted considerable cultural influence on the Palaung.

8.6. Rumai woman [Scott and Hardiman 1900, I/I: plate 15, f.pg. 569]

In general, the Golden Palaung live at higher elevations and grow little rice, while the Silver Palaung or Pale live at lower elevations and grow more rice than those at higher elevations. The Palaung grow both swidden and irrigated rice. By the early twentieth century many Palaung in Taungbaing, especially those at higher elevations, were also tea cultivators and tea was being exported to the Shan and Burmese (see Milne 1924: 224). The Palaung have a reputation as peaceful people. The Palaung are Buddhists who also worship a variety of spirits or nats. There is a hereditary priest of nats known as a *damada sawbwa*.

Scott and Hardiman (1900, I/II: 486) mention that one Palaung clan, the Pato Ru, or the "tribe of the centre," lay claim to being the Rumai proper. They inhabit the village of Tawng Ma, south of Namhsan, and this village is said to be the oldest in the state. Apparently at one time this clan was comprised entirely of relatives of the rulers of Taungbeing and practiced clan endogamy: and among the exclusive privileges claimed was the right of their male members alone among Rumai men to wear colored clothing. Men of other Rumai clans were allowed to wear only plain black and white clothing. Scott and Hardiman (1900, I/II: 486) note, however, that at the time of their writing "these differences have vanished. There are no such restrictions, and members of all clans intermarry so freely that seemingly the old distinctions have vanished."

The traditional dress of Palaung men consists of jackets and trousers more or less like those of Shan men. Palaung women, however, have a distinctive style of traditional dress. Scott and Hardiman (1900, I/II: 487) describe the dress of Silver Palaung or Pale women as comprised of "a hood which is entirely white, with a short dark-blue coat and a skirt striped horizontally with red and blue." Milne (1910: 135) briefly describes the jacket and dress of Palaung women. The jacket is loose fitting and generally made of "home-woven stuff" that is usually "dull of colour" except at festivals when it is "made of bright blue velvet faced with scarlet." Stevensen (1944: 14) describes these jackets as being blue with red collars. The skirts are relatively short and Milne remarks (1910: 135) that "the clan to which they belong may be known by the width and colour of the stripes running horizontally round the dress." There are, however, no examples provided identifying skirts with clans. Lowis (1919:

38) also notes that "there are numerous sub-tribes or clans of Palaungs clearly distinguishable from each other in dress," but provides no details. The skirts are worn with cane hoops around the waist and sometimes a silver belt. Women may also wear indigo gaiters. Davies (1909: 376) remarks that the turban worn by Palaung women "is different from that of the Kachin women, and does not stick up so high."

Scott (1921: 132) notes that differences between other Palaung and Rumai include variations in women's dress and proceeds to describe Rumai dress. The men's dress is like that of the Shan. The women's dress is described as follows (Scott 1921: 132-133):

> The women wear a picturesque costume, which includes a hood, a coat, and a skirt, with leggings of cloth. The hood is brought to a point at the back of the head, and comes down over the shoulders. The border is white, with an inner patchwork pattern of blue, scarlet, and black cotton velvet. The skirt is

often composed of panels of cotton velvet of these various colours, with garters to match, and the general effect is very gay.... The ordinary working dress is a dark blue cut-away jacket and a skirt, and blue leggings.

Scott and Hardiman (1900, I/II: 489) describe the use of certain items of cloth in the wooing activities of young Palaung. Three days after young men draw lots giving the names of eligible young women, the young man will send the woman named on the lot he draws gifts that include a silk handkerchief. Three days later the woman reciprocates with gifts consisting of "a tasseled cloth, a sort of connecting link between a towel and a handkerchief, and a belt worked by herself." The receipt of these gifts indicates that the young man may go ahead and "press his suit in person."

Based on early twentieth century sources, Lebar, Hickey, and Musgrave (1964: 123) report that men's clothing was already made of imported cloth. In regard to women's clothing, they note that some

8.7. Group of Yang Lam Riang women [Scott 1911: f.pg. 141]

women still wove their own cloth, but that even the handmade cloth usually came from the Shan, although Palaung women did embroider the cloth.

The Riang include the Riang themselves (known also as Black Karen) and the closely related Yinchia (also called Striped Karen or Black Riang). The Riang live in southern Shan State. There are three Riang clans identified by Shan names: Yang Lam, Yang Sek, and Yang Wan-hkun. The 1901 census enumerated 4,990 Riang, and in 1955 there were an estimated 20,000 Riang. The Yang Lam were closest to the Shan and Scott (1921: 139) observed that all Yang Lam men wore Shan dress and that an increasing number of the women did so as well. The traditional female dress of the Yang Lam is described (1921: 139) as consisting of an ankle-length dark indigo tubeskirt made of homespun cotton and a jacket with no front or side openings of the same color and material. The only additional color is "an insertion of scarlet at the bosom." He also notes that they sometimes wear no head-dress.

Yang Sek and Yang Wan-hkun women are de-scribed as having distinctive and more colorful dress than Yang Lam women. Yang Wan-hkun women's dress is described (Scott 1921: 140) as follows:

The skirt is of the same dark blue homespun, but it is elaborately flounced—the only instance of this feature of dressmaking among the milliners of Burma, and probably in the East generally. The dress is much shorter, probably to show the black-lacquer garters below the knee. The basis of the jacket is also indigo-blue cloth, but it is elaborately embroidered, and ornamented with beads and scarlet *appliqué*. Coils of thin bamboo or cane rings, varnished with wood oil, are worn round the waist.

Yang Sek women are described as wearing a Karen-like poncho "with perpendicular red and white stripes" and "garter rings of brass wire" by Scott (1921: 140). Woodthorpe (1897: 27) refers to the

8.8. Group of Yang Sek Riang women [Scott 1911: f.pg. 140]

ponchos as "curious long coats like sacks with holes for head and arms with very short sleeves with alternate white and red longitudinal stripes."

Göteborg's Ethnographical Museum has a few Riang textiles in its collection. Hansen (1960) describes two Yang Sek and four Yang Lam textiles. The Yang Sek textiles include: (1) a woman's sleeveless gown that is described as being made of red and white vertical striped cotton (the red stripes are broader than the white ones), decorated in the center with tassels made of lace and cords in green and purple (Ac# 35.39.492); and (2) a man's jacket with sleeves made of plain white cotton, with a collar and nine buttons (Ac# 35.39.494). The Yang Lam textiles include: (1) a woman's tubeskirt made of black cotton (Ac#35.39.530); (2) a woman's sleeveless blouse made of plain black cotton cloth with a border of bright red cloth added at the bottom, with decorations of tassles, ribbons, and fringe added on the sides, center, and across the bottom (Ac#35.39.529); (3) a woman's headcloth made of orange colored cotton with red horizontal stripes (Ac#35.39.531); and (4) a man's trousers made of indigo dyed cotton cloth (Ac#35.39.495). There are photos of the Yang Lam blouse (p. 19) and of Yang Lam and Yang Sek mannequins in costumes as well as drawings of several of the textiles.

The Danau can be included with the Palaung and Riang. There were an estimated 10,000 Danau in 1984. Scott (1921: 141) refers to them as the Danaw and remarks that "they wear a dress corresponding to the Taungthu, but cannot be said to have Taungthu affinities." In this regard, Lowis (1919: 41) writes:

> There is nothing in the outward appearance of the Danaws to distinguish them from the Shans among whom they live. It is stated that the women used formerly to wear a short *thindaing* and petticoat like the Taungthus and Taungyos. This is not an usual form of Mon Khmer dress, but the Yanghseks afford an example of its adoption by a tribe of Khmer origin, and there is nothing intrinsically improbable in the statement.

All of these peoples are placed within the De'ang nationality in China. There are about 12,000 members of the De'ang nationality in China widely scattered in western Yunnan, with the largest number living in the Dehong region. De'ang dress is described in *Ethnic Costumes and Clothing Decorations from China* (1986: 216-221) and appears to be more elaborately decorated and colorful than the dress of the De'ang living in Burma described much earlier by Scott. Chinese De'ang men wear indigo or brown jackets that open from the side, short indigo trousers, and a white turban with colorful woolen balls at the ends. Women of the different groups within the De'ang nationality can be distinguished by the characteristics of their skirts: red horizontal stripes, red and black or red and blue horizontal stripes, and black with fine red and white stripes. The women's jackets feature a variety of silver decorations as well as variously colored wool balls. They also wear black turbans with colored wool balls at the ends. The authors also comment

8.9. Yinchia woman from Mongnai area (also known as Striped Karen) [Stevenson 1944: f.pg. 19]

on the rattan hoops still worn by De'ang women: "to the De'angs, rattan hoops are a sign of beauty, without which a woman will be sneered at" (p. 217).

Samtao and Thai Loi

There are a couple of thousand Samtao and Thai Loi living in the northeastern corner of Burma near the border with Laos and China. The Thai Loi were also sometimes referred to as "hill Shans" and at times associated with the Wa (Scott and Hardiman 1900, I/II: 517; Davies 1909: 373-374). Some observers consider the Thai Loi to be Wa who have adopted many aspects of Thai culture. The 1901 census enumerated 15,660 Thai Loi living in Burma. In Laos the Thai Loi are known as Doi.

According to Chazee there are 320 Doi living in three villages (1995: 51) and 2,500 Samtao living in six villages (1995: 91) in Laos.

Davies (1909: 374-375) reports that Thai Loi "men dress in the universal dark blue of the Chinaman" and that the women possess a more distinctive dress comprised of "dark blue jackets ornamented with a little red, and with shell ornaments hanging down the front" and skirts that are "usually striped with red, blue, or yellow." Chazee (1995: 51) states that the traditional dress of the Thai Loi in Laos disappeared generations ago and that they have adopted the dress of the Lu and Lao. Chazee (1995: 91) reports that the Samtao are strongly influenced by the Lu, but notes that cloth is still woven by older women and that the designs employed resemble those of the Lu.

9

The Hmong Njua, Mien, Nungish Groups, and Kado

The Hmong Njua

The Hmong Njua, also known as Blue Hmong or Green Hmong, are one of many distinctive groups of Hmong. The original homeland of the Hmong is probably on the banks of the Yellow River where they lived about 3,000 years ago. Chinese attempts to subjugate the Hmong led them to migrate south. Today there are over five million Hmong living in various provinces of China. In China they are known as Miao and recognized as a nationality. The Hmong Njua in China are known as Tak Miao. Hmong costumes in China have been well documented. Thus, a chapter is devoted to the Miao in *Ethnic Costumes and Clothing Decorations from China* (1986: 232-241) and the Textiles and the Clothing Culture Center of Fu Jen Catholic University has produced a large, lavishly illustrated volume, *Miao Textile Design* (1993), about their cloth.

The Hmong who migrated farthest south and west into northern Mainland Southeast Asia were the Hmong Njua and Hmong Deaw (White Hmong). They are found from northern Vietnam, across northern Laos and northern Thailand, and into northeastern Burma. There are a small number of Hmong Njua in northern Vietnam, and around 120,000 in several parts of Laos. Some of the studies of the Hmong Njua in Laos have paid attention to clothing (see Lemoine 1972: 114-124). There are about 35,000 of them in northern and central Thailand. Their clothing in Thailand has been documented in Paul and Elaine Lewis (1984: 100-133). War in Laos in the 1960s and early 1970s resulted in many Hmong refugees leaving Laos for Thailand and for North America and Europe. The textiles produced by these refugees have also received considerable attention.

There is only a small Hmong Njua population in Burma, living in Kengtung State. Scott and Hardiman (1900, I/II: 599) state that "such villages as exist in British territory are of recent settlement" and comment that they subsist primarily on maize and also grow poppies. A group of Hmong Njua moved from China and settled in Kengtung in 1917. Some of these Hmong have since migrated to northern Thailand.

Though there are numerous studies of Hmong Njua textiles (see Bühler 1972, Cohen 1987, John Michael Kohler Arts Center 1986, Mallinson and Ly 1988, White 1982), this is not the case for the Hmong in Burma. As written descriptions of Hmong Njua costumes from Burma are lacking, a brief summary of the costumes of Hmong Njua living across the border in Thailand and Laos is provided. Among the features of Hmong Njua clothing is their use of embroidery and indigo-dyed batik designs. They employ cross-stitching techniques in their needlework. Their embroidery features striking color contrasts and bold rectilinear designs and is not as intricate as the embroidery of the White Hmong. The clothing of Hmong Njua women includes a finely pleated skirt with three horizontal design sections: a band of white hemp or cotton on top, batik designs with strips of appliqué in the middle, and a band with cross-stitch embroidery on the bottom. They wear indigo blouses with blue cuffs, with the front closures edged with pieces of multicolored fabrics. Their costume also includes meters of indigo fabric wrapped around the waist. Hmong Njua women also wear a plain indigo apron in the front suspended from a long red sash that is wound twice around the waist and tied in the back. Hmong Njua men wear indigo pants that are baggy, cut low in the crotch, which fit tightly at the ankles. They wear short shirts with rounded necklines. Men also wear short jackets and vests. A red sash is tied around the waist and an indigo skullcap is worn on the heads. It is important to note that there are regional variations and an individual's wardrobe can contain relatively plain clothing for everyday wear as well as highly decorated items of clothing for festive occasions.

The Mien

Very few Mien (also called Yao) live in Burma. Their language is known as Mien. One distinct group of Mien is known as Lantien (or Lantène). Many other subgroups of Mien are found in China and Vietnam. The Mien migrated in a southwesterly direction from southeastern China into Southeast Asia, first settling in northern Vietnam and then later in Laos, Thailand, and Burma. In all there are around one million Mien scattered across southern China and northern Mainland Southeast Asia.

Scott and Hardiman (1900, I/II: 602), writing at the beginning of the twentieth century, report that "very few [Mien] have yet crossed the Mèkhong … but the westward movement is still going on and the two or three villages on the Kengtung borders seem likely to draw more after them." In the same work (1900: I/I: 603-604), however, they note in reference to the few Mien villages found in Kengtung that "so far it is uncertain whether their number will increase or not." In fact, they virtually disappear from the literature after these early references to them in Burma.

In its basic form, the clothing of the Mien living in neighboring Laos and Thailand is fairly uniform, while there is a great deal more variety among the Mien living further east in Vietnam and China.

The woman's costume consists of loose-fitting pants, a tunic, a sash, and a headcloth. All of these items are made of cotton that is dyed indigo or black. The distinguishing feature of these items of clothing is the embroidery that is especially noteworthy on the pants. In the past silk thread was used for this embroidery and natural dyes. In recent years silk thread has been replaced with pre-dyed commercial cotton or acrylic yarn. There are also special items of clothing produced for brides, including a head-covering, an apron-cape (this includes appliqué as well and is used for other special occasions), and other specially-embroidered clothing.

Men's clothing includes a loose-fitting jacket and pants. These are made of cotton and dyed indigo or black. The jacket may have metal buttons and sometimes is embellished with colored piping along the edges. Turbans are sometimes worn on ceremonial occasions.

A variety of other decorated types of cloth is produced as well. Hats are made for boys and girls with embroidered and appliqué decorations and red pompoms on top. There are small embroidered bags used for storing valuables and a variety of shoulder bags with embroidered or appliqué designs. Special clothing is also made for priests and shamans, featuring different types of decorative robes.

9.1. Hmong Njua husband and wife
[Scott 1911: f.pg. 97]

9.2. Group of Hmong Njua
men and women
[Scott and Hardiman 1900,
I/I: plate 16, f.pg. 597]

9.3. Group of Mien men and
women (also known as Yao)
[Scott and Hardiman 1900,
I/II: plate 18, f.pg. 85]

9.4. Drawing of Nung,
described as "Kioutse types"
[d'Orléans 1898: 260]

The Nungish Peoples

This group includes the Rawang (or Nung Rawang), the Nung (or Lutzu), the Norra, and the Lama. They live in the Upper Salween valley, with the Lisu to the south and Tibet to the north. According to Leach (1954: 45, 59), the Nung in the Kachin Hills are culturally much like the Jingpho, while in the north they are influenced by Tibetans. They belong to the Nu nationality in China. There are over 20,000 Nu living in the Nujuang River valley in northwestern Yunnan. Many of the Nu in China were dominated by the Nashi at Weihsi but more recently they came directly under Chinese domination.

Ward (1924: 139) describes the village of Bahang as being typically Nung: small and scattered with "twenty or more huts included in the name, a hut here and a hut there; but they are not, as a rule, within shouting distance of each other, and frequently not even in view." The various Nungish groups are traditionally shifting cultivators, their primary crop being maize. They also produced

9.5. Drawing of Nung, described as "Loutse types." [d'Orléans 1898: 262]

opium and in the past bartered opium and skins for goods that included cloth. They had a reputation as peaceful people, unlike their Tibetan and Lisu neighbors. Rock (1947: 334) remarks in his description of the Nung of Bahang: "to the north of Bahang are hostile Tibetans amd to the south savage Black Li-su." For the most part the various Nungish societies in Burma and across the border in China were relatively egalitarian, though they possessed village headmen and slaves were known to exist. Their religion in China was a modified form of Lamaism derived from Tibet, blended with animism, and they had their own priest/exorcists. There was also some Catholic missionary activity among them.

Rock (1947: 334-335) cites older Chinese sources that describe the Nung as wearing clothing made of hemp, the men wearing trousers and women skirts. In his caption to Plate 189, Rock describes the women as weaving hemp cloth, indicating that Nung clothing continued to be made of hemp in the 1930s. Prince Henri d'Orléans (1898: 263) says that "in dress the men follow the Thibetan fashion" and describes women's attire as consisting of "two garments—one fitted to the figure, the other looped from under the left arm to the right shoulder." He notes (1898: 262) that among the gifts given by a young man at the betrothal feast is "a tchaupa (Thibetan garment)."

Ward (1924: 213) remarks about Nung of the Tazu valley that "the people are hard up for clothes" and describes their dress as follows:

> … the men invariably go about naked except for a truss tied round the waist with string: this from the day they can toddle. Women and girls wear a short skirt, and decorate themselves with hoops of rattan, worn round the waist and round the calf…. Everybody possesses a striped towel, homewoven, but this is not worn in the daytime—at least not during working hours. When in use it is wrapped round the shoulders or fastened diagonally across the chest.

Ward (1924: 214) also mentions that one of his guides engaged in trade with the Nung of Tazu, carrying "a great roll of Tibetan cloth" for this purpose in his bedding. He also remarks (1924: 222) that as he traveled further westward towards the

Nam Tamai "the Nungs grew more and more like the Kachins—at least outwardly" and that in the vicinity of Nok-Mung their houses begin to look like those of the neighboring Shan and the men dress "in *lone-gyi* and jacket" (1924: 240).

The Pitt Rivers Museum has five Nung textiles donated by Colonel Green in 1934, collected in the 1920s: (1) hemp shawl (65.5cm width and 160cm length), features a plain body with supplementary weft patterns at the ends in cotton threads in various colors (Ac# 1934.81.94); (2) hemp blanket (72cm width and 184cm lenth plus fringe) from the upper Nmai valley, the central portion is ornamented with blue tufts and bands with blue and black zigzags at the edges, there is a broad border at the ends in part made of dog's hair dyed red with a border above it of variously colored lozenges (Ac# 1934.81.92); (3) skirt made of hemp worn by males and females (68cm width and 160cm lenth plus fringe) from the upper Nmai valley, fringed and bordered at both ends with red thread and features lines of embroidery in a variety of colors and patterns (Ac# 1934.81.93); (4) bag made of hemp (23cm width and 27cm length) from Upper Nmai valley, embrodered patterns with cotton yarn in various colors (Ac# 1934.81.97); and (5) bag made of hemp from the upper Sumprabum between the Mali river and the Kumon range, embroidery of cotton yarn in several colors with designs including animals and people (Ac# 1934.81.96).

The Kado

The Kado (also called Kadu or Kudo) call themselves Sak. They are Buddhists and live in western Burma, mainly in the Katha area near the border with the Indian state of Manipur. They grow glutinous rice on irrigated terraces, and also grow cotton. Prior to the Second World War they intermarried with Jingpho, Burmese, and others. As a result, the Kado for the most part lost any distinctive culture.

9.6. Group of Nung women [Ward 1924: f.pg. 192]

Scott and Hardiman (1900, I/II: 570) list six divisions of Kado and note that only one, the Ganan, "have resisted the temptation to Burmanize themselves as their dress." They also report (Scott and Hardiman 1900, I/II: 364) that "in Katha, the Kachins and Kadus still very generally make their own clothing," but remark that even at the time of their writing "the threads made from home-grown cotton are being rapidly ousted by the common threads of European manufacture. Threads equally cheap and dyed more brilliantly can be had in nearly all the bazaars." Unfortunately, the authors provide only a very brief description of Kado dress (Scott and Hardiman 1900, I/II: 570-571): "properly the dress of a married Kadu woman is all black. The unmarried girls dress in 'all colours.'"

The Pitt Rivers Museum has seven Ganan textiles donated by Major R.C. Temple in 1894. These include: (1) a plain indigo woman's jacket with long sleeves and no collar (Ac# 1894.27.6.1); (2) another indigo woman's jacket (Ac# 1894.27.6.2); (3) an indigo skirt with woven borders in yellow, green, and white (Ac# 1894.27.5); (4/5) two pieces of cotton material (one plaid, the other plain dark blue) (Ac# 1894.27.6.3-.4); and (6/7) two shoulder-bags (Ac# 1894.27.2 and Ac# 1894.27.4).

9.7. Rawang woman, Myitkyina, Kachin State (1997) [photo by Laura Kan]

10

Textiles Illustrated in the Color Plates

This chapter describes in detail the numbered color plates, as each photo includes only a brief caption to identify the textile illustrated. All photographs in the plates are by the author.

As a caution, it is important to point out that identification of textiles from Burma is often difficult. There are several problems associated with the pieces in museum collections. For example, in the Bankfield Museum collection, the term Shan is generally used in a geopolitical sense in identifying textiles and includes most of the various ethnolinguistic groups found within Shan State. In the case of the Denison University collection, textiles are generally identified according to general ethnic group only and not according to subgroup. The problem is perhaps even more acute in the case of pieces in private collections. Such pieces frequently have been obtained from dealers in Thailand or urban areas of Burma. The information provided by these dealers is usually confined to giving the name of the general ethnic group from which the textiles came, and even this may be inaccurate.

The source of the pieces photographed is indicated as follows:

(BM)	Bankfield Museum
(DU)	Denison University
(NHM)	Natural History Museum
(FM)	Field Museum of Natural History
(PC)	Private Collection.

In the case of The Bankfield Museum, use of the designations GB and GK in the accession numbers indicated that the pieces were loaned to the museum by E.C.S. George in 1900 and subsequently given to the museum in 1937. The dates in the accession numbers from the Denison University collection generally indicate when the pieces were catalogued and do not reflect the age of the particular piece or even, necessarily, when it was obtained by the university.

Burmish

1. Intha, tubeskirt, made of two pieces sewn together, silk, plain red ground with white and gold-colored stripes, some with simple weft ikat patterning, 72cm x 102cm. (PC)
2. Intha, from Inpawkhon village, tubeskirt, plain black cotton hem piece sewn on to body made of silk with some metallic weft yarns, weft ikat woven in *zin me* pattern, striped section forming an inside pleat, 84cm x 104cm, see Fraser-Lu (1988: 96-97). (PC)
3. Intha, tubeskirt, silk, plain pink and red horizontal stripes as well as grey horizontal stripes with weft ikat patterning, 85cm x 88cm. (PC)
4. Taungyo, colored drawing of a *thingdaing* (woman's smock) from Scott and Hardiman (1900, I/II: facing p. 370).
5. Taungyo, *thingdaing,* cotton, with Job's tears attached for decoration, 78cm x 83cm, see drawing of this piece in Start (1917: figure 7, p. 7). (BM: GS57)
6. Taungyo, from Pindaya district, western Shan State, *thingdaing,* thin horizontal stripes made of silk and metallic thread, Job's tears around neck, buttons at sleeve holes, and metal disks down the center of the front and back attached as decorations, 69cm x 78cm. (PC)
7. Taungyo, colored drawing of a *tabet* (woman's headdress) from Scott and Hardiman (1900, I/II: facing p. 370).
8. Taungyo, *tabet,* plain white cotton with red silk thread stitched along the sides, near the ends

are three thin stripes of red and yellow silk thread as well as a broad band of silk thread nearer the center, 26.5cm x 348cm plus fringe, see drawing of this piece in Start (1917: fig. 6, p. 6) and Innes (1957: fig. 33, p. 38, described on p. 39). (BM: GS84)

Tai

9. Shan, man's shirt, made from commercial cloth, w. 64cm at back. (DU: 1974.3)

10. Shan, woman's jacket, Color plate I in Innes (1957: frontispiece) features a model wearing this jacket. It is described in some detail on p. 3. It is made of a combination of local cotton and commercial European cotton. The body measures 69cm x 65cm, and the sleeves are 36cm long, with a width of 23cm at the cuff. (BM: GS19)

11. Shan, bag, the shoulder strap is made of cotton that is left plain except where it is attached to the side of the body, this portion is over-stitched with silk and metallic thread with Job's tears added as decorations, the central part of the body has a cotton base that is entirely over-stitched with silk and metallic thread. The body measures 11.5cm x 12.5cm. (FM: 235656)

12. Shan, bag, the construction is similar to #23 except that additional Job's tears are attached as decorations where the shoulder strap and central body pieces are joined. The body measures 22cm x 23cm. The piece dates from the early twentieth century. (PC)

13. Shan, bag, a cotton base with extensive embroidery covering the body and a portion of the shoulder-strap also of cotton, Job's tears attached above the fringe as decorations. The body measures 28.5cm x 28cm. (DU: 1969.9)

14. Shan, piece of cloth used for a skirt, cotton, made of two pieces sewn together, thin plain bands and broad bands with supplementary weft patterning, 58.5cm x 121cm. The piece was collected by Alleyne Ireland, a British government official, around the turn of the century and sold to the museum in 1905. (FM: 87169)

15. Shan, piece of cloth for a skirt, cotton, made of two pieces sewn together, thin plain bands and broad bands with supplementary weft patterning, 66cm x 113.5cm. The piece was collected by Alleyne Ireland around the turn of the century and sold to the museum in 1905. (FM: 87171)

16. Shan, skirt, plain black and blue cotton hem piece, plain black upper portion, a wide band of cloth attached as decoration featuring vertical stripes of plain weave and with supplementary weft patterning and strips of plain velvet and leather, 27cm x 96.5cm. (DU: 1974.4)

17. Shan, skirt, plain black and blue cotton hem piece, plain black upper portion, with wide patterned pieces of cloth attached as decorations to lower portion, these consist of two pieces of cloth attached horizontally, one of silk and metallic thread with supplementary weft pattering and the other of plain red velvet, additional strips of decorated cloth made of silk are attached vertically. The piece is described by Innes (1957: 5) as showing strong Chinese influence. The skirt measures 33cm x 134cm. (BM: GS20)

18. Shan, skirt, plain black and blue hem piece, a plain black upper portion made of cotton, and a decorative band of cloth attached to the lower portion. The piece is described by Start (1917: 29-30) and a drawing of it appears as Fig. 22 p. 28 (with additional details in Fig. 23 p. 29). Start considers the piece interesting because of "the great variety of imported material used in decoration, and the beautiful border of folded cloth appliqué." The skirt measures 77cm x 94cm. (BM: GS24)

19. Thai Nua or Chinese Shan, skirt, similar to those worn by the Shan, features a plain black and blue hem piece, plain black upper portion, and a band of patterned cloth attached to the lower portion. The decorated band shows strong Chinese influence and the patterning includes the use of metallic thread. It measures 77cm x 93.5cm. (FM: 87174)

20. Shan, Thai Mao subgroup, piece of cloth for a skirt, geometric patterning in various colors using aniline dyes, 23.5cm x 35cm. This piece is described by Start (1917: 29) and a drawing of it appears on page 26 as Fig. 21 (a detail appears on p. 27). (BM: GS21)

21. Shan, possibly Thai Mao subgroup, decorative cloth used in religious settings, center consists

of a piece of handspun white cotton cloth with geometric supplementary weft patterning in red and black, around this are sewn a band of plain blue cotton cloth and a band of plain red cotton cloth, 58cm x 93cm.(PC)

22. Shan, blanket, handspun cotton, made of two pieces sewn together, twill weave, indigo-dyed, 112cm x 202cm. (PC)

23. Lu, Mong Yawng, Shan State, tubeskirt, handspun cotton, made of three pieces sewn together, plain white waistband (turned pink by running dye), below this a plain red piece, and the bottom portion with a plain white stripe at the top and a plain black band at the bottom with center featuring thin red and black lines with occasional spots of white, 61cm x 93cm. (PC)

24. Lu, Kengtung, tubeskirt, cotton, made of two pieces sewn together, a plain dark indigo portion and a portion with plain stripes, 64cm x 103cm. (BM: GS54)

25. Lu, ceremonial cloth, cotton, discontinuous supplementary weft patterning (elephants with mahouts, horses with riders, and human figures), 47cm x 88cm. (PC)

26. Lu, Kengtung State, *pha chet* (man's shoulder-cloth), cotton, continuous supplementary woven patterns, 20cm x 77cm. (DU: no accession number)

27. Lu, Kengtung State, *pha chiwon* (altar decoration), cotton, continuous supplementary weft woven patterns, 41cm x 88cm plus 20-24cm fringe. (DU: 1969.248)

Chin

Northern Chin

28. Thado, body wrap, made of two pieces sewn together, commercial cotton, black with horizontal white lines with red and black lozenge-shaped decorations, yellow zig-zag patterned bands towards the ends, 138cm x 185cm. Thado blankets such as the three shown here (nos. 26-28) are also sometimes identified as being Tangkhol Naga. (PC)

29. Thado, body wrap, made of two pieces sewn together, cotton, large plain horizontal stripes in red, green, and black, with four thin white lines decorated with chevrons, two vertical bands with triangular patterns towards ends, 117cm x 182cm. (PC)

30. Thado, body wrap, similar to #27, 114cm x 152cm. (DU: 1967.8)

31. Probably Mara (Lakher), body cloth, made of two pieces sewn together, commercial cotton, black with three sets of thin red and white horizontal lines and two sets of horizontal lines of geometric supplementary weft patterning, 104cm x 157cm. (PC)

32. Anal, blanket (detail), made of two pieces sewn together, cotton, plain purple with thin white double woven bands with geometric patterning in purple, male and female figures made of cowries added as decoration, 153cm x 120cm. These pieces (nos. 32-34) are said to come from "Naga-Chin", which probably means the Anal. (PC)

33. Anal, body wrap, commercial cotton, made of two pieces sewn together, black with thin white horizontal lines featuring fine geometric patterning, 128cm x 171cm. (PC)

34. Anal, blanket, made of two pieces sewn together, handspun cotton, plain blue with thin vertical white double woven bands with geometric supplementary weft patterning in red and green, thin plain red horizontal stripes near each end, 102cm x 159cm. (PC)

35. Lushai, *puan pui* (quilted body wrap), handspun cotton, made of three pieces sewn together, plain weave with shag carpet like strips on one side, white with black stripes in the center and thin red and black stripes near the edge, also thin red and black stripes near the ends, 68cm x 136cm. See Shakespear (1912: 30) and Stevenson (1943: 122). Spearman (1880, II: 66) describes a similar blanket for the Khumi of the Southern Chin. These cloths (nos. 32-35) are sometimes said to be from the Wa. (PC)

36. Reverse of #35.

37. Lushai, *puan pui* (quilted body wrap), handspun cotton center made of three pieces sewn together and two commercial cotton pieces sewn along the sides, plain weave with shag carpet-like strips on one side of center, center portion plain white with black and white stripes at edges of each piece of cloth and red and black lines near the ends, side pieces black with black and white lines along edges, 122cm x 162cm. (PC)

Michael C. Howard

38. Lushai, *puan pui* (quilted body wrap), dark indigo-dyed handspun cotton, made of three pieces sewn together, plain weave with shag carpet-like strips on one side, thin red lines near sides and edges, 117cm x 162cm. (PC)

39. Haka, *cawng-nak* (body wrap for man), made of two pieces sewn together, silk, alternating horizontal plain and supplementary weft patterned bands, 125cm x 196cm. (PC)

40. Lushai, possibly Thangur subgroup, body wrap,, made of two pieces sewn together, handspun cotton, plain white with two plain black horizontal bands, 115cm x 195cm. (PC)

41. Falam, Za Hau subgroup, man's longyi, cotton, plain checks, 152cm x 112cm (open). (PC)

42. Falam, *pawr* (loincloth), from the Biar Dum group of Northern Chin, consisting of the Laizo and Zahao Falam as well as Ngawm, Bawm, and Tawr, commercial cotton, plain black with thin red stripes, a band of supplementary weft geometric patterning made of silk thread at each end, 34cm x 323cm plus fringe. (PC)

43. Mara (Lakher), *dua ah* (ceremonial loincloth), made of three pieces sewn together, the center is of plain white cotton cloth, the ends are made of cotton with silk supplementary weft weave geometric patterning, white center 42cm x 624cm, one end 42cm x 72cm and the other end 42cm x 75cm. (PC)

44. Haka Subdivision, woman's blouse, sleeveless with V-neck, made from four pieces sewn together vertically, upper portion plain black with short bands of geometric supplementary weft patterning in yellow and red silk thread, a row of embroidered patterns also in red and yellow silk thread, and rows of white beds of buttons added as decoration, the lower portion is on a black ground with geometric supplementary weft patterning in red and yellow silk thread throughout and a row of white beads and buttons across the bottom, 83cm x 82cm. (PC)

45. Haka Subdivision, woman's blouse, sleeveless with V-neck, made from four pieces sewn together vertically, upper portion plain indigo-dyed cloth with short bands of geometric supplementary weft patterning in yellow and red silk thread and a row of embroidered patterns also in red and yellow silk thread, the lower portion is on an indigo ground with

geometric supplementary weft patterning in red silk thread throughout, 87cm x 92cm. (PC)

46. Haka Subdivision, woman's blouse, sleeveless with V-neck, made from four pieces sewn together vertically, plain red vertical bands divided by thin plain yellow and black stripes, a wide section towards the top featuring supplementary weft patterning (largely geometric, but also a row of birds) using yellow thread, 91cm x 102cm. (PC)

47. Haka Subdivision, woman's blouse, sleeveless with V-neck, made from four pieces sewn together vertically, plain red vertical bands divided by thin plain yellow and black stripes, a wide section towards the top featuring supplementary weft patterning (largely geometric, but also a row of birds) using yellow thread, 91cm x 102cm. (PC)

48. Thado, woman's blouse, sleeveless, cotton, black ground with horizontal and vertical geometric patterning in various colors, 44cm x 46cm. (PC)

49. Probably from Haka Subdivision and could be Lautu from southern Haka area around Hnaring (said to be "Lethu"), woman's blouse, sleeveless with V-neck, made of two pieces sewn together vertically, upper portion featured plain black vertical bands divided by thin colored stripes and two bands with supplementary weft geometric patterning, lower portion continues the pattern from the upper portion and adds several horizontal bands with supplementary weft geometric patterning, white buttons attached as a clasp near the top of the V-neck and around the edges of the bottom portion as decoration, 39cm x 44cm. (PC)

50. Probably from Haka Subdivision, woman's blouse, sleeveless with V-neck, made of two pieces sewn together vertically, warp of indigo-dyed handspun cotton, upper portion features short bands of geometric supplementary weft patterning in green, red, and white thread, lower portion decorated throughout in geometric supplementary weft patterning, 48cm x 51cm. (PC)

51. Probably from Tidim Subdivision, woman's blouse, sleeveless with V-neck, made of three pieces sewn together vertically, the back and sides of the front are one piece, this is made of

plain indigo-dyed handspun cotton with a thin band of purple and white geometric patterning along the bottom, the center of the front is made of two pieces of silk cloth with plain vertical bands in black, white, purple, green, and yellow, the white lines have fine geometric patterning and one of the lack lines has zig-zag patterning, 52cm x 42cm. (PC)

52. Possibly Mara (Lakher), woman's blouse, sleeveless with V-neck, made of two pieces sewn together vertically, cotton base with silk supplementary weft weave patterning, top portion covered in geometric patterning, the center of the lower portion is covered in small red beads arranged in bands with diamond patterning flanked by two vertical rows of supplementary weft weave geometric patterning and then, at the outside, by three plain weave vertical rows decorated with three horizontal rows of red beads and clusters of four cowrie shells, 40cm x 40cm. (PC)

53. Possibly Mara (Lakher), woman's blouse, sleeveless with V-neck, made of two pieces sewn together vertically, cotton base with silk supplementary weft weave patterning, top portion covered in geometric patterning, the center of the lower portion is covered in small red beads arranged in bands with diamond patterning flanked by two vertical rows of supplementary weft weave geometric patterning and then, at the outside, by three plain weave vertical rows decorated with three horizontal rows of red beads and clusters of four cowrie shells, 47cm x 50cm. (PC)

54. Probably Haka, woman's blouse, sleeveless and opens at the front, made of two pieces sewn together vertically, silk, top is plain black, followed by a band of geometric supplementary weft patterning, then a zig-zag twill weave band, the lower portion has two thin bands of patterning and a wide plain red band, 45cm x 32cm. (PC)

55. Haka, woman's blouse, sleeveless with V-neck, made of two pieces sewn together vertically, silk, top features vertical alternating plain red and patterned bands, below this a zig-zag twill weave band, the lower portion has two thin bands of patterning and a wide plain red band, 52cm x 37cm. (PC)

56. Probably from far north of the Chin area, woman's skirt, made of two pieces sewn together, handspun cotton, plain horizontal stripes in light and dark blue as well as purple, green, and yellow, 118cm x 66cm. (PC)

57. Probably from far north of the Chin area, woman's skirt, made of two pieces sewn together, handspun cotton, plain indigo-dyed with supplementary weft geometric patterning at ends and thin red, green, and yellow stripes along the center, 123cm x 66cm. (PC)

58. Falam, woman's skirt, made of two pieces sewn together, upper piece plain black cotton with some decoration near the edges, bottom piece woven in silk with a plain green and purple band and two bands with geometric supplementary weft weave patterning, a row of cowrie shells and hanging beads and bells added across the center, 108cm x 80cm. (PC)

59. Falam, woman's skirt, made of two pieces sewn together, upper piece plain black cotton with some decoration near the edges, bottom piece woven in silk with a plain green and purple band and two bands with geometric supplementary weft weave patterning, 140cm x 77cm. (PC)

60. Haka or Falam, woman's skirt, made of two pieces sewn together, silk, the narrow top pieces mainly on a black ground and is plain at the top with rows of supplementary weft geometric decorations across the rest of it, the larger lower portion features alternating plain purple bands with green and black bands featuring geometric supplementary weft patterning, 121cm x 89cm. (PC)

61. Lushai (Mizo), woman's skirt, handspun cotton, white ground with blue thread woven as an extra weft over the white, two bands of white and blue patterns known as *kwakpuizigzial* (*kwakpui*=bud of a fern plant), 100cm x 50cm. An old style of skirt rarely worn during the past few decades, see Shirali 1983: 73. (PC)

62. Haka, tubeskirt, made of two pieces sewn together, silk, covered entirely in bands of supplementary weft weave geometric patterning, 65cm x 94cm. (PC)

63. Haka Subdivision and could be Lautu from southern Haka area around Hnaring (said to be Lethu), apron hung on front in front of skirt, made of two pieces of cloth sewn together, plain black horizontal bands separated by single lines of colored thread and four small bands with

supplementary weft decorations, three vertical bands of decoration, the outer two of these feature geometric supplementary weft patterning, 52cm x 47cm. (PC)

64. Tedim, bag, silk, vertical stripes with green base, body 32cm x 25.5cm. (DU: 1967.11)

65. Tedim, bag, cotton, vertical stripes with red base, body 34cm x 26.5cm. (DU: 1967.16)

Southern Chin

66. Daai (Makue U Nu subgroup), body wrap, made of three pieces of handspun cotton, plain stripes of different shades of indigo, 115cm x 158cm. (PC)

67. Daai (Makue U Nu subgroup), body wrap, made of three pieces of hemp cloth sewn together, the only decoration consists of brown stripes near the edges, 121cm x 169cm. (PC)

68. Daai (Makue U Nu subgroup), body wrap, made of three pieces of very rough hemp cloth sewn together, the only decoration consists of brown stripes near the edges, 104cm x 158cm. (PC)

69. Daai (Makue U Nu subgroup), body wrap, made of three pieces of handspun cotton, plain white and indigo stripes, 101cm x 149cm. (PC)

70. Kanpetlet area (said to be Ma Lan Na), body wrap, made of two pieces of handspun cotton, plain brown, black, and yellow stripes, 98cm x 157cm. (PC)

71. Daai (probably Makue U Nu subgroup), body wrap, made of four pieces of very rough handspun cotton sewn together, dyed black with thin red and blue stripes, 135cm x 144cm. (PC)

72. Man's sitting cloth, commercial cotton, collected 1958-60, 36cm x 63cm. See Lehman 1962: 84. (NHM 70.2/2434)

73. Khumi, loincloth, made of two pieces (one very long and a short piece at one end) sewn together, double weave, front of long piece has a center that is all black with small embroidered decorations in various colors scattered throughout and sides with black and red warp threads and black and white weft threads that produce a zig-zag pattern, the back of the long piece has a black center woven so as to produce a diamond pattern and red and black sides, a small part of the center of the long piece next to where the short piece is attached is covered

in small rows of embroidered decorations, the small end-piece has a center that has a black background covered with rows of embroidered decorations in different colors, the sides are similar to the long piece but the pattern is more compressed, the back of the end-piece has a red center and red and black sides, small yellow beads are attached along the sides of the entire cloth, 15cm x 426cm. (PC)

74. Khumi, loincloth, made of three pieces (one very long center piece and two short end pieces) sewn together, front of center piece has black warp threads, the center of this piece is plain black and woven so as to create diamond-shaped patterns, at the ends the center features small rows of supplementary weft geometric patterning, the edges use red, white, and yellow weft threads to create zig-zag patterns, the back of the center piece has a plain black center and red edges, the end pieces have a black ground that is covered both front and back by other threads, at the center of the front of the end pieces are small rows of supplementary weft geometric patterning in red, yellow, and white, and the edges are smaller versions of the zig-zag pattern, the back of the end pieces has a light red center and darker red sides, 15cm x 442cm. (PC)

75. Khumi, dance shoulder cloth, made of a single piece of double woven cotton cloth, plain black with narrow red striped down the center and along the edges with three narrow rows of supplementary weft geometric patterning at the ends, strands made of two small white beads and a clear plastic tube with a tuft of purple yarn at the end attached along the edges and in a row down the center, longer strands (with green and purple tufts at the ends) used to decorate the ends, 13cm x 72cm plus fringe. See Brauns and Löffler 1990: 35. (PC)

76. Khumi, Arakan/Rakhine State, shoulder cloth, made of a single piece of double woven cotton cloth, yellow and brown warp threads and brown plus a few orange weft threads to create rows of geometric patterns in three wide bands, the back is largely yellow, 43cm x 159cm. (PC)

77. Khumi, woman's chest covering for dances, made of a single piece of double woven cotton cloth, warp consists of clusters of three black threads interspersed with two red threads, weft

includes yellow, purple, white, and orange silk threads to create a large field of diamond-shaped patterns in the center and rows of smaller diamonds along the sides, in addition there are two bands with narrow rows of supplementary weft patterning, the back is red and black, 72cm x 42cm. (PC)

78. Khumi, woman's chest covering for dances, made of a single piece of double woven cotton cloth, warp consists of clusters of three black threads and two red threads, weft includes yellow, orange, white, and green silk threads to create a large field of diamond-shaped patterns in the center and rows of smaller diamonds along the sides, in addition there are two bands with two distinct sets of patterning, the central part has green and black supplementary weft patterns and at the ends are narrow rows of embroidered patterns, 71cm x 34cm. (PC)

79. Khumi, woman's chest covering for dances, made of a single piece of double woven cotton cloth, the warp consists of sets of three black threads and a single purple thread, the weft includes white, yellow, green, and orange threads to create diamond patterns with representations of airplanes inside of them, the back is plain black and purple, 71cm x 32cm. (PC)

80. Khumi, woman's chest covering for dances, made of a single piece of double woven cotton cloth, warp consists of clusters of four brown threads interspersed with single red threads, weft includes yellow, purple, white, and green silk threads to create zig-zag shaped patterns in the center and along the sides, in addition there are two bands with narrow rows of supplementary weft patterning, the back is red and black, 60cm x 31cm. (PC)

81. Khumi, woman's chest covering for dances, made of a single piece of double woven cotton cloth, warp consists of clusters of three brown threads interspersed with two red threads, weft includes yellow, purple, orange, and green silk threads to create diamond shaped patterns in the center and along the sides, in addition there are two bands with two distinct sets of patterning, the central portion features black warp threads and purple weft threads to create zig-zag patterns and a narrow band of diamond

shaped patterns, the ends feature rows of embroidered patterns, the back is red and black, 60cm x 31cm. (PC)

82. Daai (Makue U Nu subgroup), woman's blouse, sleeveless with V-neck, made of four pieces of handspun cotton sewn together, plain white, black and red stripes, beads, brass bells, and other objects attached to front as ornaments, 61cm x 64cm. (PC)

83. Daai, Makue U Nu subgroup, woman's sleeveless blouse, made of two pieces sewn together, handspun cotton, indigo-dyed with thin plain stripes, 53cm x 74cm. (PC)

84. Woman's blouse, cotton, buttons attached as decorations, 62cm x 73cm. This piece is identified as Plains Chin or Asho, but may in fact be from the Haka area. (DU P67.12)

85. Asho, from Thayetmyo, woman's blouse, cotton, 61cm x 107cm. (DU P67.146)

86. Khumi, skirt, cotton, black warp threads with green supplementary weft triangular patterning throughout, double weave that produces a plain black back, 117cm x 62cm. (PC)

87. Khumi, tubeskirt, cotton, black warp threads with red supplementary weft patterning throughout on the front and vertical lines on the rear, thin vertical lines of green and yellow supplementary weft patterning near the edges of the front, double weave that produces a plain black inside/back, glass beads added along top and bottom as accessories, 88cm x 44cm. See photograph in Brauns & Löffler 1990: 35. (PC)

88. Reverse of #87.

89. Khumi, skirt, cotton, black with pink and white threads added to the weft to create small squares in rows, double weave that produces a plain black back, 113cm x 61cm. (PC)

90. Kanpetlet area (said to be Yak Kai), woman's skirt, made of a single piece of commercial cotton cloth, black weft threads, warp threads in black, purple, and yellow to create thin stripes, evidence that round metal disks were attached in a vertical row down the center as with #37 but they have been removed, strands of three white beads attached as decorations along the top and bottom, 117cm x 59cm. (PC)

91. Kanpetlet area (said to be Ma Lan Na), tubeskirt, made of two pieces of commercial cotton cloth sewn together, upper portion plain black, center

with black, red, and white horizontal stripes, lower portion plain black with scattered small supplementary weft geometric patterns made of various colors of thread, 76cm x 93cm. (PC)

92. Woman's blouse, commercial cotton, collected between 1958 and 1960, 60cm x 63cm. (NHM 70.2/2430)

Naga

93. Khiamnungan or Yimchungru, body wrap, handspun cotton, made of two pieces sewn together, black center with ten rows of eight red squares as decoration, edges feature red, black, and yellow stripes, 109cm x 151cm plus fringe. (PC)

94. Khiamnungan, *nyechet* (man's body wrap), cotton, made of three pieces sewn together, black center piece with eight rows of seven red squares as decoration, edges are black with four white stripes, 93cm x 145cm plus fringe. See Sardeshpande 1987: 71. (PC)

95. Tangkhol, *changkham* or *kairao* style *phi* (man's body wrap), made of two pieces sewn together, wide red and black stripes with white and green lozenge-shaped patterns and thin white and blue lines towards ends, two white and one green line of thread also used as decoration across a portion of the cloth near the center, 95cm x 177cm plus fringe. (PC)

96. Probably Tangkhol, made of two pieces sewn together, commercial cotton, red, white and black horizontal stripes with geometric supplementary weft patterning in the large red stripes, 181cm x 110cm plus fringe. (PC)

97. Obtained in Singkaling near Hkampti (subgroup unknown), skirt, cotton, 74cm x 165cm.. (DU: 1968.151)

98. Described as coming from Kettha on the upper Chindwin near Homalin (subgroup unknown), tubeskirt, cotton, 72cm x 114cm. (DU: 1968.163)

99. Konyak, woman's rain cloak/skirt, made of shredded palm leaves, width at top 46cm x length at center 79cm. See Elwin 1959: 9, 13. (PC)

100. Described as coming from Hahti, Upper Chindwin (subgroup unknown), loincloth end piece, cotton, plain indigo-dyed base with thin

vertical stripes, job's tears sewn in rows, 26cm x 49cm. Obtained by Vernay Hopwood and H.C. Raven in 1935 in the course of an expedition sponsored by the Natural History Museum. (NHM: 70.0/6373)

101. man's chest cloth, cotton, double weave with supplementary weft diamond patterning, 17cm x 154cm plus fringe. (PC)

Mru

102. *Wan-klai* (skirt), cotton, most of the skirt is plain black with thin red and yellow stripes along the edges, there is also a section featuring red, yellow, and green geometric patterned embroidery, 75cm x 27cm. See Brauns and Löffler 1990: 137. (PC)

Jingpho

103. Woman's blouse, commercial velvet with metal ornaments attached as decoration, body 43cm x 40cm, sleeve 18cm x 40cm. (PC)

104. Jacket, black cotton ground with extensive supplementary weft and embroidered patterning in red and other colors, also pieces of plain red cloth sewn onto sleeves and down the front, thin white and red bordering, body 45cm x 35cm, sleeve 16cm x 39cm. (PC)

105. Sleeveless blouse, made of three pieces sewn together, indigo dyed cotton base with patterning at bottom (ends) made of dog hair dyed red, a piece of cloth of the type made for a skirt folded in half, joined at the center of each side with a piece of yarn, and a V-neck opening cut at the center of the top and lined with red commercial cotton cloth, small brass bells, beads, and cowrie shells added as decorations, 70cm x 75cm, extensive patching. (PC)

106. *Pukhang* (skirt), made of two pieces sewn together, red (plus small amounts of other colors) wool weft on black handspun cotton warp, red geometric patterns cover entire cloth, 139cm x 61cm, dates from 1910-30. (PC)

107. *Pukhang* (skirt), made of three pieces sewn together, plain horizontal stripes woven with handspun cotton thread and supplementary weft

weave patterning at ends made of dog hair and made out of cotton thread along the bottom, 145cm x 73cm., possibly mary. (PC)

108. *Pukhang* (skirt), made of three pieces sewn together, plain horizontal stripes woven with handspun cotton thread and supplementary weft weave patterning at ends made of dog hair and cotton thread, natural dyes, 164cm x 66cm. (PC)

109. From Myitkyina, Kachin State, *pukhang* (skirt), made of three pieces sewn together, plain handspun indigo-dyed cotton center with thin light blue horizontal lines, geometric supplementary weft weave patterning at ends made of cotton yarn dyed rust and other colors, 147cm x 90cm. (PC)

110. *Pukhang* (skirt), made of three pieces sewn together, dark indigo-dyed handspun cotton warp and weft, plain center, supplementary weft geometric patterning at ends of wool dyed red and other colors, 152cm x 60cm. (PC)

111. From Myitkyina, Kachin State, *pukhang* (skirt), made of three pieces sewn together, commercial cotton plain weave base dyed black, three panels with supplementary weft geometric patterning made of yarn dyed rust and other colors, 155cm x 65cm. (PC)

112. *Pukhang* (skirt), made of three pieces sewn together, red (plus small amounts of other colors) wool weft on indigo-dyed cotton warp, relatively solid patterning at ends and on bottom center section with loose patterns in middle of center, top center section plain, 145cm x 70cm. (PC)

113. Tubeskirt, commercial cotton, plain black and purple horizontal stripes and a vertical band with supplementary weft patterning, 60cm x 170cm. (PC)

114. Pair of tube-leggings with rattan hoops, cotton warp threads and supplementary weft weave patterns in colored wool yarn, each legging 15cm x 28cm. (DU: P67.5)

115. Pair of tube-leggings, plain black cotton ground with extensive wool supplementary weft weave patterning (largely in red, but small amounts of white, yellow, and green as well), 14.5cm x 25cm. (PC)

116. Pair of tube-leggings, plain black cotton ground with red-dyed dog hair used extensively in the weft, also small amounts of colored wool geometric supplementary weft weave patterning, 18cm x 32cm. (PC)

117. Uma Lakhum or Lana subgroup, *n'hpye* (shoulder bag), body made of indigo-dyed cotton with supplementary weft patterning made of wool dyed red and other colors, appliquéed decorations made of oblong pieces of red flannel with small embroidered decorative squares in the center of each piece, Job's tears attached as decoration, and tassels hanging in bunches added as accessories. (BM: GK11)

118. Uma Lakhum or Lana sub-group, *n'hpye* (shoulder bag), body made of black cotton with supplementary weft patterning made of wool dyed red and other colors, appliquéed decorations made of oblong pieces of red flannel with small embroidered decorative squares in the center of each piece, Job's tears and glass beads attached as decoration, and tassels hanging in bunches added as accessories, 35.5cm x 27cm. This piece is described by Innes (1957: 21; and see Fig. 22 p. 28). Start (1917: 47) has a drawing (Fig. 38) of a similar piece. (BM: GK9)

119. *N'hpye* (shoulder bag), the body is made of white cotton cloth with a few thin red and blue stripes, there are small embroidered geometric patterns throughout the body, 28cm x 27.5cm. A drawing of this piece appears as Fig. 40 in Start (1917: 50) and the piece is described on page 51. (BM: GK42)

120. *N'hpye* (shoulder bag), plaited cotton strap, body made of plain white cotton warp thread with the weft made of various colors and including some patterning near the top of the bag, body 26cm x 32cm. Innes (1957: 19) reports that, according to E.R. Leach, such bags with plaited straps "probably came from the Maru or Lashi region which lies between the N'mai Hka river and the Yunnan border." (BM: GK1)

121. *N'hpye* (shoulder bag), black cotton base with supplementary weft geometric patterning, white glass beads and Job's tears added as decorations, tassels made of red commercial cloth, white glass beads, and gold-colored plastic beads added as accessories, body 25cm x 28cm. (PC)

122. Reverse of #121.

123. *N'hpye* (shoulder-bag), plaited cotton strap, red cotton warp, supplementary weft weave with geometric patterns, tassels made of bunches of red commercial cloth and red glass beads added as accessories along the sides, lined with commercial cotton cloth, body 30cm x 29cm. Such bags are said to have been used only by men of higher status. (PC)

124. Reverse of #123.

125. *N'hpye* (shoulder-bag), cotton body with pieces of red felt and metal attached as decorations, strands of commercial cloth attached as fringe at the bottom, body 25cm x 29cm, said to date from the 1920s. (DU: 1968.281)

126. *N'hpye* (shoulder-bag), cotton with geometric patterning, newer plain commercial cotton back and shoulder strap added, cowrie shells added as decorations, body 27cm x 31cm. (PC)

127. Man's headcloth, plain white cotton, embroidered geometric patterns at ends, 45cm x 93cm plus tassels. (PC)

Karen

128. Sgaw, from Bassein area, tubeskirt, made of two pieces sewn together, handspun cotton, plain and weft ikat stripes, wide band of weft ikat patterning in center, 82cm x 132cm. Purchased from Mrs. G.E. Blackwell in 1962. (FM: 235647)

129. Sgaw, Nim Lan village (near Hsipaw), tubeskirt, cotton, plain waistband plus body made of three pieces sewn together vertically, plain and warp ikat patterned stripes, 103cm x 104cm. (PC)

130. Paku, tubeskirt, cotton, made of two pieces sewn together, plain with thin plain stripes near ends and at center, 70.5cm x 94cm. Obtained from Mrs. G.E. Blackwell in 1943. (NHM: 70.0/8684)

131. Bwe, tubeskirt, made of two pieces sewn together, commercial cotton, plain stripes, 76.5cm x 94.5cm. (DU: 1969.246)

132. Sgaw, Papun area, tubeskirt, cotton, made of three pieces sewn together, top portion features plain stripes, middle portion features supplementary weft patterned stripes, bottom portion features a zig-zag pattern, 96cm x 132cm. (DU: P67.78)

133. Padaung, tubeskirt, handspun cotton, plain black top, lower portion features lines created by variously colored warp threads, 55cm x 47cm. (PC)

134. Padaung, from Baptist mission in the Bassein District, tubeskirt, handspun cotton, plain stripes and three broader stripes featuring supplementary weft patterning, 59.5cm x 44.5cm. The piece was part of the Baptist missionary collection obtained in 1900. (NHM: 1/5834)

135. Sgaw, from Baptist mission in the Bassein District, woman's tunic, handspun cotton, Job's tears attached for decoration, 76cm x 90.5cm. The piece was part of the Baptist missionary collection obtained in 1900. (NHM: 70/1712)

136. Sgaw, Bassein area, woman's tunic, handspun and commercial cotton, Job's tears attached for decoration, 73cm x 79cm. (FM: 235645)

137. Sgaw, Bassein area, man's tunic, cotton, largely plain, but with small stripes of embroidered decoration using wool yarn, 77cm x 104cm. (FM: 235644)

138. Paku, man's tunic, plain white cotton with colored wool yarn decorations along bottom and as edging along the v-neck collar and sleeve holes, colored pom-poms attached, 76cm x 96.5cm. Obtained from Mrs. G.E. Blackwell in 1943. (NHM: 70.0/8682)

139. Paku, boy's tunic, plain white handspun cotton with colored wool yarn decorations in the lower portion and along the bottom and as edging along the v-neck collar and sleeve holes, colored pom-poms attached, 54cm x 70cm. (FM: 235638)

140. Paku, woman's tunic, body made of plain black commercial cotton, embroidered decorations made of red felt and variously colored wool yarns, 63cm x 74cm. (FM: 235641)

141. Paku, woman's tunic, body made of plain black velvet, embroidered decorations made of red felt and variously colored wool yarns, 63.5cm x 76cm. (DU: 1968.260)

142. Paku, from Baptist mission in the Bassein District, woman's wedding tunic, plain black commercial cotton base, decorations made of strips of plain red velvet and embroidered patterns of variously colored cotton thread, 56cm x 86cm. From the Baptist missionary

collection obtained in 1900. (NHM: 1/5838)

143. Paku, woman's blouse for special occasions, plain cotton base with decorations made of colored wool yarn and Job's tears, 68.5cm x 63.5cm. (DU: P67.117)

144. Paku, woman's blouse for special occasions, plain cotton base with decorations made of colored wool yarn and Job's tears, 76cm x 66cm. (DU: 1971.506)

145. Paku, child's tunic, body made of plain black commercial cotton, strips of plain red commercial cotton attached to lower portion of body, decorations made of wool yarn and Job's tears, 54cm x 71cm. (FM: 235639)

146. Pwo, *hse* or *thingdaing* (woman's blouse), handspun cotton, top portion features supplementary weft geometric patterning made of variously colored threads, plain indigo-dyed lower portion with thin plain white stripes, 55cm x 61cm. (PC)

147. Pwo, woman's tunic, body made of plain black handspun cotton, strips of plain red commercial cotton attached to lower portion of body, decorations made of wool yarn and Job's tears, 70cm x 83.5cm. Obtained from Mrs. William Ivens in 1946. (NHM: 70.2/397)

148. Bwe, man's tunic, cotton, handspun cotton with plain red and white vertical stripes, embroidered decorations made of silk thread, 74cm x 97cm. Obtained from Mrs. G.E. Blackwell in 1943. (NHM: 70.0/8687)

149. Bwe, Toungoo hills, man's tunic, handwoven cotton with plain red and white vertical stripes, lower portion features supplementary weft decorations made of silk thread and wool yarn, 69.5cm x 76.5cm. (FM: 235637)

150. Bwe, burial robe, handspun cotton with supplementary weft geometric decorations throughout, 71cm x 90cm plus fringe. From Bwe Karen Baptist mission, Toungoo, made and laid aside for years prior to burial. (DU: 1968.286)

151. Padaung, woman's tunic, plain white cotton, thin vertical stripes along edges and brightly colored pieces of commercial cotton yarn attached at bottom as decorations, 52cm x 71cm. (PC)

152. Sgaw, *hse* or *thingdaing* (woman's blouse), plain black cotton upper portion, lower portion with supplementary weft weave decorations using red, yellow, and blue cotton yarn over a black base, tassels attached to sides and center, 61cm x 63cm. (PC)

153. Sgaw, *hse* or *thingdaing* (woman's blouse), plain black cotton upper portion, lower portion with supplementary weft weave decorations using red, yellow, blue, and white cotton yarn over a black base, tassels attached to sides and center, 66cm x 66cm. (DU: 1969: 256)

154. Sgaw, *hse* or *thingdaing* (woman's blouse), plain indigo dyed handspun cotton base with decorations made of red and yellow cotton yarn and Job's tears as well as a strip of plain red cloth near the bottom, tassels attached to sides, 65cm x 56cm. (PC)

155. Sgaw, Shan State, *hse* or *thingdaing* (woman's blouse), black commercial cotton base with supplementary weft weave stripes in lower portion for decoration, red cotton thread edging around v-neck and attached as tassels at the end of the neck opening, tassels attached to sides, 56cm x 58cm, collected in the mid-1980s. (PC)

156. Paku, Toungoo Hills District, sash/headcloth, plain red cotton with thin plain white stripes and a few scattered embroidered decorations of yellow thread, 34cm x 228cm. (DU: P67.113)

157. Sgaw, Bassein area, headcloth, plain red handwoven cotton with supplementary weft geometric patterning and tassels made of variously colored wool yarn at both ends, 27.5cm x 158cm plus fringe. (FM: 235646)

158. Paku, woman's headcloth, plain white handspun cotton with supplementary weft geometric patterning (largely in red) at both ends, 38cm x 164cm plus fringe. Obtained from Mrs. G.E. Blackwell in 1943. (NHM: 70.8685)

159. Subgroup unknown, Rangoon District, bag, cotton, dark red ground with variously colored thing horizontal and vertical lines forming a checked pattern, supplementary weft lines across the top of the body and towards the side at the bottom, also a small supplementary weft geometric pattern in the center, 25.5cm x 26cm. (DU: P67.94)

160. Sgaw, bag, cotton, plain red ground interspersed with bands comprised of thin plain green stripes and wider stripes featuring weft ikat patterning, tassels attached at the top of the body, 27cm x 27cm, said to date from the 1920s. (DU: 1967.160)

161. Subgroup unknown, bag, plain red cotton ground with diamond-shaped supplementary weft patterns in white and other colors and thin horizontal stripes across the top of the body and on the sides towards the bottom, 26cm x 26cm. (DU: P67.86)

162. Subgroup unknown, bag, cotton, plain vertical stripes and bands of stripes made of silk thread across the top of the body and the sides of the bottom, lines of small metal disks and pom-poms attached as decorations, 22.5cm x 28.5cm. (FM: 235662)

163. Subgroup unknown, bag, handwoven cotton, plain and geometrically patterned vertical stripes, thin horizontal stripes across the top of the body and the sides of the bottom, tufts of brightly colored wool yarn sewn across the top of the body, pom-poms attached as decorations, 37cm x 33cm. (FM: 235653)

Akha

164. Lomi, *pah hon ali* (man's jacket), handspun cotton base with commercial cotton appliqué, appliqué patterns with couched thread, *loimisa* patterns on back of jacket from top to bottom (centipede, bamboo wall, mountain, chicken legs, butterfly wings, poppy flower, mountain, chicken feet, mountain), body 47cm x 50cm, sleeves 18cm x 42cm. (PC)

165. Subgroup unknown (possibly Ulo), bag, handspun cotton base with commercial cotton appliqué, top with appliqué patterns, plain black bottom, 26.5cm x 32cm. (DU: P67.2)

166. Ulo, shoulder-bag, handspun cotton base with commercial cotton appliqué, appliqué patterns with couched thread with metal spheres and Burmese coins attached, 33cm x 23cm. (PC)

167. Ulo, *pah hon abu* (woman's jacket), cotton, appliqué patterns with couched thread and sequins, lettering on the back ("1987/ THNIQLATHQO/THINANGMITSAQHE-TAAPHEMIYEZA/SOHAZAESHABYM NA ZALEMANGN/EMALIADOLEHOBOOR LRRMRTHEN"), 50cm x 51cm. (PC)

Lahu

168. Lahu Na, woman's coat, plain black cotton base, appliqué patterns using commercial cotton around the collar, down the center, along the sides, and on the sleeves, 47cm (at bottom) x 112cm (at back). (DU: 1968.11)

169. Lahu Na, from Venbo near Kengtung, woman's coat used for weddings, plain black handspun cotton base, commercial cotton appliqué down the center, along the sides, and on the sleeves, metal disks attached as decoration around the collar and down the upper portion of the center of the front, 58.5cm (at bottom) x 130cm (at back). This piece made to order for Dr. Anna Gray, said to have been made by one of the few women in the community still able to make such a coat. (DU: P67.110)

170. Lahu Na, bag, cotton, bands with black and white geometric patterning interspersed with thin plain vertical stripes, short tassels attached to lower portion on the sides, 30cm x 30.5cm. (DU: 1968.9)

171. Lahu Na, bag, cotton, appliqué patterns at top, plain bottom, tassels attached along the sides, 21cm x 27cm. (DU: 1967.148)

Lisu

172. Woman's apron, made of three pieces of plain black commercial cotton sewn together (body, flap, and waistband), strips of variously colored commercial cotton appliqué and used as edging, small embroidered patterns of variously colored thread along outer edges, cowries and buttons attached as decorations, body 57cm top and 71cm bottom x 52cm, flap 23cm x 59cm, waistband 14cm x 96cm. (PC)

Wa

173. Skirt, handspun cotton featuring plain horizontal stripes, 122cm x 48cm. (DU: 1968.6)

174. Tubeskirt, handspun cotton with plain vertical stripes interspersed with thin stripes of metallic thread, occasional supplementary weft

geometric patterning on the black stripes, 81cm x 102cm, dates from early 1990s. (PC)

175. Woman's blouse, plain dark indigo cotton with red piping on edges and center, length 41cm. (DU: 1968.5)

176. From Si Kehn No (also known as Yaong Raok), bag, plain dark indigo cotton with thin red line near top and red piping, 35cm x 35cm. (DU: 1968.3)

177. Tubeskirt, plain black commercial cotton base with a few thin plain horizontal stripes and thin vertical stripes in the lower part featuring geometrical patterning, also some supplementary weft geometrical patterning of cotton and metallic thread, 85.5cm x 104cm, dates from early 1990s. (PC)

178. Bag, plain black cotton base, zig-zag patterned horizontal stripes on shoulder strap and across top and bottom of body, small diamond-shaped supplementary weft patterns in the center of the body, 27cm x 27cm. (DU: 1968.4)

179. Bag, plain black cotton base, zig-zag patterned horizontal stripes on shoulder strap and across top and bottom of body as well as a stripe with diamond-shaped supplementary weft patterns in the lower portion, small diamond shaped supplementary weft patterns in the center of the body, 27cm x 28.5cm. (DU: 1968.7)

Palaung

180. Subgroup unknown, tubeskirt, made of three pieces sewn together, plain black cotton base interspersed with thin horizontal lines, vertical band with supplementary weft geometric patterning, 80cm x 49cm. (BM: 1955.56)

181. Maingkwim clan, tubeskirt, plain black cotton base interspersed with thin horizontal lines, vertical band with supplementary weft geometric patterning. (BM: 1955.72.2)

182. Maingkwim clan, tubeskirt, made of three pieces sewn together, plain black cotton base interspersed with thin horizontal lines, vertical band with supplementary weft geometric patterning, 80.5cm x 51cm. (BM: 1955.71.2)

183. Manton clan, tubeskirt, made of three pieces sewn together, plain red and black horizontal stripes, 90cm x 52.5cm. (BM: 1955.43.1)

184. Yarbon clan, tubeskirt, made of three pieces sewn together, plain red and black horizontal stripes, 83.5cm x 53.5cm. (BM: 1955.70.2)

185. Silver Palaung, Kengtung, tubeskirt, made of three pieces sewn together, commercial fiber thread, plain stripes, the thin stripes at each end are the fashion favored by younger unmarried women, 60cm x 101cm. (PC)

186. Silver Palaung, Kengtung, tubeskirt, made of three pieces sewn together, commercial cotton, plain stripes, the plain yellow and white bands at each end are the fashion favored by older married women, 63cm x 108cm. (PC)

187. Yarbon clan, jacket, plain black cotton, a strip of plain red cotton attached around the collar, a thin strip of plain white cotton attached as edging along the bottom, variously colored threads with dangling strands used as edging along the sides of the body and sleeve ends, body 37cm x 32cm, sleeve 37cm x 16cm. (BM: 1955.70.1)

188. Reverse of #187.

189. Maingkwim clan, jacket, plain black cotton, a strip of plain red cotton attached around the collar, a thin line of white cotton thread used as edging for the body, body 39cm x 29cm, sleeve 62cm x 17cm. (BM: 1955.72.2)

190. Maingkwim clan, headcloth, plain indigo dyed cotton with embroidered patterning at the corners and thin red edging, 53cm x 48cm. (BM: 1955.71.5)

191. Maingkwin clan, headcloth, plain black cotton with thin embroidered lines of colored thread at ends as decoration, fringe made of variously colored thread, 213cm plus fringe x 26cm. (BM: 1955.71.3)

192. Yarbon clan, woman's headcoth, plain white cotton with thing lines of colored thread along the seam and embroidered as decoration at the ends, 44cm x 24.5cm. (BM: 1955.70.4)

Riang

193. Yang Lam, southern Shan State, woman's blouse, plain black cotton base, a piece of plain red cotton cloth attached along the bottom,

above this is a thin line of variously colored thread, a horizontal row of tassels in the center of the back and front made of Job's tears, glass beads, and red and green thread, 43cm x 26.5cm. Descriptions of this piece appear in Start (1917: 17-18) and Innes (1957: 35) along with drawings of it (Start 1917: Fig. 10, p. 10; Innes 1957: Fig. 30, p. 36). (BM: GS63)

Hmong Njua

194. Apron, front is made of pieces of plain red and blue-green commercial cotton with appliqué work and cross-stitch embroidered geometric patterns, back is made of plain black commercial cotton, frontpiece 17cm x 60cm, each side piece 8.5cm x 165cm plus fringe. (PC)

1. Intha, tubeskirt, 72cm x 102cm. (PC)

2. Intha, Inpawkhon village, tubeskirt, 84cm x 104cm. (PC)

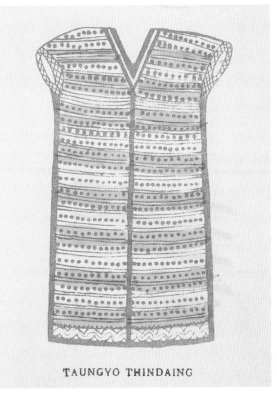

TAUNGYO THINDAING

3. Intha, tubeskirt 85cm x 88cm. (PC)

4. Taungyo, *thingdaing* (woman's smock). From Scott and Hardiman (1900, I/II: f. pg. 370).

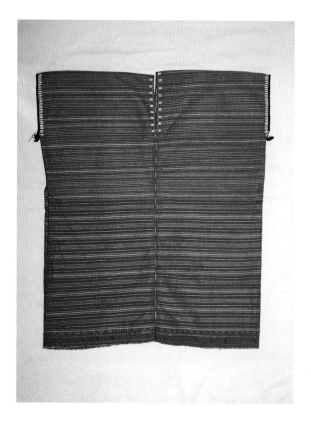

5. Taungyo, *thingdaing,* 78cm x 83cm.
(BM: GS57)

6. Taungyo, Pindaya district, western Shan State
thingdaing, 69cm x 78cm. (PC)

7. Taungyo, *tabet* (woman's headdress).
From Scott and Hardiman (1900, I/II: f. pg. 370).

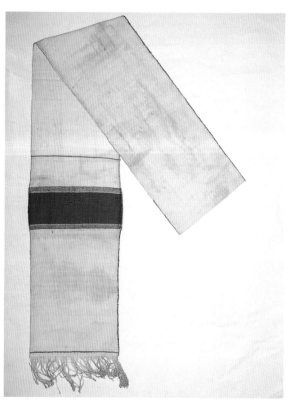

8. Taungyo, *tabet,* 26.5cm x 348cm plus fringe.
(BM: GS84)

9. Shan, man's shirt, w. 64cm at back. (DU: 1974.3)

10. Shan, woman's jacket, body 69cm x 65cm, sleeves 23cm x 36cm. (BM: GS19)

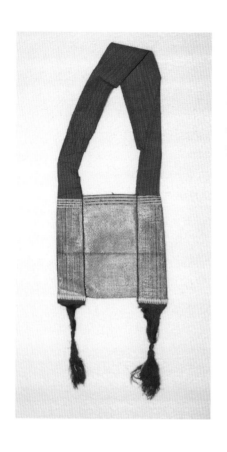

11. Shan, bag,
11.5cm x 12.5cm
(FM: 235656)

12. Shan, bag,
22cm x 23cm
(PC)

13. Shan, bag,
28.5cm x 28cm
(DU: 1969.9)

14. Shan, cloth for skirt, 58.5cm x 121cm. (FM: 87169)

15. Shan, cloth for skirt, 66cm x 113.5cm. (FM: 87171)

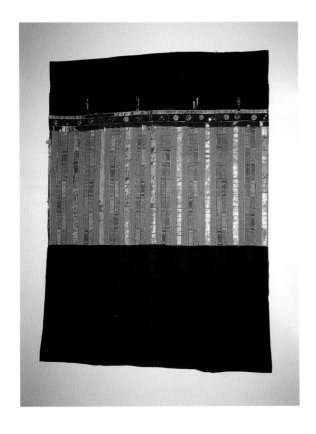

16. Shan, skirt, 27cm x 96.5cm.
(DU: 1974.4)

17. Shan, skirt, 33cm x 134cm.
(BM: GS20)

18. Shan, skirt, 77cm x 94cm.
(BM: GS24)

19. Thai Nua, skirt, 77cm x 93.5cm.
(FM: 87174)

20. Shan, Thai Mao, cloth for skirt, 23.5cm x 35cm. (BM: GS21)

21. Shan, ceremonial cloth, 58cm x 93cm.(PC)

22. Shan, blanket, 112cm x 202cm.
(PC)

23. Lu, Mong Yawng, Shan State, tubeskirt,
61cm x 93cm. (PC)

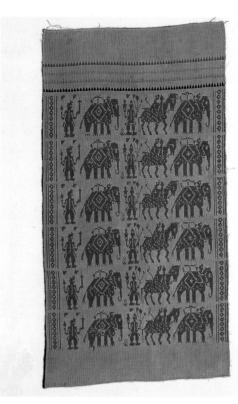

24. Lu, Kengtung, tubeskirt, 64cm x 103cm.
(BM: GS54)

25. Lu, ceremonial cloth, 47cm x 88cm. (PC)

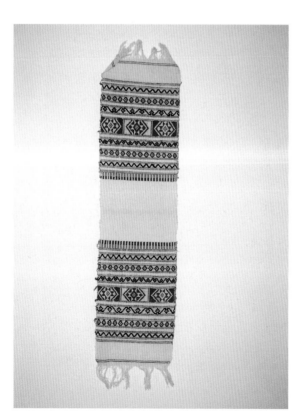

26. Lu, Kengtung state, *pha chet* (man's
shoulder-cloth), 20cm x 77cm.
(DU: no accession number)

27. Lu, Kengtung state, *pha chiwon*
(altar decoration), 41cm x 88cm
plus 20-24cm fringe. (DU: 1969.248)

28. Thado, body wrap, 138cm x 185cm. (PC)

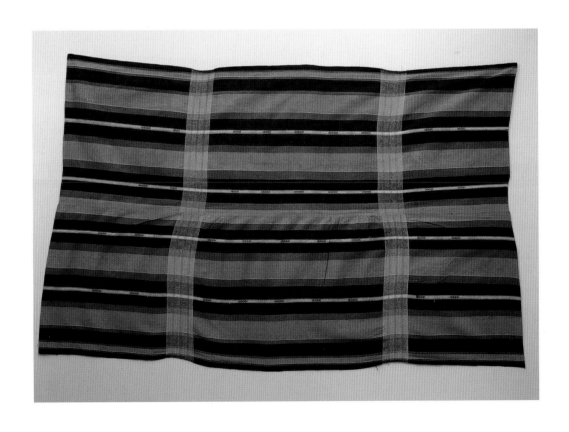

29. Thado, body wrap, 117cm x 182cm. (PC)

131

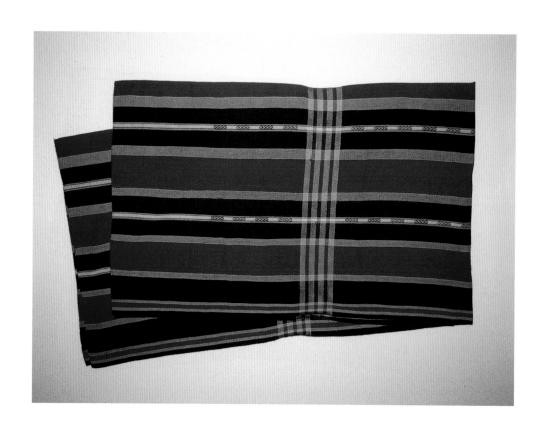

30. Thado, body wrap, 114cm x 152cm. (DU: 1967.8)

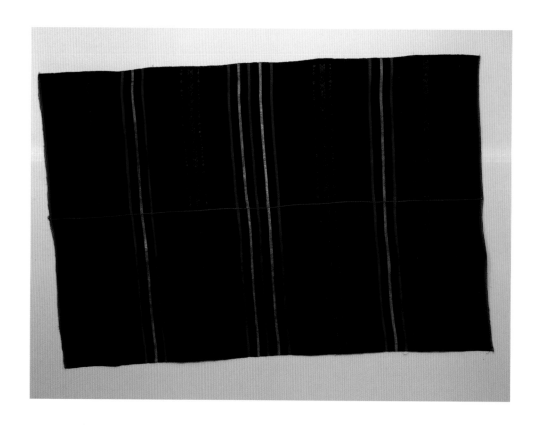

31. Probably Mara (Lakher), body wrap, 104cm x 157cm. (PC)

32. Anal, body wrap (detail), 153cm x 120cm. (PC)

33. Anal, body wrap,
128cm x 171cm. (PC)

34. Anal, body wrap,
102cm x 159cm. (PC)

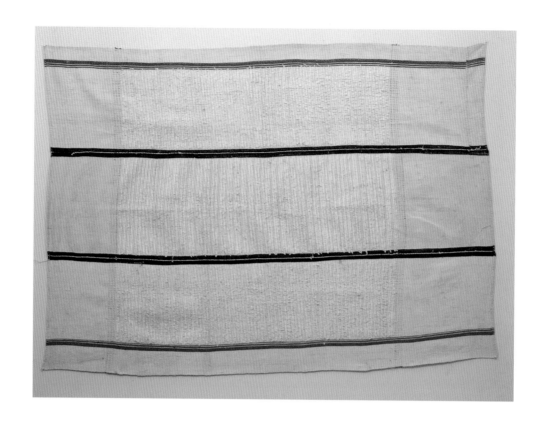

35. Lushai, *puan pui* (quilted body wrap), 68cm x 136cm. (PC)

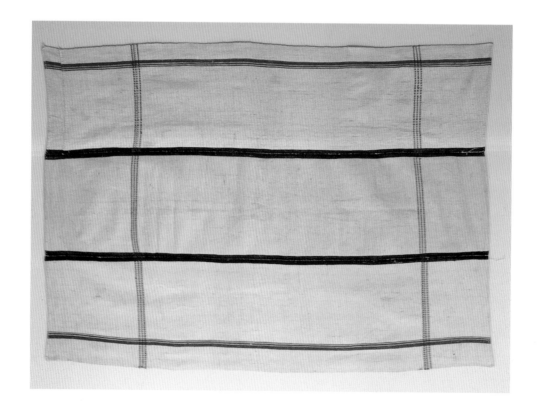

36. Reverse of #35.

37. Lushai, *puan pui* (quilted body wrap), 122cm x 162cm. (PC)

38. Lushai, *puan pui* (quilted body wrap), 117cm x 162cm. (PC)

39. Haka, *cawng-nak* (body wrap for man), 125cm x 196cm. (PC)

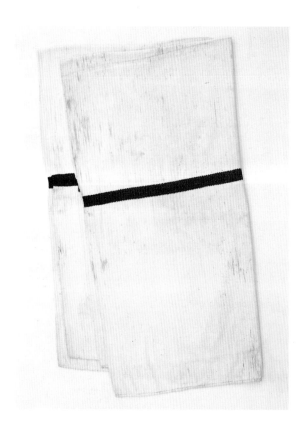

40. Lushai, man's body wrap,
115cm x 195cm. (PC)

41. Falam (Za Hau subgroup), man's longyi,
152cm x 112cm (open). (PC)

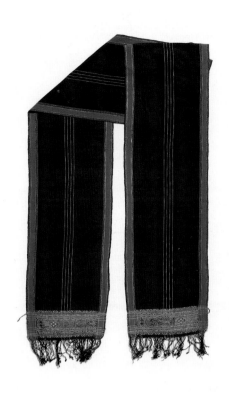

42. Falam, *pawr* (loincloth),
34cm x 323cm plus fringe. (PC)

43. Mara (Lakher), *dua ah* (ceremonial loincloth),
white center 42cm x 624cm, ends 42cm x
72cm and 42cm x 75cm. (PC)

44. Haka Subdivision, woman's blouse,
83cm x 82cm. (PC)

45. Haka Subdivision, woman's blouse,
87cm x 92cm. (PC)

46. Haka Subdivision, woman's blouse,
91cm x 102cm. (PC)

47. Haka Subdivision, woman's blouse,
91cm x 102cm. (PC)

48. Thado, woman's blouse,
44cm x 46cm. (PC)

49. Haka Subdivision, woman's blouse,
39cm x 44cm. (PC)

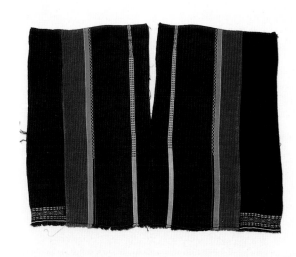

50. Probably from Haka Subdivision,
woman's blouse, 48cm x 51cm. (PC)

51. Probably from Tidim Subdivision,
woman's blouse, 52cm x 42cm. (PC)

52. Possibly Mara (Lakher),
woman's blouse, 40cm x 40cm. (PC)

53. Possibly Mara (Lakher),
woman's blouse, 47cm x 50cm. (PC)

54. Probably Haka, woman's blouse,
45cm x 32cm. (PC)

55. Haka, woman's blouse,
52cm x 37cm. (PC)

56. Probably from far north of the Chin area, woman's skirt, 118cm x 66cm. (PC)

57. Probably from far north of the Chin area, woman's skirt, 123cm x 66cm. (PC)

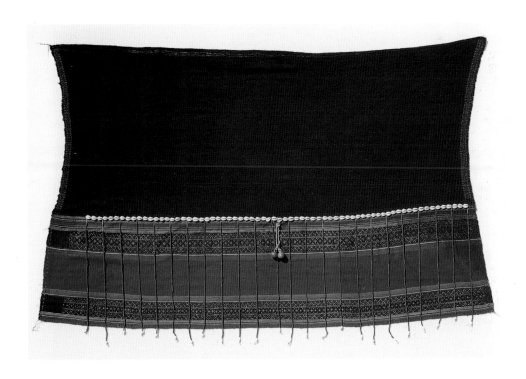

58. Falam, woman's skirt, 108cm x 80cm. (PC)

59. Falam, woman's skirt, 140cm x 77cm. (PC)

60. Haka or Falam, woman's skirt, 121cm x 89cm. (PC)

61. Lushai (Mizo), woman's skirt, 100cm x 56cm. (PC)

62. Haka, tubeskirt,
65cm x 94cm. (PC)

63. Haka Subdivision, possibly Lautu,
decorative apron, 52cm x 47cm. (PC)

64. Tedim, bag, body 32cm x 25.5cm.
(DU: 1967.11)

65. Tedim, bag, body 34cm x 26.5cm.
(DU: 1967.16)

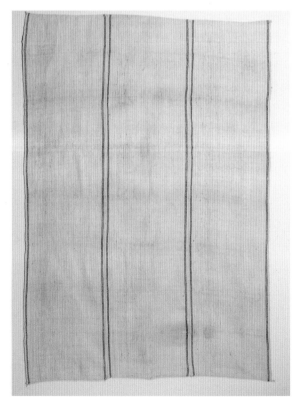

66. Daai (Makue U Nu subgroup),
body wrap, 115cm x 158cm. (PC)

67. Daai (Makue U Nu subgroup),
body wrap, 121cm x 169cm. (PC)

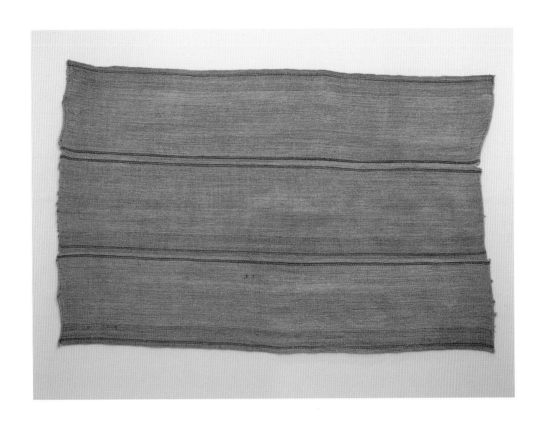

68. Daai (Makue U Nu subgroup), body wrap, 104cm x 158cm. (PC)

69. Daai (Makue U Nu subgroup), body wrap, 101cm x 149cm. (PC)

70. Kanpetlet area (said to be Ma Lan Na), body wrap, 98cm x 157cm. (PC)

71. Daai (probably Makue U Nu subgroup),
body wrap, 135cm x 144cm. (PC)

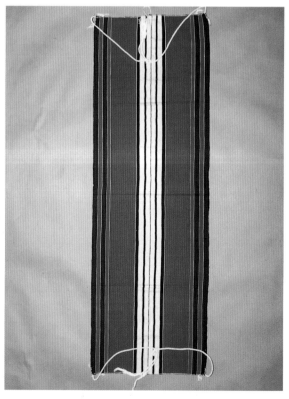

72. Man's sitting cloth,
36cm x 63cm. (NHM 70.2/2434)

73. Khumi, loincloth,
15cm x 426cm. (PC)

74. Khumi, loincloth,
15cm x 442cm. (PC)

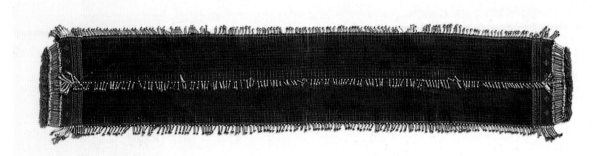

75. Khumi, woman's chest covering for dances, 60cm x 31cm. (PC)

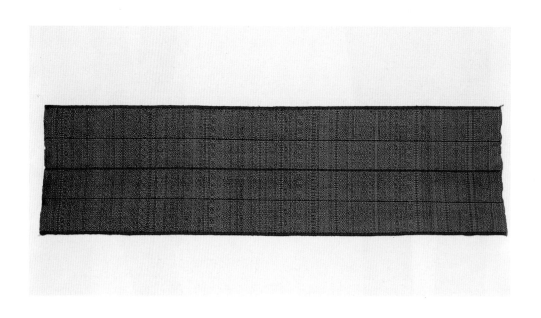

76. Khumi, Arakan/Rakhine State, shoulder-cloth, 43cm x 159cm. (PC)

77. Khumi, woman's chest covering for dances, 72cm x 42cm. (PC)

78. Khumi, woman's chest covering for dances, 71cm x 34cm. (PC)

79. Khumi, woman's chest covering for dances, 71cm x 32cm. (PC)

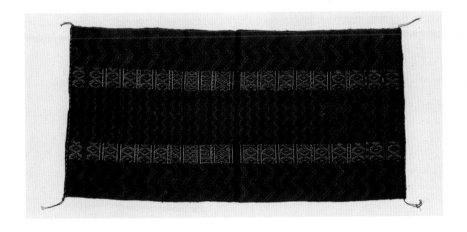

80. Khumi, woman's chest covering for dances, 60cm x 31cm. (PC)

81. Khumi, woman's chest covering for dances, 60cm x 31cm. (PC)

82. Daai (Makue U Nu subgroup),
woman's blouse, 61cm x 64cm. (PC)

83. Daai (Makue U Nu subgroup),
woman's blouse, 53cm x 74cm. (PC)

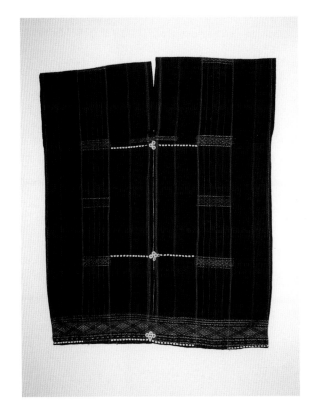

84. Asho or Haka area, woman's blouse,
62cm x 73cm. (DU P67.12)

85. Asho, Thayetmyo,
61cm x 107cm. (DU P67.146)

86. Khumi, skirt, 117cm x 62cm. (PC)

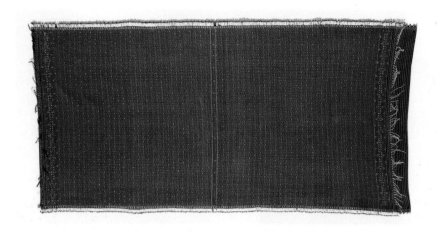

87. Khumi, tubeskirt, 88cm x 44cm. (PC)

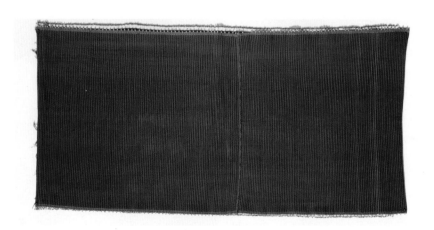

88. Back of #87.

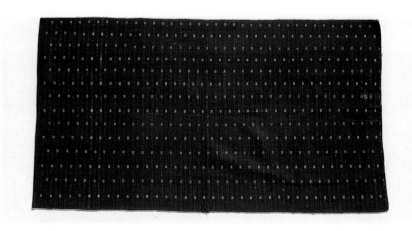

89. Khumi, skirt, 113cm x 61cm. (PC)

90. Kanpetlet area (said to be Yak Kai), skirt, 117cm x 59cm. (PC)

91. Kanpetlet area (Ma Lan Na), tubeskirt,
76cm x 93cm. (PC)

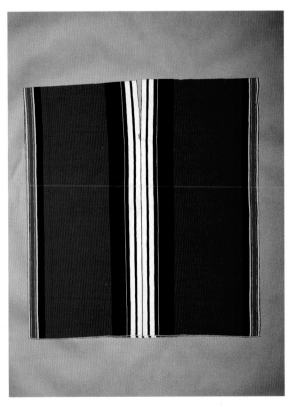

92. Woman's blouse,
60cm x 63cm. (NHM 70.2/2430)

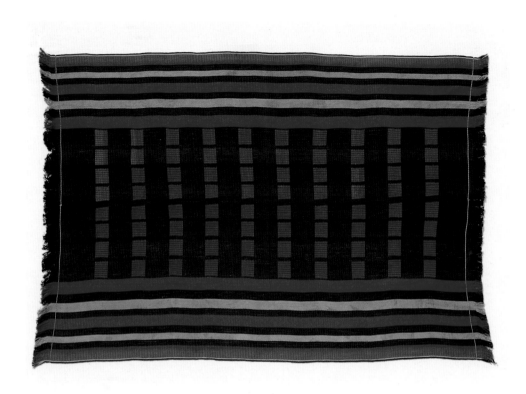

93. Khiamnungan or Yimchungru, body wrap, 109cm x 151cm plus fringe. (PC)

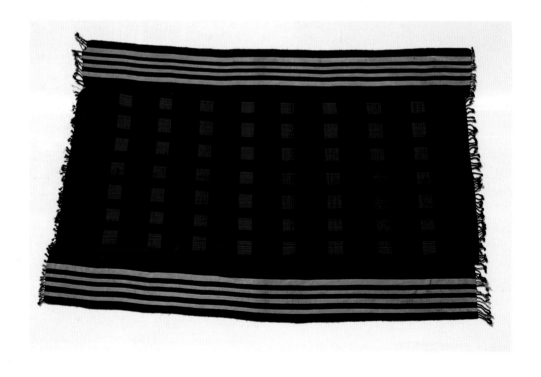

94. Khiamnungan, *nyechet* (man's body wrap), 93cm x 145cm plus fringe. (PC)

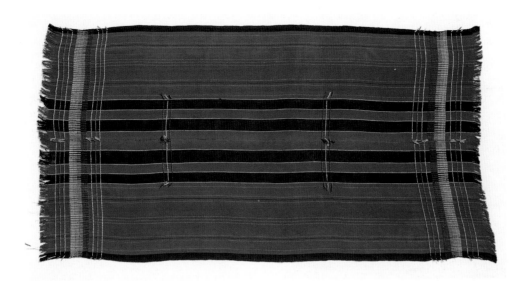

95. Tangkhol, *changkham* or *kairao* style *phi* (man's body wrap),
95cm x 177cm plus fringe. (PC)

96. Probably Tangkhol, 181cm x 110cm plus fringe. (PC)

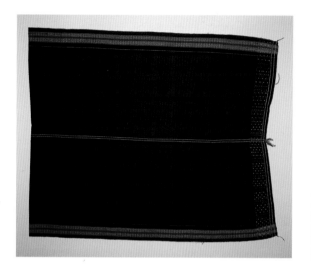

97. Obtained in Singkaling near Hkampti
(subgroup unknown), skirt, 74cm x 165cm.
(DU: 1968.151)

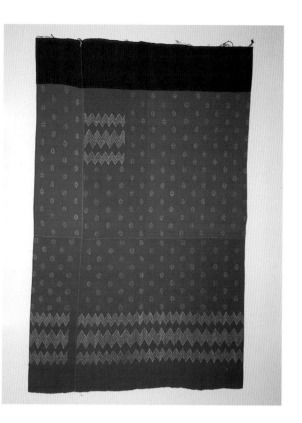

98. From Kettha, upper Chindwin
(subgroup unknown), tubeskirt, 72cm x 114cm.
(DU: 1968.163)

99. Konyak, woman's rain cloak/skirt,
46cm x 79cm. (PC)

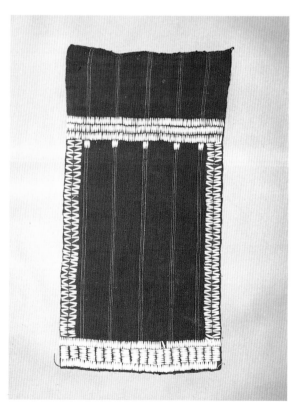

100. From Hahti, Upper Chindwin
(subgroup unknown), loincloth end piece,
26cm x 49cm. (NHM: 70.0/6373)

101. Man's chest cloth, 17cm x 154cm plus fringe. (PC)

102. *Wan-klai* (skirt), 75cm x 27cm. (PC)

103. Woman's blouse, body 43cm x 40cm, sleeve 18cm x 40cm. (PC)

104. Jacket, body 45cm x 35cm, sleeve 16cm x 39cm. (PC)

105. Woman's blouse, 70cm x 75cm. (PC)

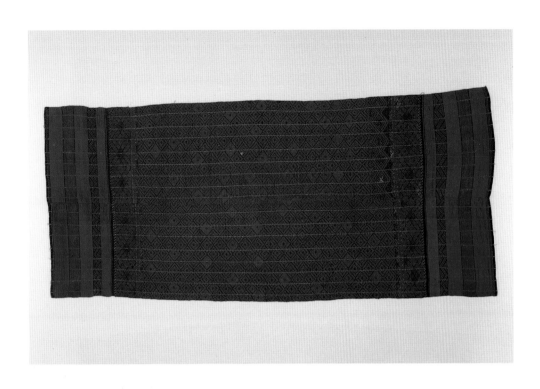

106. *Pukhang* (skirt), 139cm x 61cm. (PC)

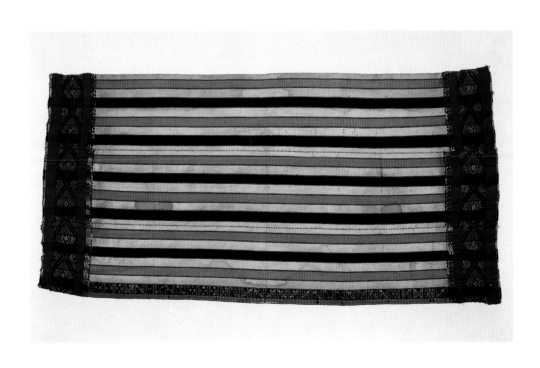

107. *Pukhang* (skirt), 145cm x 73cm. (PC)

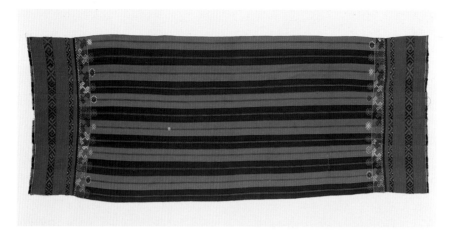

108. *Pukhang* (skirt), 164cm x 66cm. (PC)

109. From Myitkyina, Kachin State, *pukhang* (skirt), 147cm x 90cm. (PC)

110. *Pukhang* (skirt), 152cm x 60cm. (PC)

111. From Myitkyina, Kachin State, *pukhang* (skirt), 155cm x 65cm. (PC)

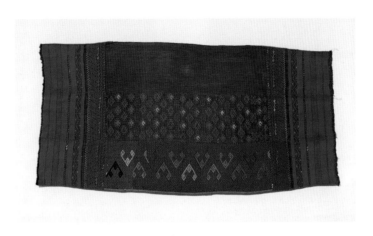

112. *Pukhang* (skirt), 145cm x 70cm. (PC)

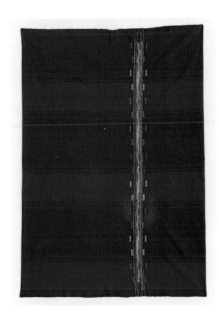

113. Tubeskirt,
60cm x 170cm. (PC)

114. Tube-leggings,
15cm x 28cm. (DU: P67.5)

115. Tube-leggings, 14.5cm x 25cm. (PC)

116. Tube-leggings, 18cm x 32cm. (PC)

117. Uma Lakhum or Lana subgroup, *n'hpye* (shoulder-bag). (BM: GK11)

118. Uma Lakhum or Lana subgroup, *n'hpye* (shoulder-bag), 35.5cm x 27cm. (BM: GK9)

119. *N'hpye* (shoulder-bag), 28cm x 27.5cm.
(BM: GK42)

120. *N'hpye* (shoulder-bag), 26cm x 32cm.
(BM: GK1)

121. *N'hpye* (shoulder-bag), 25cm x 28cm.
(PC)

122. Back of #121.

123. *N'hpye* (shoulder-bag), 30cm x 29cm. (PC)

124. Back of #123.

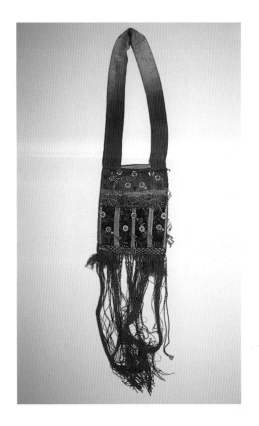

125. *N'hpye* (shoulder-bag), 25cm x 29cm.
(DU: 1968.281)

126. Shoulder-bag, body 27cm x 31cm.
(PC)

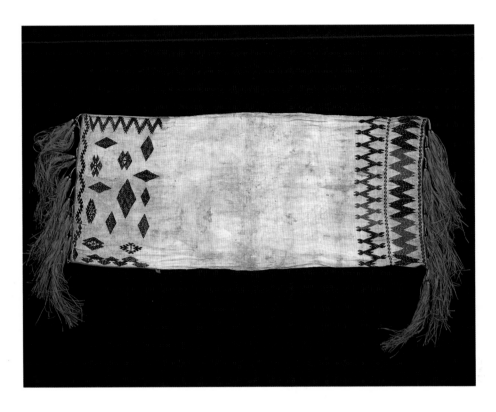

127. Man's headcloth, 45cm x 93cm plus tassels. (PC)

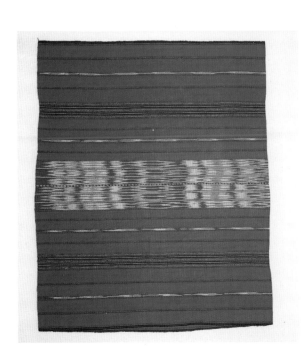

128. Sgaw, Bassein area, tubeskirt,
82cm x 132cm. (FM: 235647)

129. Sgaw, Nim Lan village (near Hsipaw),
tubeskirt, 103cm x 104cm. (PC)

130. Paku, tubeskirt, 70.5cm x 94cm.
(NHM: 70.0/8684)

131. Bwe, tubeskirt, 76.5cm x 94.5cm.
(DU: 1969.246)

132. Sgaw, Papun area, tubeskirt,
96cm x 132cm. (DU: P67.78)

133. Padaung, tubeskirt, 55cm x 47cm.
(PC)

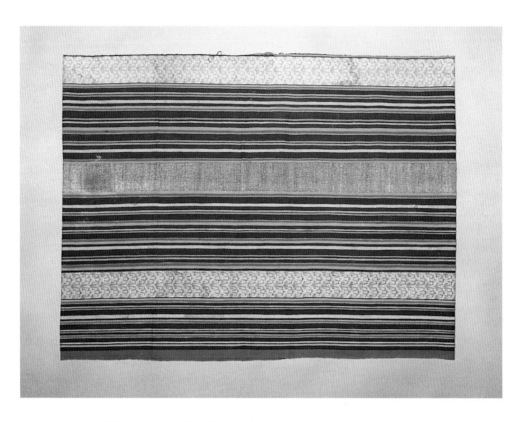

134. Padaung, Baptist mission, Bassein district, tubeskirt,
59.5cm x 44.5cm. (NHM: 1/5834)

135. Sgaw, Baptist mission, Bassein district, woman's tunic,
76cm x 90.5cm. (NHM: 70/1712)

136. Sgaw, Bassein area, woman's tunic, 73cm x 79cm. (FM: 235645)

137. Sgaw, Bassein area, man's tunic, 77cm x 104cm. (FM: 235644)

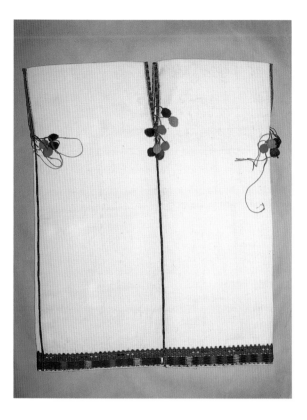

138. Paku, man's tunic, 76cm x 96.5cm.
(NHM: 70.0/8682)

139. Paku, boy's tunic, 54cm x 70cm.
(FM: 235638)

140. Paku, woman's tunic, 63cm x 74cm.
(FM: 235641)

141. Paku, woman's tunic, 63.5cm x 76cm.
(DU: 1968.260)

142. Paku, Baptist mission, Bassein district, woman's wedding tunic,
56cm x 86cm. (NHM: 1/5838)

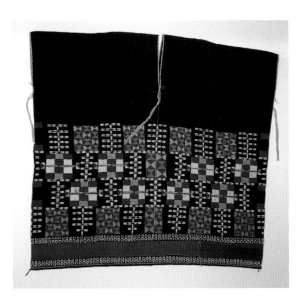

143. Paku, woman's blouse,
68.5cm x 63.5cm. (DU: P67.117)

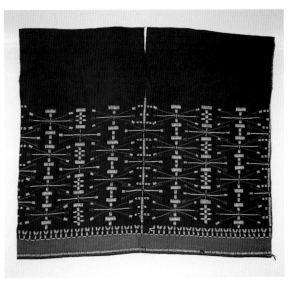

144. Paku, woman's blouse,
76cm x 66cm. (DU: 1971.506)

145. Paku, child's tunic,
54cm x 71cm. (FM: 235639)

146. Pwo, *hse* or *thingdaing* (woman's blouse),
55cm x 61cm. (PC)

147. Pwo, woman's tunic, 70cm x 83.5cm. (NHM: 70.2/397)

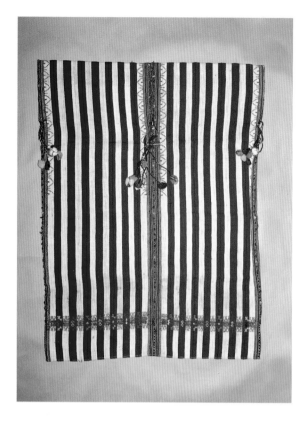

148. Bwe, man's tunic, 74cm x 97cm.
(NHM: 70.0/8687)

149. Bwe, Toungoo hills, man's tunic,
69.5cm x 76.5cm. (FM: 235637)

150. Bwe, Bwe Karen Baptist mission, Toungoo, burial robe,
71cm x 90cm plus fringe. (DU: 1968.286)

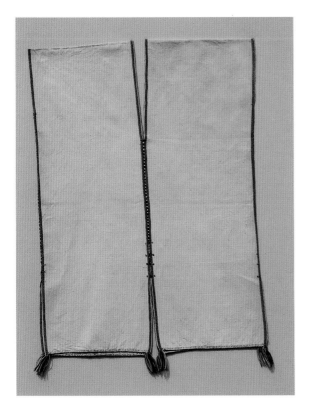

151. Padaung, woman's tunic,
52cm x 71cm. (PC)

152. Sgaw, *hse* or *thingdaing* (woman's
blouse), 61cm x 63cm. (PC)

153. Sgaw, *hse* or *thingdaing* (woman's
blouse), 66cm x 66cm. (DU: 1969.256)

154. Sgaw, *hse* or *thingdaing* (woman's
blouse), 65cm x 56cm. (PC)

155. Sgaw, Shan State, *hse* or *thingdaing* (woman's blouse), 56cm x 58cm. (PC)

156. Paku, Toungoo Hills district, sash/headcloth, 34cm x 228cm. (DU: P67.113)

157. Sgaw, Bassein area, headcloth, 27.5cm x 158cm plus fringe. (FM: 235646)

158. Paku, woman's headcloth, 38cm x 164cm plus fringe. (NHM: 70.8685)

159. Subgroup unknown,
Rangoon district, bag,
25.5cm x 26cm. (DU: P67.94)

160. Sgaw, bag,
27cm x 27cm
(DU: 1967.160)

161. Subgroup unknown, bag,
26cm x 26cm.
(DU: P67.86)

162. Subgroup unknown, bag,
22.5cm x 28.5cm. (FM: 235662)

163. Subgroup unknown, bag,
37cm x 33cm. (FM: 235653)

164. Lomi, *pah hon ali* (man's jacket), body 47cm x 50cm, sleeves 18cm x 42cm. (PC)

165. Subgroup unknown (possibly Ulo), bag, 26.5cm x 32cm. (DU: P67.2)

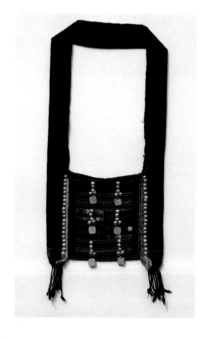

166. Ulo, shoulder-bag, 33cm x 23cm. (PC)

167. Ulo, *pah hon abu* (woman's jacket), 50cm x 51cm. (PC)

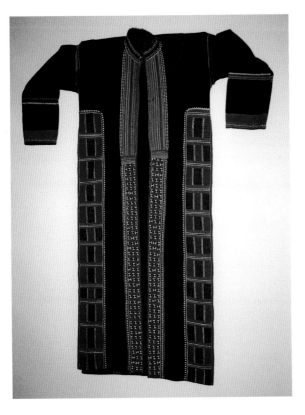

168. Lahu Na, woman's coat,
47cm x 112cm. (DU: 1968.11)

169. Lahu Na, Venbo (near Kengtung),
woman's coat, 58.5cm x 130cm. (DU: P67.110)

170. Lahu Na, bag, 30cm x 30.5cm.
(DU: 1968.9)

171. Lahu Na, bag, 21cm x 27cm.
(DU: 1967.148)

172. Woman's apron, body 57cm top and 71cm bottom x 52cm,
flap 23cm x 59cm, waistband 14cm x 96cm. (PC)

173. Skirt, 122cm x 48cm. (DU: 1968.6)

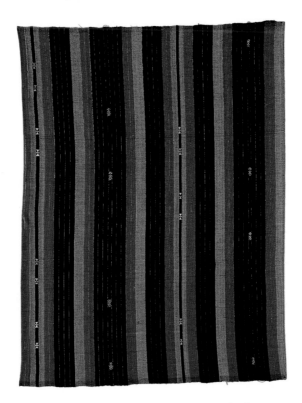

174. Tubeskirt, 81cm x 102cm. (PC)

175. Woman's blouse,
length 41cm. (DU: 1968.5)

176. From Si Kehn Nö, bag,
35cm x 35cm. (DU: 1968.3)

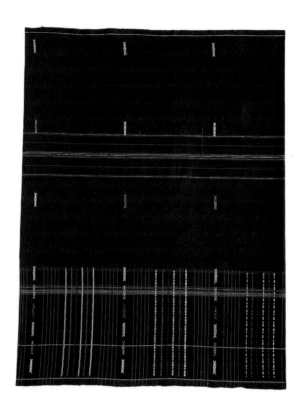

177. Tubeskirt, 85.5cm x 104cm. (PC)

178. Bag, 27cm x 27cm.
(DU: 1968.4)

179. Bag, 27cm x 28.5cm.
(DU: 1968.7)

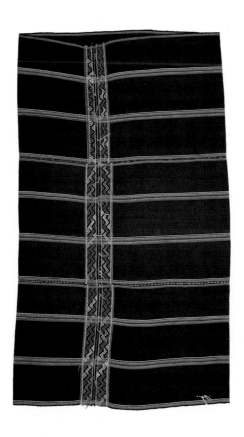

180. Subgroup unknown, tubeskirt, 80cm x 49cm. (BM: 1955.56)

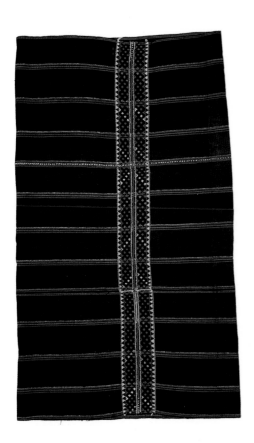

181. Maingkwim clan, tubeskirt.
(BM: 1955.72.2)

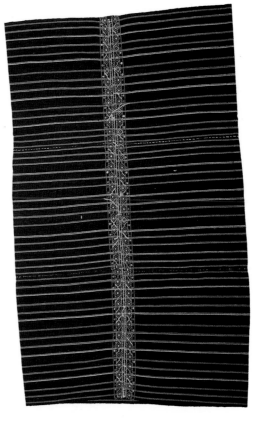

182. Maingkwim clan, tubeskirt,
80.5cm x 51cm. (BM: 1955.71.2)

183. Manton clan, tubeskirt, 90cm x 52.5cm.
(BM: 1955.43.1)

184. Yarbon clan, tubeskirt, 83.5cm x 53.5cm.
(BM: 1955.70.2)

185. Silver Palaung, Kengtung State,
tubeskirt, 60cm x 101cm. (PC)

186. Silver Palaung, Kengtung State,
tubeskirt, 63cm x 108cm. (PC)

187. Yarbon clan, jacket, body 37cm x 32cm,
sleeve 37cm x 16cm. (BM: 1955.70.1)

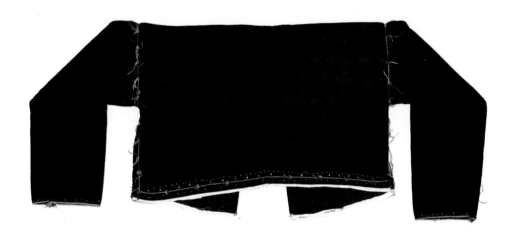

188. Back of #187.

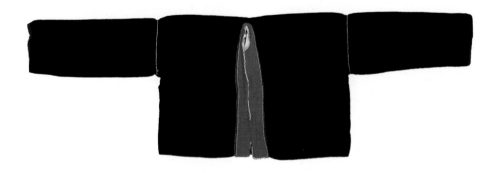

189. Maingkwim clan, jacket, body 39cm x 29cm,
sleeve 62cm x 17cm. (BM: 1955.72.2)

190. Maingkwim clan, headcloth, 53cm x 48cm. (BM: 1955.71.5)

191. Maingkwin clan, headcloth,
213cm plus fringe x 26cm. (BM: 1955.71.3)

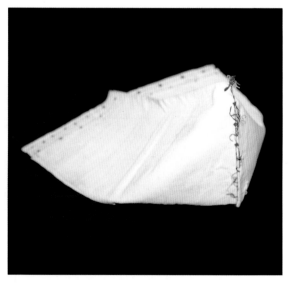

192. Yarbon clan, woman's headcoth,
44cm x 24.5cm. (BM: 1955.70.4)

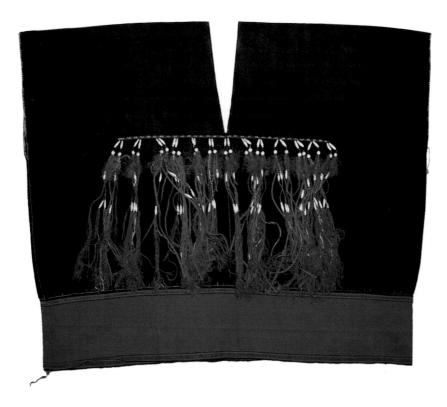

193. Yang Lam, woman's blouse, 43cm x 26.5cm. (BM: GS63)

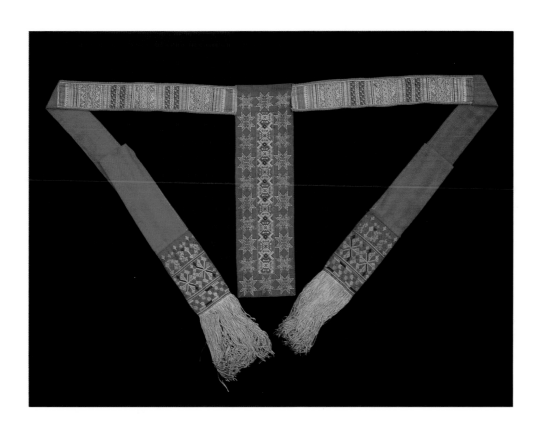

194. Apron, 17cm x 60cm, each side piece 8.5cm x 165cm plus fringe. (PC)

References

Adams, Marie, "Dress and design among the peoples of highland Southeast Asia," *Textile Museum Journal,* vol. 4, no. 1, 1974, pp. 51-66.

Anderson, John, *A Report on the Expedition to Yunnan via Bhamo* (Calcutta, 1871).

_____, *Mandalay to Momien: A Narrative of Two Expeditions to Western China of 1868 and 1875* (London, 1876).

Athamasar, Raynou, "The effects of socio-cultural change on the textiles of the T'ai Mao of Muang Mou Luang, Burma," in M.C. Howard, W. Wattanapun, and A. Gordon (eds.), *Traditional T'ai Arts in Contemporary Perspective* (Bangkok: White Lotus Press, 1997, pp. 139-47

Barua, S.N., *Tribes of Indo-Burma Border* (New Delhi: Mittal Publications, 1991).

Bernatzik, Hugo Adolf, *Akha und Meau: Probleme der Angewandten Völkerkunde in Hinterindien* (Innsbruck: Wagnerische Universitäts Buchdrükerei, 1947).

Brauns, Claus-Dieter and Lorenz G. Löffler, *Mru: Hill People on the Border of Bangladesh* (Basel: Birkhäuser Verlag, 1990).

Bühler, Alfred, "Hanfverarbeitung und Batik bei den Meau in Nordthailand," *Ethnologische Zeitschrift,* vol. 1, 1972, pp. 61-81.

Burmese Art Newsletter, vol. 1, no. 4, June, 1969 (Museum of Burmese Art and Culture, Denison University, Granville, Ohio).

Carpenter, C.H., *Self-support, Illustrated in the History of the Bassein Karen Mission from 1840 to 1880* (Boston: Rand, Avery, and Company/The Franklin Press, 1883).

Carrapiett, W.J.S. *The Kachin Tribes of Burma* (Rangoon: Superintendent, Government Printing and Stationery, Burma, 1929).

Chazee, Laurent, *Atlas des Ethnies et des Sous-Ethnies du Laos* (Bangkok: Privately printed, 1995).

Clothing Culture Center, *Miao Textile Design* (Taipei: Fu Jen University Press, 1993).

Cohen, Erik, "The Hmong cross: A cosmic symbol in Hmong (Meo) textile designs," *Res,* Autumn, 1987, pp. 27-45.

Das, N.K., "The Naga movement," in K.S. Singh (ed.) *Tribal Movements in India* (Delhi: Manohar, 1982), vol. 1, pp. 39-52.

Davies, H.R. *Yünnan: The Link Between India and the Yangtze* (Cambridge: Cambridge University Press, 1909).

D'Orléans, Henri, *From Tonkin to India by the Sources of the Irawadi, January '95-January '96* (London: Methuen, 1898).

Dudley, Sandra, "Burmese collections in the Pitt Rivers Museum: An introduction," *Journal of Museum Ethnography,* no. 5, 1996, pp. 57-64.

Elwin, Verrier, *The Art of the North-East Frontier of India* (Shillong: North-East Frontier Agency, 1959).

_____, *The Tribal World of Verrier Elwin: An Autobiography* (Oxford: Oxford University Press, 1964).

Ferrars, Max and Bertha, *Burma* (London: Sampson Low, Marston, 1901).

Fraser-Lu, Sylvia, *Handwoven Textiles of South-East Asia* (Singapore: Oxford University Press, 1988).

_____, *Burmese Crafts Past and Present* (Kuala Lumpur: Oxford University Press, 1994).

Fürer-Haimendorf, Christoph von, *The Naked Nagas* (London: Methuen, 1939).

_____, *The Konyak Nagas: An Indian Frontier Tribe* (New York: Holt, Rinehart & Winston, 1969).

_____, *Return to the Naked Nagas: An Anthropologist's View of Nagaland 1936-1970* (Delhi: Vikas Publishing House, 1976).

Gilhodes, P. Ch., "La culture matérielle de Katchins (Birmanie)," *Anthropos,* vol. 5, 1910, pp. 615-634.

_____, *The Kachins: Religion and Customs* (originally published 1922, reprinted 1996 by White Lotus Press, Bangkok).

Gogoi, Puspadhar, *Tai of North-east India: Ahom, Khamti, Phake, Aiton, Turung, Khamyang* (Dhemaji, Assam: Chumpra Printers and Publications, 1996).

Goodman, Jim, *Meet the Akhas* (Bangkok: White Lotus Press, 1996).

Grant Brown, G.E.R., *Burma Gazetteer: Upper Chindwin District* (Rangoon: Superintendent, Government Printing and Stationery, Union of Burma, 1911).

Hansen, Henny Harald, *Some Costumes of Highland Burma at the Ethnographical Museum of Gothenburg* (Göteborg: Elanders Boktryckeri Aktiebolag, 1960).

Hanson, O., *The Kachins: Their Customs and Traditions* (Rangoon: American Baptist Mission Press, 1913).

Hinton, E.M., "The dress of the Pwo Karen of north Thailand," *Journal of the Siam Society,* vol. 62, 1974, pp. 27-34.

Hodson, T.C., *The Naga Tribes of Manipur* (originally published 1911; reprinted 1974 by B.R. Publishing Company, Delhi)

Hutton, J.H., *The Angami Nagas, with Some Notes on Neighbouring Tribes* (London: Macmillan, 1921a).

_____, *The Sema Nagas* (London: Macmillan, 1921b).

Innes, R.A., *Costumes of Upper Burma and the Shan States in the collections of the Bankfield Museum, Halifax* (Halifax: Bankfield Museum, 1957).

Izikowitz, Karl Gustav, *Över Dimmornas Berg: Djungelfärder i Franska Indokina* (Stockholm: Aler Bonniers Förlag, 1944).

Jacobs, Julian, *The Nagas: Hill Peoples of Northeast India* (London: Thames and Hudson, 1990).

John Michael Kohler Arts Center, *Hmong Art: Tradition and Change* (Sheboygan, WI: John Michael Kohler Arts Center, 1986).

Kauffmann, H.E., "Das Weben in den Naga-Bergen (Assam)," *Zeitschrift für Ethnologie,* vol. 69, 1938, pp. 113-135.

Leach, E.R., *Political Systems of Highland Burma* (Cambridge, MA: Harvard University Press, 1954).

Lebar, Frank M., Gerald C. Hickey, and John K. Musgrave, *Ethnic Groups of Mainland Southeast Asia* (New Haven, CT: Human Relations Area Files, 1964).

Lehman, F.K., *The Structure of Chin Society: A Tribal People of Burma Adapted to a Non-Western Civilization* (Urbana, IL: University of Illinois Press, 1963).

Lemoine, Jacques, *Un Village Hmong Vert du Haut-Laos* (Paris: Editions du Centre National de la Recherche Scientifique, 1972).

Lewin, T.H., *Wild Races of South Eastern India* (London: Wm. H. Allen, 1870).

Lewis, Paul, and Elaine Lewis, *Peoples of the Golden Triangle: Six Tribes in Thailand* (London: Thames and Hudson, 1984).

Ling Roth, Henry, *Studies in Primitive Looms* (Halifax: Bankfield Museum, 1918).

Lowis, C.C., *The Tribes of Burma* (Rangoon: Superintendent, Government Printing, 1919).

Mallinson, Jane, Nancy Donnelly, and Ly Hang, *Hmong Batik: A Textile Technique from Laos* (Seattle: Mallinson/Information Services, 1988).

Marshall, Harry I., *The Karen People of Burma: A Study in Anthropology and Ethnology, Ohio State University Bulletin 26* (13) (Columbus, OH: Ohio State University, 1922).

McMahon, A.R., *The Karens of Golden Chersonese* (London: Walter W.G. Beatson, 1876).

Mills, J.P., *The Lhota Nagas* (London: Macmillan, 1922).

_____, *The Ao Naga* (London: Macmillan, 1926).

_____, *The Rengma Nagas* (London: Macmillan, 1937).

Milne, Mary Lewis, *Shans at Home,* by Mrs. Leslie Milne (London: John Murray, 1910).

_____, *The Home of an Eastern Clan: A Study of the Palaungs of the Shan States,* by Mrs. Leslie Milne (Oxford: Clarendon Press, 1924).

Nabholz-Kartaschoff, Marie-Louise, "De bijzondere plaats van een gewone kleur," in L. Oei (ed.) *Indigo* (Amsterdam: Stichting Indigo, 1985), pp. 155-162.

Naga Institute of Culture, *The Arts and Crafts of Nagaland* (Kohima: Naga Institute of Culture, Government of Nagaland, 1968).

Parry, N.E., *The Lakhers* (originally published 1932; reprinted in 1976 by the Tribal Research Institute, Aizawl, Mizoram).

Reid, Robert, "The excluded areas of Assam," *The Geographical Journal,* vol. 103, nos. 1/2, 1944, pp. 18-29.

Rock, Joseph F., *The Ancient Na-Khi Kingdom of Southwest China* (Cambridge, MA: Harvard University Press, 1947).

Rose, Archibald, and J. Coggin Brown, "Lisu (Yawyin) tribes of the Burma-China frontier," *Memoirs of the Royal Asiatic Society of Bengal,* vol. 3, 1911, pp. 249-277.

Rowney, Horatio Bickerstaffe, *The Wild Tribes of India* (London: Thos. de la Rue, 1882).

Roy, Nilima, *Art of Manipur* (Delhi: Agam Kala Prakashan, 1979).

Sardeshpande, S.C., *The Patkoi Nagas* (Delhi: Daya Publishing House, 1987).

Scott, James George, *Burma: A Handbook of Practical Information* (London: Alexander Moring, 1911).

_____ and J.P. Hardiman, *Gazetteer of Upper Burma and the Shan States* (Rangoon: Superintendent of Government Printing and Stationery, 1900)

Seidenfaden, Erik, *The Thai Peoples: Book I: The Origins and Habitats of the Thai Peoples with a Sketch of their Material and Spiritual Culture* (Bangkok: The Siam Society, 1967).

Shakespear, John B., *The Lushei Kuki Clans* (London: Macmillan, 1912).

Shanghai Theatrical College, *Ethnic Costumes and Clothing Decorations from China* (Hong Kong: Hai Feng Publishing Co./Chengdu: Sichian People's Publishing House, 1986).

Shirali, Aditi, *Textile and Bamboo Crafts of the Northeastern Region* (Ahmendabad: National Institute of Design, 1983).

Smith, Martin, *Burma: Insurgency and the Politics of Ethnicity* (London: Zed Press, 1991).

Spearman, H.R., *British Burma Gazetteer* (Rangoon: Government Press, 1880).

Start, Laura E., *Burmese Textiles from the Shan and Kachin Districts,* Bankfield Museum Notes, Social Series No. 7 (Halifax: Bankfield Museum, 1917).

Stevenson, H.N.C., *The Economics of the Central Chin Tribes* (Bombay: The Times of India Press, 1943).

_____, *The Hill Peoples of Burma* (London: Longmans, Green, 1944).

Telford, J.H., "Animism in Kengtung State," *Journal of the Burma Research Society,* vol. 27, pt. II, 1937, pp. 86-238.

Ward, F. Kingdon, *In Farthest Burma: The Record of an Arduous Journey of Exploration and Research Through the unknown Frontier Territory of Burma and Tibet* (London: Seeley, Service, 1921)

_____. *From China to Hkamti Long* (London: Edward Arnold, 1924).

White, Virginia, *Pa Ndau: The Needlework of the Hmong* (Cheney, WA: Cheney Free Press, 1982).

Woodthorpe, R.G., "Some accounts of the Shans and hill tribes of the states on the Mekong," *Journal of the Royal Anthropological Institute of Great Britain and Ireland,* vol. 26, 1897, pp. 13-28.

Yunuo, A., *The Rising Nagas* (Delhi: Vivek Publishing House, 1974).